IFIP Advances in Information and Communication Technology 763

IFIP Advances in Information and Communication Technology

The IFIP AICT series publishes state-of-the-art results in the sciences and technologies of information and communication. The scope of the series includes: foundations of computer science; software theory and practice; education; computer applications in technology; communication systems; systems modeling and optimization; information systems; ICT and society; computer systems technology; security and protection in information processing systems; artificial intelligence; and human-computer interaction.

Edited volumes and proceedings of refereed international conferences in computer science and interdisciplinary fields are featured. These results often precede journal publication and represent the most current research.

The principal aim of the IFIP AICT series is to encourage education and the dissemination and exchange of information about all aspects of computing.

More information about this series at https://link.springer.com/bookseries/6102

Jason Staggs · Sujeet Shenoi
Editors

Critical Infrastructure Protection XIX

19th IFIP WG 11.10 International Conference, ICCIP 2025
Arlington, VA, USA, March 17–18, 2025
Revised Selected Papers

Springer

Editors
Jason Staggs
University of Tulsa
Tulsa, OK, USA

Sujeet Shenoi
University of Tulsa
Tulsa, OK, USA

ISSN 1868-4238 ISSN 1868-422X (electronic)
IFIP Advances in Information and Communication Technology
ISBN 978-3-032-11913-1 ISBN 978-3-032-11914-8 (eBook)
https://doi.org/10.1007/978-3-032-11914-8

This Springer imprint is published by the registered company Springer Nature Switzerland AG
The registered company address is: Gewerbestrasse 11, 6330 Cham, Switzerland

Preface

The cyber infrastructure – comprising computers, embedded devices, networks and software systems – is vital to operations in every sector: chemicals, commercial facilities, communications, critical manufacturing, dams, defense industrial base, emergency services, energy, financial services, food and agriculture, government facilities, healthcare and public health, information technology, nuclear reactors, materials and waste, transportation systems, and water and wastewater systems. Global business and industry, governments, indeed society itself, cannot function if major components of the critical infrastructure are degraded, disabled or destroyed.

This book, *Critical Infrastructure Protection XIX*, is the nineteenth volume in the annual series produced by IFIP Working Group 11.10 on Critical Infrastructure Protection, an active international community of scientists, engineers, practitioners and policy makers dedicated to advancing research, development and implementation efforts related to critical infrastructure protection. The book presents original research results and innovative applications in the area of critical infrastructure protection. Also, it highlights the importance of weaving science, technology and policy in crafting sophisticated, yet practical, solutions that will help secure information, computer and network assets in the various critical infrastructure sectors.

This volume contains seven selected papers from the Nineteenth Annual IFIP Working Group 11.10 International Conference on Critical Infrastructure Protection, which was held at SRI International in Arlington, Virginia, USA on March 17–18, 2025. A total of 18 full-length papers were submitted for presentation at the conference. The papers were refereed in a single-blind manner by members of the conference program committee and other individuals, all of them internationally recognized experts in critical infrastructure protection, and submissions received an average of three reviews each. The seven accepted papers were rewritten by the authors after the conference to accommodate the suggestions provided by the referees and by the conference attendees. The post-conference manuscripts were subsequently revised by the editors to produce the final chapters published in this volume.

The chapters are organized into four thematic sections: (i) Themes and Issues; (ii) Industrial Control System Security; (iii) Infrastructure Modeling and Simulation; and (iv) Infrastructure Communications Security. The coverage of topics showcases the richness and vitality of the discipline, and offers promising avenues for future research in critical infrastructure protection.

This book is the result of the combined efforts of several individuals and organizations. In particular, we thank Laura Tinnel for her tireless work on behalf of IFIP Working Group 11.10. We also thank the National Science Foundation, U.S. Department of Homeland Security, National Security Agency and SRI International for their support of IFIP Working Group 11.10 and its activities. Finally, we wish to note that all opinions, findings, conclusions and recommendations in the chapters of this book are those of the authors and do not necessarily reflect the views of their employers or funding agencies.

October 2025

Jason Staggs
Sujeet Shenoi

Organization

General Chair

Laura Tinnel	SRI International, USA

Program Chairs

Jason Staggs	University of Tulsa, USA
Sujeet Shenoi	University of Tulsa, USA

Program Committee

Irfan Ahmed	Virginia Commonwealth University, USA
Stefan Axelsson	Stockholm University, Sweden
Raymond Chan	Singapore Institute of Technology, Singapore
Kam-Pui Chow	University of Hong Kong, China
Chiara Foglietta	Università Roma Tre, Italy
Richard George	Johns Hopkins University Applied Physics Laboratory, USA
Janne Hagen	Norwegian Water Resources and Energy Directorate, Norway; and University of Oslo, Norway
Elizabeth Kurkowski	Johns Hopkins University Applied Physics Laboratory, USA
Stefano Panzieri	Università Roma Tre, Italy
Mason Rice	Oak Ridge National Laboratory, USA
Leon Strous	De Nederlandsche Bank, The Netherlands
Øyvind Toftegaard	Norwegian University of Science and Technology, Norway; and Norwegian Energy Regulatory Authority, Norway
Zachary Tudor	Idaho National Laboratory, USA

Contents

Contributors

Hayretdin Bahsi Tallinn University of Technology, Tallinn, Estonia;
Northern Arizona University, Flagstaff, AZ, USA

Raymond Chan Singapore Institute of Technology, Singapore, Singapore

Sebastian Chlup Austrian Institute of Technology, Vienna, Austria

Manuel Egger Austrian Institute of Technology, Vienna, Austria

Sye Loong Keoh University of Glasgow, Glasgow, UK

Shaymaa Mamdouh Khalil Tallinn University of Technology, Tallinn, Estonia

Christl Korbinian Austrian Institute of Technology, Vienna, Austria

Tarmo Korotko Tallinn University of Technology, Tallinn, Estonia

Antoine Lemay Hitachi Energy Research, Montreal, Canada

Michal Ostoja-Gajewski Hitachi Energy Research, Krakow, Poland

Ewa Piatkowska Hitachi Energy Research, Krakow, Poland

Benjamin Rainer Austrian Institute of Technology, Vienna, Austria

Stefan Rass Johannes Kepler University Linz, Linz, Austria

Stefan Schauer Austrian Institute of Technology, Vienna, Austria

Christoph Schmittner Austrian Institute of Technology, Vienna, Austria

Øyvind Toftegaard Norwegian University of Science and Technology, Gjøvik, Nor way;
Norwegian Energy Regulatory Authority, Oslo, Norway

Arzhan Tong Royal Holloway, University of London, Egham, UK

Rongqi Wang University of Glasgow, Glasgow, UK;
Singapore Institute of Technology, Singapore, Singapore

Stephen Wolthusen Royal Holloway, University of London, Egham, UK;
Norwegian University of Science and Technology, Gjøvik, Norway

Themes and Issues

Effects of Hard and Soft Measures in the First European Network and Information Security Directive

Øyvind Toftegaard[1,2(✉)]

[1] Norwegian University of Science and Technology, Gjøvik, Norway
[2] Norwegian Energy Regulatory Authority, Oslo, Norway
oyat@nve.no

Abstract. The 2016 Network and Information Security Directive was the first piece of cyber security legislation in the European Union. The directive sought to establish a high common security level across European critical infrastructures and services.

This chapter examines how the use of compulsory (hard) measures and optional (soft) measures in the Network and Information Security Directive have impacted cyber security in the European Union energy sector. An interrupted time series methodology was employed to analyze cyber security benchmark data pertaining to European Union states collected between 2015 and 2023. The results reveal that the hard measures achieved 100% compliance by 2018 when the directive came into force. However, the implementation of the hard measures crowded out the implementation of soft measures. Thus, the directive did not necessarily engender a high common security level. Instead, it led to the prioritization of cyber security measures. Hard measures at the strategic level were prioritized upward whereas soft measures at the tactical level were prioritized downward. The key result is that governmental authorities planning to stipulate hard and soft cyber security measures in legislation must ensure that their prioritizations are correct.

Keywords: Network Security · Information Security · Critical Infrastructure · Critical Services · Energy Sector · European Union · Law and Policy

1 Introduction

Effective cyber security regulation is important to protect critical infrastructures and services such as energy, communications and healthcare from cyber threats. The threats include denial of service and ransomware attacks that disrupt service delivery, as well as cyber espionage and data manipulation with financial or political goals. Regulations support critical infrastructure and service operators by incorporating key cyber security measures in legislation. Compulsory measures require operator cyber security teams with direction and mandate. Additionally, when regulations stipulate cyber security audits, operators tend to give their

Published by Springer Nature Switzerland AG 2026
J. Staggs and S. Shenoi (Eds.): ICCIP 2025, IFIP AICT 763, pp. 3–22, 2026.
https://doi.org/10.1007/978-3-032-11914-8_1

cyber security teams adequate resources to reduce the risk of non-compliance. Compliance is about conformance to the requirements imposed by laws, policies, procedures and conduct [3]. However, where regulation is concerned, compliance is not just about conformance with legal rules – it may also involve compliance with regulatory goals. Specifically, although a set of legal rules has been satisfied by an entity, it may not necessarily be in a state of compliance with a regulatory goal. In fact, if fulfilling the rules in a regulation does not fulfill the policy goal underlying the regulation, the implementation may be viewed as being rules-specific or compliance-oriented, but not in compliance with the regulatory goal.

Cyber security regulatory goals may be met in several ways. Compliance theories explain how decisions are made based on gains, costs and other constraints [4]. One of the main approaches is to engage a psycho-economic theory that explains what increases the motivation to fulfill a regulatory goal as well as what reduces the motivation. Due to the complexity of psycho-economic mechanisms, using different regulatory approaches may result in different levels of fulfillment of the regulatory goals. Unfortunately, little information is available on the effectiveness of cyber security legislation at reducing cyber risk. Also, there is limited understanding about the effects that central regulatory measures – such as hard (compulsory) laws and soft (optional) laws – have on cyber security regulations.

Efforts at creating the content of the European Union (EU) Network and Information Security (NIS) Directive [7] had proceeded for several years before the directive was published in 2016. In fact, as far back as June 2001, the European Commission, the executive arm of the European Union, communicated a network and information security proposal for consideration as an EU policy [5]. The NIS Directive was the first EU-wide cyber security legislation – it required operators of critical infrastructures and services to take appropriate security measures and report security incidents.

The principal objective of the study described in this chapter was to investigate how the hard and soft measures in the NIS Directive have impacted cyber security maturity in the EU energy sector. The study draws on data pertaining to the cyber security maturity of several EU states collected over a period of eight years. It attempts to identify whether legal compliance was achieved and whether compliance with the main regulatory goal was achieved. It also discusses why certain regulatory goals were achieved or not achieved.

2 Background

This section discusses the EU Network and Information Security (NIS) Directive of 2016 with an emphasis on its hard and soft measures (laws).

2.1 Network and Information Security Directive

The Network and Information Security Directive, which was published in 2016 and came into force in 2018, was the first EU-wide cyber security legislation.

Its main goal was to establish a high common security level across EU critical infrastructures and services. The directive applied to critical sectors such as energy, transportation, water and healthcare. It required authorities to work strategically on – and to administer – national cyber security. It also required operators of essential services to take appropriate security measures and report security incidents. A revised version of the NIS Directive, commonly referred to as NIS2 [9], was published in 2022. This study focuses on the first NIS Directive and the effects of its requirements.

NIS was a directive, which means that its implementation as national law was up to each EU member state. For example, if a member state already had similar rules in place, the corresponding rules in the NIS Directive could be disregarded. However, all the requirements in the directive had to be covered somehow by national legislation. Non-compliance with the rules in the NIS Directive could have led to penalties imposed by governmental authorities or the EU. The EU penalties ranged from a formal notice or opinion by the European Commission to a referral of the case to the EU Court of Justice [6]. The latter could result in a lump sum fine or daily fines until the required measure was implemented in a satisfactory manner.

The NIS Directive required each EU state to establish a national strategy on the security of network and information systems, exchange security information within the EU, create a computer security incident response team (CSIRT) and establish national requirements for cyber security and related notifications [7]. These measures were compulsory and were considered to be hard laws. Other measures in the NIS Directive were optional and considered to be soft laws.

Article 7 in the NIS Directive contained a mix of hard measures and soft measures:

> *Each Member State shall adopt a national strategy. ... The national strategy ... shall address, in particular, the following issues:*
> 1. *the objectives and priorities of the national strategy,*
> 2. *a governance framework to achieve the objectives and priorities of the national strategy,*
> 3. *the identification of measures relating to preparedness, response and recovery, including cooperation between the public and private sectors,*
> 4. *an indication of the education, awareness-raising and training programmes relating to the national strategy,*
> 5. *an indication of the research and development plans relating to the national strategy,*
> 6. *a risk assessment plan to identify risks,*
> 7. *a list of the various actors involved in the implementation of the national strategy.*

According to Article 7, it was compulsory to adopt a national strategy, which made it a hard law. It was also compulsory that the national strategy have objectives and priorities. However, it was not compulsory to implement the objectives and priorities. The implementation was implicit because it was clearly the regulatory objective, but because it was not stated as a direct requirement, it was a soft law. The same can be said about the requirement to identify

Table 1. Four variations of hard and soft laws [13].

Form	Substance
Hard	Hard
Hard	Soft
Soft	Hard
Soft	Soft

awareness-raising programs related to national security. Identifying such programs in national strategies was compulsory and the clear regulatory goal was to implement them. However, because its implementation was not required, the measure could be considered to be a soft law.

2.2 Hard and Soft Laws

Hard laws are traditionally seen as legally binding laws whereas soft laws normally refer to non-binding instruments. Examples of legally binding laws are regulations, directives, decrees and orders. Examples of non-binding instruments are strategies, communications, standards and recommendations. A hard law involves a thorough democratic process with multiple stakeholders and the process increases the likelihood of an effective outcome. Additionally, a hard law may be enforced by penalizing non-compliance.

A soft law, on the other hand, has the advantages of speed of release and the ability to rapidly change its requirements. Also, a soft law is beneficial to policy makers if they are uncertain of its effects. Additionally, because soft law compliance is voluntary, any lack of results is the responsibility of the regulated entity, not the governmental authority.

It is important to note that hard laws and soft laws are not as binary as the strict statements above. According to Pronto [13] a rule can be a soft law even if it is presented as a hard law. Also, a rule may be deemed hard although it is presented as a soft law.

Table 1 shows the four variations of hard laws and soft laws specified by Pronto [13]. According to Pronto, what is traditionally referred to as a hard law is a law that is hard in form as well as hard in substance. This means that the law is legally binding and contains compulsory provisions.

At the other end of the spectrum, is a law that is soft in form as well as soft in substance. This is traditionally referred to as a soft law. In the case of a soft law, the legal instrument and its content are non-binding.

A law can be soft in form but hard in substance. An example is a non-binding instrument such as a cyber security standard that contains rules that are compulsory. This may occur, for example, when a governmental authority enacts a hard law that requires entities to be compliant with, say, one chapter of a cyber security standard. In this case, the chapter is hard in substance for the regulated entities although the standard is a non-binding instrument.

Finally, a legally binding law may contain non-binding provisions. This may occur, for example, if a provision requires certain entities to consider the use of specific security measures or to implement certain measures on a voluntary basis.

The NIS Directive has hard hard laws and hard soft laws. This study examines the effects of using the two variations of hard and soft laws. In the study, the term hard law refers to a legal requirement that is hard in form and hard in substance. The term soft law refers to a legal requirement that is hard in form but soft in substance.

3 Literature Review

Several studies have been conducted on the application of hard laws and soft laws in the legal domain as well as a few in the cyber security discipline. The studies considered in this section are relevant to the work discussed in this chapter.

In a non-academic report evaluating the implementation of the 2016 EU NIS Directive, the Centre for European Policy Studies (CEPS) [1] stated that the implementation of the NIS Directive posed a risk of limited consistency and unnecessary complexity to its stakeholders. In addition, CEPS reported under-achievement when it came to cooperation on information exchange and the harmonization of cyber security maturity. The shortcomings were perceived to be due to the lack of financial resources, staff and knowledge.

Storm et al. [15] noted that legislation that is not followed by some sort of control is less likely to be implemented by entities subject to the legislation. This conclusion was based on the observations of large increases in the numbers of compliant entities after the completion of audits.

Toftegaard [16] found significant positive effects resulting from the imposition of ISO/IEC 27001 Certification as a hard measure. The positive effects were seen in the case of small electric grid operators whose technical security performance improved. However, Toftegaard also found indications of negative effects from the same hard measure related to the technical security performance of large grid operators. A reduction in internal motivation when exposed to strict rules was suggested as the reason for the negative effects. This conclusion was based on the fact that large operators already had highly motivated security staff. The positive effects observed for small operators were perceived as being due to their initial lack of security focus. Therefore, just about any cyber security intervention would have increased the security performance.

Massacci et al. [12] investigated the economic impacts of rules-based cyber security regulations versus risk-based cyber security regulations. Rules-based regulations involve detailed compliance requirements as well as penalties for non-compliance. In contrast, risk-based regulations have governmental authorities intervening with fines for security breaches, but operators may define their own security investments based on their risk assessments and potential losses. A hybrid version involving both types of regulations is common in EU states, although the tendency is to have mostly risk-based regulations.

Massacci and colleagues attempted to determine whether a rules-based regime or a risk-based regime was the best way to regulate cyber security for electricity transmission operators. Upon modeling and analyzing the policy implications, they concluded that a cyber security maturity threshold would be beneficial. Operators falling below the threshold due to low maturity could be subjected to rules-based regulations to help them rise above the threshold. Mature operators could be subject to risk-based regulations, fostering innovation and efficiency gains. While rules-based regulations are similar to hard measures, risk-based regulations are not directly comparable with soft measures because there would still be penalties for non-compliance.

The literature review reveals that research has focused on the effects of applying hard and soft laws in the cyber security domain. However, the research efforts have not evaluated the effects of hard and soft cyber security measures over extended periods of time. The time series research methodology employed to address this open question is described in the following section.

4 Research Methodology

This section describes the research questions and hypotheses, the interrupted time series methodology and the motivation crowding theory employed in this study.

4.1 Research Questions and Hypotheses

The main objective of the study was to investigate how the use of hard (compulsory) and soft (non-compulsory) measures in the NIS Directive have impacted cyber security in the EU energy sector. To achieve the objective, one main research question (Q 1) and three sub-questions (SQ 1.a, SQ 1.b and SQ 1.c) were formulated:

Q1: *How does the use of hard and soft measures in the NIS Directive impact cyber security maturity?*
- SQ 1.a: *Was regulatory compliance achieved?*
- SQ 1.b: *Was regulatory goal compliance achieved?*
- SQ 1.c: *Why was compliance achieved or not achieved?*

In sub-question SQ 1.a, regulatory compliance refers to conformance with the rules in a legislative act (NIS Directive). In sub-question SQ 1.b, compliance with the regulatory goal refers to conformance with the goal that the policy makers wanted to achieve with the legislative act. In this case, the NIS Directive goal was a high common security level across the EU critical infrastructures and services. In sub-question SQ 1.c, compliance refers to regulatory compliance as well as regulatory goal compliance.

Table 2. Time series design with the numbers of EU states observed.

Group	2015 (N)	2016	2017 (N)	2018	2018 (N)	2021 (N)	2022	2023 (N)
EU States (Exposure)	Obs. (11)	NIS Pub.	Obs. (13)	NIS in Force	Obs. (15)	Obs. (20)	NIS2 Pub.	Obs. (21)
Non-EU States (Control)	–	–	–	–	–	Obs. (4)	–	Obs. (3)

Based on the main research question, the following hypotheses were specified:

> **Main Hypothesis ($\mathbf{H_1}$)** : *A hard measure has a different impact on cyber security maturity than a soft measure.*
> **Null Hypothesis ($\mathbf{H_0}$)** : *Whether a measure is hard or soft does not impact cyber security maturity.*

Although one of the two hypotheses would turn out to be true, the research sub-questions were used to explain in more detail how hard and soft measures affect cyber security maturity. The concerns were not merely regulatory compliance and regulatory goals, but also the potential mechanisms that led to the result.

4.2 Interrupted Time Series Methodology

An interrupted time series methodology that utilizes quasi-experimental logic was applied to answer research sub-questions SQ 1.a and SQ 1.b. As in any experimental design, an exposure group is exposed to a treatment. The exposure group in the study comprised several EU states subject to the NIS Directive. The treatment was the NIS Directive and the year when the NIS Directive came into force (2018) was the interruption in the time series methodology. The control group that was not exposed to the treatment comprised non-EU states that were either EU observer states or were from the European Economic Area. Time series data was extracted from five cyber security benchmark questionnaires answered in 2015, 2017, 2018, 2021 and 2023 by 14 to 24 EU states and three to four non-EU states, depending on the year. Table 2 summarizes the research methodology along with the numbers of states included in the annual analyses.

In the study, 12 questions from the benchmarks were compared over time. Five questions were related to hard measures and seven questions were related to soft measures. The questions were created so that the answers would be "Implemented" or "Not Implemented."

Some answers to the benchmarks were identified as being reported incorrectly. For example, one measure was reported as not implemented, although it was reported as implemented in the previous year. Incorrect answers were corrected in instances where mistakes were obvious – for example, if online information confirmed that the measure was indeed implemented. However, when there was uncertainty, the data for the question for the country was disregarded. Three types of answers were always disregarded – "Not Applicable," "Don't Know" and "Blank" (no answer provided). Furthermore, the answer "In Progress" was treated as "Not Implemented" because the measure was not yet implemented.

The treatment in the quasi-experimental design used in the study can be viewed as a series of treatments. The first treatment was in 2016 when the NIS Directive was published. The second – and main – treatment was in 2018 when the NIS Directive came into force and compliance was required on the part of all EU states. The third treatment was in 2022 when the NIS2 Directive was published. Table 2 covers the three treatments.

The data used in the study was drawn from the Council of European Energy Regulators (CEER) cyber security benchmarks corresponding to the years 2015, 2017, 2018, 2021 and 2023. Only the 2018 benchmark was published [2]; the other four benchmarks are unpublished.

To validate the data drawn from the CEER benchmarks, corresponding data was collected from the Global Cybersecurity Index of the International Telecommunications Union (ITU). The ITU data did not separate EU states and non-EU states, but provided an overall European status (Eur). The ITU data was used to visually validate the benchmark data.

The implementation rates of soft and hard measures were analyzed individually and combined. The method for computing the combined implementation rate for hard and soft measures involved adding the average implementation percentages for the soft measures with the average implementation percentages for the hard measures and dividing the result by two. An alternative method would be to add the implementation rate of each of the measures (hard and soft) and divide the result by the total number of measures. However, the first computational method was selected because it weighted the hard and soft measures equally.

4.3 Motivation Crowding Theory

To answer the research sub-question SQ 1.c, the study applied Frey's motivation crowding theory [10] to analyze the results of research sub-questions SQ 1.a and SQ 1.b. According to the theory, motivation is an important factor that drives compliance. However, some measures may have negative impacts on compliance. For example, if a governmental authority were to apply a monetary incentive to purchase firewalls and monitor network traffic, it would be good for cyber security, but it would not foster holistic cyber security. The reason is that there would be increased focus on firewalls and network traffic monitoring due to the monetary incentive. The monetary incentive would, however, crowd out the intrinsic motivation for components without governmental support, reducing the focus on key measures such as security updates and patching.

Figure 1 illustrates Frey's motivation crowding theory. The theory is applied in the discussion section to explain the results presented below.

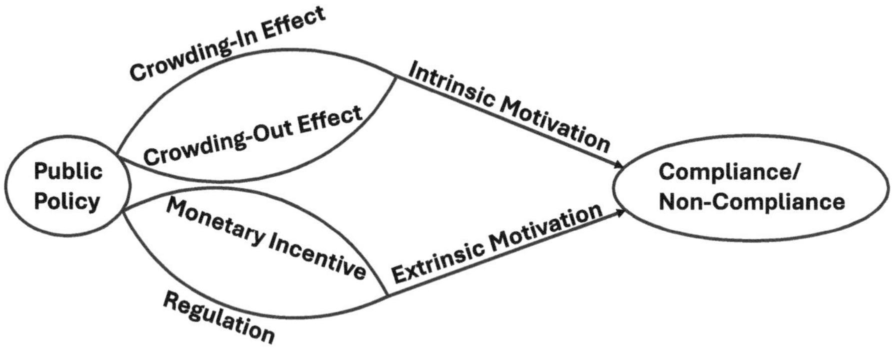

Fig. 1. Motivation crowding theory (based on [4]).

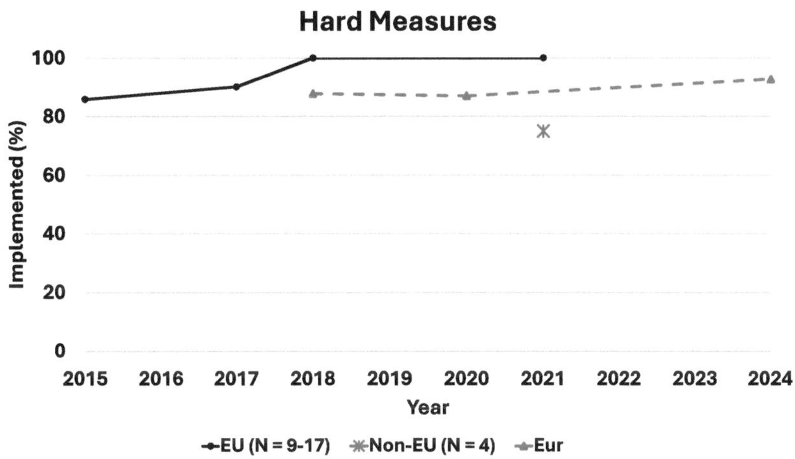

Fig. 2. Implementation of hard measures in the NIS Directive.

5 Results

Fig. 2 shows the implementation of the hard measures in the NIS Directive based on the data obtained for the study. According to the data, the use of hard measures in the NIS Directive resulted in 100% compliance in the EU when the NIS Directive came into force in 2018.

Table 3 shows that all the measures included in Fig. 2 are deemed to be compulsory by the NIS Directive due to the use of the word "shall." Note that column "EU" refers to whether (✓) or not benchmark data was available from EU states, column "Non-EU" refers to whether (✓) or not benchmark data was available from non-EU states and column "Eur" identifies whether (✓) or not data collected by ITU was available for European states. "Strategy" refers to a national cyber security strategy. "NCA CS" refers to the required establishment of a national competent authority on cyber security. "SPoC" refers to the sin-

Table 3. Hard measures included in Fig. 2.

Article	Wording	Measure	EU	Non-EU	Eur
7,1	"Shall"	Strategy	✓		✓
8,1	"Shall"	NCA CS	✓		✓
8,3	"Shall"	SPoC	✓	✓	
9,1	"Shall"	CERT/CSIRT	✓		✓
14,3	"Shall"	Notification	✓	✓	✓

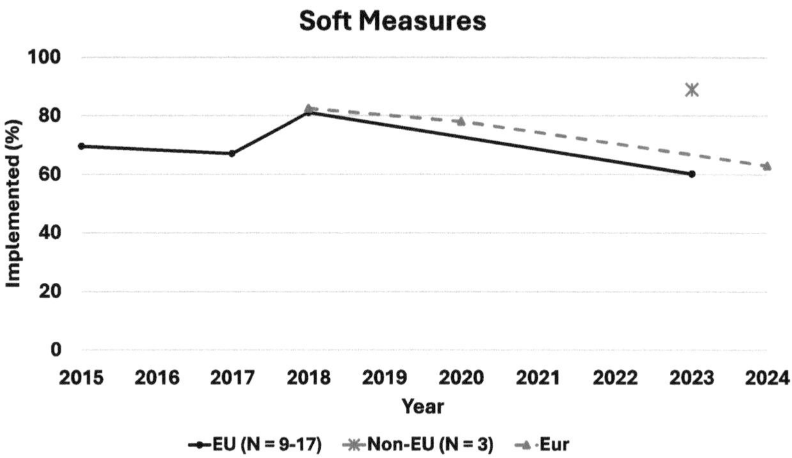

Fig. 3. Implementation of soft measures in the NIS Directive.

gle point of contact – the national entity responsible for information collection and dissemination. "CERT/CSIRT" refers to a national computer emergency response team/computer security incident response team. Finally, "Notification" refers to the duty to provide notifications of threats and vulnerabilities.

Figure 3 shows the implementation of the hard measures in the NIS Directive based on the data employed in the study. According to the data, the use of soft measures in the directive resulted in a compliance level in EU states between 60% and 80% during the 2015 to 2023 time period.

Table 4 shows the NIS Directive had wording such as "on a voluntary basis," "encourage" and "necessary" for several measures. This wording is much weaker than "shall" used for the hard measures. Therefore, the measures in Table 4 are deemed to be soft.

Note that "Status Report" refers to a cyber security incident report published on a voluntary basis by a national authority. "Certification" refers to the implementation of cyber security certification schemes at the national level. "Awareness" implies that the national cyber security strategy implements cyber security awareness programs. "Risk Assessment" implies that assessments are performed when appropriate and are conducted proportionately. "Audit" implies that cyber

Table 4. Soft measures included in Fig. 3.

Article	Wording	Measure	EU	Non-EU	Eur
12,3(c)	"On a voluntary basis"	Status Report	✓	✓	
19,1	"Encourage"	Certification	✓	✓	
7(d)	"An indication"	Awareness	✓	✓	✓
14,1	"Appropriate and proportionate"	Risk Assessment	✓		✓
15,1	"Necessary"	Audit	✓	✓	✓
12,3(h)	"Discussing"	Exercise	✓	✓	✓
14,1	"Appropriate and proportionate"	Baseline Security	✓	✓	

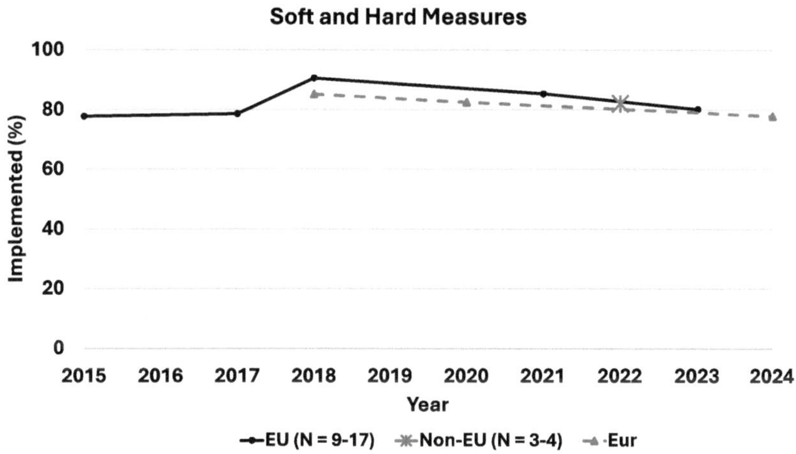

Fig. 4. Combined implementation of hard and soft measures.

security audits are performed when necessary. "Exercise" implies that cyber security exercises are performed. Finally, "Baseline Security" refers to establishing an appropriate and proportionate minimum cyber security level on a national basis. Note that a checkmark (✓) denotes that the associated measure applied to EU, non-EU or European states.

Data from the control group of non-EU states was only available in 2021 for hard measures and in 2023 for soft measures. Examination of the control groups in Figs. 2 and 3 reveals that the EU states scored better on implementing hard measures in 2021. However, the non-EU states scored better than the EU states on implementing soft measures in 2023. Graphs based on the data collected by ITU are also included in Figs. 2 and 3. The graphs reveal that the European (Eur) average is between the averages of the EU states and non-EU states in 2021 as well as in 2023. The ITU data validates the results of this study because the data represents European states overall (i.e., EU and non-EU).

Figure 4 shows the combined implementation results for hard and soft measures. The EU states and non-EU states had roughly the same levels of cyber

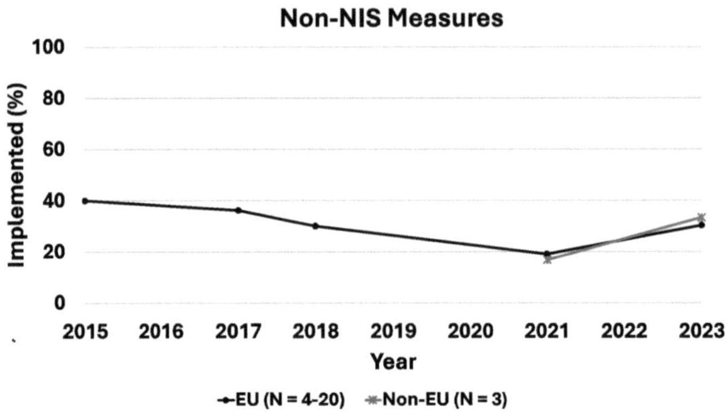

Fig. 5. Implementation of measures not included in the NIS Directive.

Table 5. Measures included in Fig. 5.

Measure	EU	Non-EU
Cross-Border Risk Assessment	✓	✓
Dedicated Energy Cyber Security Strategy	✓	✓
Dedicated Energy CERT/CSIRT	✓	✓
Cyber Security Laboratory Testing	✓	✓

security maturity from 2021 through 2023. The ITU results again indicate that the results are valid because the results from the European states (Eur) follow the benchmark results.

Figure 5 shows the implementation results of measures not included in the NIS Directive. Note that the NIS Directive did not have any spillover effect on cyber security measures unrelated to those listed in the directive. This statement is based on the fact that the implementation rates of EU states and non-EU states are roughly the same. Also relevant is the absence of a spike in cyber security compliance in 2018 when the NIS Directive came into force. Spikes are seen in 2018 for hard measures and soft measures in Figs. 2 and 3, respectively.

Table 5 lists the measures that were not included in the NIS Directive. "Cross-Border Risk Assessment" refers to the cross border risks to the energy system that are part of a risk assessment. "Dedicated Energy Cyber Security Strategy" refers to a strategy that exists in addition to the national cyber security strategy. "Dedicated Energy CERT/CSIRT" implies that a separate CERT or CSIRT exists exclusively for the energy sector. Finally, "Cyber Security Laboratory Testing" refers to the existence of a national testing regime for confirming the cyber security of hardware and/or software. Note that a checkmark (✓) denotes that the associated measure applied to EU or non-EU states.

6 Discussion

This section provides answers to the three sub-questions. The sub-question answers are used to answer the main research question: *How does the use of hard and soft measures in the NIS Directive impact cyber security maturity?* The section also discusses the results in light of previous work and provides recommendations for policy makers.

6.1 Research Sub-Questions

SQ 1.a: Was Regulatory Compliance Achieved? The implementation rate for hard measures was 100% and the implementation rate for soft measures was 60%. Despite the low implementation rate for soft measures, EU states were fully compliant with the legislative rules. This is because the implementation of soft measures in the NIS Directive was non-compulsory. In particular, EU states could decide for themselves if and to what extent they should implement the soft measures. This is true when it comes to the measures that are "on a voluntary basis" and "if necessary." However, some soft measures have wording such as "encourage" and "discussing." In these cases, an EU state had to demonstrate that it encouraged cyber security certification and discussed cyber security exercises. Of course, this does not mean that certification and exercises actually occurred, although it is clear that they were regulatory goals.

This study did not have access to data pertaining to (for example) whether cyber security certification was encouraged or exercises were discussed. Instead, the data focused on whether or not certification and exercises were conducted. Therefore, this study cannot provide complete insights into whether or not regulatory compliance was fully achieved. However, based on the available data, full compliance with the legislative rules was achieved.

SQ 1.b: Was Regulatory Goal Compliance Achieved? The regulatory goal of the NIS Directive was a high common security level. However, while the implementation rate of hard measures was 100%, the implementation rate of soft measures was just 60%. When the implementation rates of hard and soft measures are combined and upon comparing EU states with non-EU states overall (Fig. 4), it becomes clear that the EU states in the exposure group did not perform better than the non-EU states in the control group. Figure 4 shows that the EU and non-EU states on average implemented just above 80% of the NIS measures. This result indicates that the desired effect of the NIS Directive, to increase the general cyber security level, was lacking.

Although this study shows the lack of an overall effect of the NIS Directive, there is a positive effect in that the directive led to the prioritization of hard measures. However, the prioritization occurred at the cost of soft measures. The regulatory goal was a high common security level across EU critical infrastructures and services, but the goal was not achieved in the energy sector. Furthermore, important measures such as cyber security audits, risk assessments, exercises and baseline security were included in the NIS Directive in soft form.

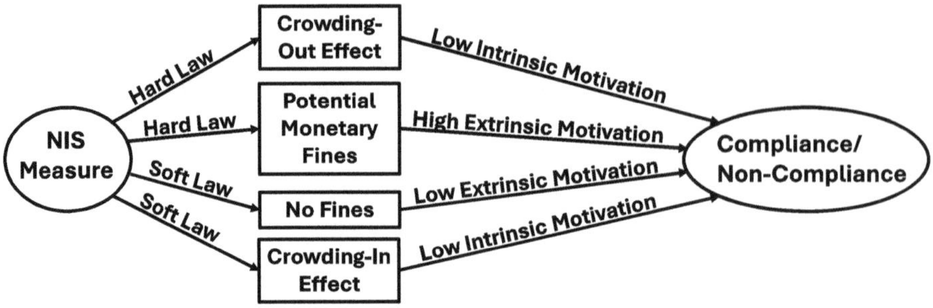

Fig. 6. Main motivational factors.

Because these soft measures were prioritized downward as hard measures were prioritized upward, the result was non-compliance with the regulatory goal.

SQ 1.c: Why Was Compliance Achieved or Not Achieved? Regulatory compliance appears to have been achieved due to threats of (mostly monetary) penalties if the hard measures were not implemented by 2018. Since the threats were confined to hard measures, there was little if any risk of reactions related to soft measures.

Non-compliance with the regulatory goal in the form of low implementation rates for soft measures is apparent. The low implementation rates for soft measures appear to have occurred because they were crowded out by the hard measures. This observation is supported by Frey's motivation crowding theory that states if external intervention is perceived to be controlling by reducing the extent to which affected entities can determine their own actions, then the external intervention crowds out intrinsic motivation [10]. This means that detailed hard measures would crowd out intrinsic motivation.

Figure 6 shows the main motivational factors that appear to have impacted the compliance results. The figure also shows that the only heavy impact on motivation was the external motivation to implement hard measures due to potential monetary fines. The lack of potential fines for soft measures and hard measures crowding out the motivation for implementing soft measures led to low internal motivation to implement the soft measures.

According to Frey, soft measures have less negative impact on intrinsic motivation than hard measures because they are perceived as less controlling. Soft measures may even increase intrinsic motivation if they are seen as being supportive. However, the positive effects of soft measures were inadequate to compete with the negative extrinsic motivation stemming from the hard measures in the NIS Directive.

The assumption that the hard measures crowded out the motivation to implement soft measures is also supported by the results of non-EU states in the control group. The control group results show that, without the NIS Directive, EU states would probably have had more common levels of cyber security, albeit not higher levels (see Fig. 4).

Figure 5, which shows the implementation levels of non-NIS measures, also supports this assumption. The figure shows that the implementations of non-NIS measures for EU and non-EU states were around the same levels from 2021 to 2023. The figure also shows the absence of the NIS Directive effect around 2018, which is seen for the hard and soft measures in Figs. 2 and 3. The lack of a spike around 2018 means that these non-NIS measures were not affected by the NIS Directive. This validates the assumption that the overall cyber security level with or without the NIS Directive would have been the same.

6.2 Main Research Question

Hard measures in the NIS Directive were implemented at the cost of soft measures in the same directive. The reason was likely due to the hard measures crowding out the soft measures. The hard measures included strategy, national competent authority, single point of contact, CERT/CSIRT functions and incident reporting. These are typically viewed as strategic cyber security measures [11]. The soft measures included status reports, certifications, awareness, risk assessments, audits, exercises and baseline security, which are typically seen as tactical cyber security measures. This means that, of the three organizational levels, strategic, tactical and operational, the NIS Directive only covered the two highest levels corresponding to management.

It is challenging to specify which measures at the strategic and tactical levels are the most important. Therefore, it is difficult to say whether the prioritization of strategic measures over tactical measures, which was the result of the NIS Directive, was a good thing or a bad thing. However, cyber security implementation at the operational level is important – these relate to daily cyber security activities such as network monitoring, firewall configuration and access management. The tactical level is also closer to the operational level than the strategic level, and is therefore especially important. On the other hand, EU law pertains to states, which is why the focus was more on the strategic level.

6.3 Results in Light of Previous Work

Toftegaard [16] discerned a positive effect imparted by the ISO/IEC 27001 Certification hard measure for small grid operators and an indication of a negative effect from the same hard measure for large grid operators. These results fit well with the assumption that hard measures crowd out motivation. The reason is that large entities may be expected to have highly motivated security staff whose motivation may suffer. Small entities, however, may have limited or no security staff and, therefore, motivation does not play the same role.

This study advances previous work [16] because it has discerned positive effects due to hard measures compared with soft measures. This means that the focus on implementing security measures was due to compliance instead of achieving holistic cyber security. This assumption also fits well with the observations of Storm et al. [15] who found that legislation not followed up by some sort of control is less likely to be implemented by entities subject to the legislation.

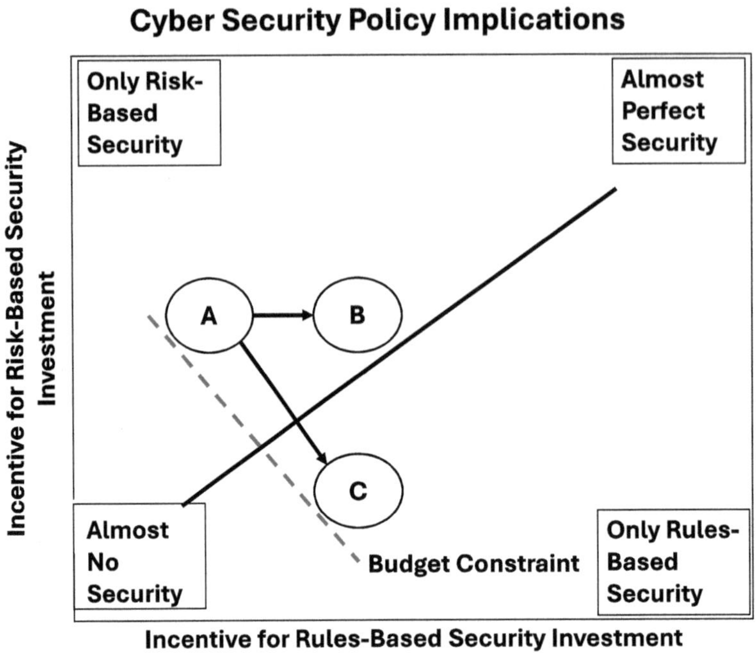

Fig. 7. Implications of adding more hard measures (based on [12]).

Therefore, the result of the NIS Directive was a high focus on hard measures at the cost of soft measures instead of achieving a high common security level.

Motivational factors may not be the only reason why hard measures were implemented at the cost of soft measures. The Centre for European Policy Studies [1] reported in 2021 that the implementation of the NIS Directive posed a risk of limited consistency and underachievement when it came to harmonization of cyber security maturity. The reasons for the shortcomings were the lack of financial resources, staff and knowledge. Because staff and knowledge also require financial resources, it is natural to look closer at budget constraints.

Massacci et al. [12] looked closer at the economic impacts of rules-based versus risk-based cyber security regulations. They observed that budget constraints could limit the effects of governmental authorities adding more security rules due to a corresponding reduction in risk-based security investments. Figure 7 illustrates the implication. A governmental authority desires to move operators from area A to area B. However, due to budget constraints, the operators are only able to move along the dashed line and end up in area C. The addition of more rules does not achieve a higher security level, but shifts from a risk-based security regime to a rules-based security regime.

The mechanism illustrated in Fig. 7 has similarities to what was observed in this study, where hard measures were implemented at the cost of soft measures. Considering the discussion in this section, hard measures may not only crowd out the motivation to implement non-compulsory security measures. Adding hard measures may also take away financial resources that would otherwise have been used to focus on non-compulsory security measures identified as important by operator personnel. Therefore, introducing hard measures is a double-edged sword. On one hand, it may be helpful to force operators with almost no security to achieve a certain security threshold. On the other hand, it may stall or even reduce the security of highly mature operators with motivated security staff.

6.4 Policy Recommendations

This study has found that hard measures negatively impact the implementation of soft measures. The negative impact could have been avoided if the NIS Directive had not mixed hard and soft measures, but instead provided either hard measures or soft measures. Because hard measures are prioritized at the cost of soft measures, the required measures should have either soft or hard substance. It is vital that all critical measures have hard substance if a legal instrument includes both hard and soft measures. Hard measures may also be treated as soft if the requirements are unclear because this would make it difficult to penalize non-compliance. Therefore, clarity when describing measures is also important.

This does not mean that policy makers should never specify soft measures. Soft measures may be used when regulatory goals could be achieved without 100% compliance. They could also be used when implementation rates just above 50% are adequate. However, if the regulatory goal is full compliance by all the entities, then the measures must be hard in substance.

7 Validity Threats

Internal validity refers to the extent to which the observed results represent the truth in a studied population and are free from methodological errors [14] This study employed a questionnaire where each respondent self-reported the implementation of hard and soft measures. A potential source of error is that some respondents may not have had complete insights about the status of the topics covered by the questions. Another source of error is that reporting inadequate implementations of hard measures could have led to penalties for non-compliance. This may be the reason why an implementation rate of 100% was reported for the hard measures.

Additionally, respondents who were uncertain about the implementation of hard measures were permitted to enter not applicable or provide no answers. Since ITU data used to compute the Global Cybersecurity Index was employed to validate respondent data, the risk of an internal validity compromise is expected to be minimal.

Of course, legislation aside from the NIS Directive could have impacted the results. A spike was seen in the 2018 data with regard to states reporting that cyber security certification was required. It is difficult to tell if the spike was due to the NIS Directive or the Cybersecurity Act [8] that focused on cyber security certification. However, since the certification requirement was soft in both frameworks, the effects of the soft measure could be viewed as being the same. Thus, the concern can be disregarded.

External validity pertains to the extent to which the study results may be generalized [14]. This study was based on a few observed states. The exposure group ranged from 11 to 21 EU states per observation. The control group had few observations – only three to four non-EU states per observation. The limited number of observations coupled with the variations in the answers provided by the states during the observation period are expected to have negative impacts on the external validity of this study.

Another consideration is whether or not the results can be compared at the corporate level and outside the energy sector. Since the NIS Directive measures were targeted at governmental authorities, it is uncertain if the results are also representative of corporate entities. However, the results should be representative of other sectors because the NIS Directive applies to multiple critical infrastructure sectors. In any case, because the results conform to Frey's motivation crowding theory, which is not restricted to cyber security, the results of this study should be transferable to other domains.

8 Conclusions

This study has assessed how the hard and soft measures stipulated in the NIS Directive have impacted cyber security maturity in EU and European states. The results demonstrate that hard measures increased cyber security maturity more than soft measures. This supports the rejection of the null hypothesis – *Whether a measure is hard or soft does not impact cyber security maturity.*

This study has also answered three sub-questions that support the analysis – *Was regulatory compliance achieved? Was regulatory goal compliance achieved? Why was compliance achieved or not achieved?* This study argues that legal compliance was achieved, but not the goal of regulatory compliance. Legal compliance was achieved because 100% of the hard measures were implemented. However, because hard measures were implemented at the cost of soft measures, the regulatory goal of establishing a high common security level across the EU critical infrastructures was not achieved.

Frey's motivation theory was employed to analyze why regulatory compliance was achieved, but not regulatory goal compliance. According to the analysis, non-compliance penalties (typically monetary fines) were the principal driver for implementing hard measures. However, the stipulation of hard measures reduced the motivation to implement soft measures due to the focus on hard measures and the low risk of penalties for soft measure non-compliance.

This study has shown that the impact of the NIS Directive on the EU energy sector was requirement-specific and compliance-oriented rather than holistic and security-oriented. Consequently, the NIS Directive impact did not result in a high common security level, but it contributed to the prioritization of strategic measures. Hard measures residing at the strategic level were prioritized upward whereas soft measures at the tactical level were prioritized downward. This means that governmental authorities that plan to incorporate hard and soft measures in legislation must be sure that their prioritizations are correct.

The study conclusions are based on limited data, especially pertaining to the control group comprising three to four non-EU states. Although the Global Cybersecurity Index data was employed to validate the results, research should be conducted using a larger volume of data to confirm the findings. The study has examined the effects of hard measures and soft measures for states at only the strategic and tactical levels. Future research should evaluate the effects of hard measures and soft measures at the enterprise level, including the operational organizational level. Future case studies should also attempt to clarify why hard measures tend to crowd out soft measures.

Acknowledgements. This research was supported by the Norwegian Energy Regulatory Authority and the Norwegian Water Resources and Energy Directorate. The author thanks the Council of European Energy Regulators (CEER) Cybersecurity Workstream for providing access to cyber security benchmark data. The author also thanks members of the Ostrom Cybersecurity and Internet Governance Program at Indiana University, Janne Hagen from the Norwegian Water Resources and Energy Directorate and members of the Critical Infrastructure Security and Resilience Research Group at the Norwegian University of Science and Technology for providing valuable comments.

References

1. Centre for European Policy Studies, Study to Support the Review of Directive (EU) 2016/1148 Concerning Measures for a High Common Level of Security of Network and Information Systems Across the Union (NIS Directive) – No. 2020-665: Final Study Report, Brussels, Belgium (cdn.ceps.eu/wp-content/uploads/2022/07/KK0921034ENN.en_compressed.pdf) (2021)
2. Council of European Energy Regulators, Cybersecurity Benchmark, Document Reference: C19-CS-56-03, Brussels, Belgium (2019). www.ceer.eu/publication/cybersecurity-benchmark
3. DiMeo Grant, P., Ballard, D.: Law for Nurse Leaders: A Comprehensive Reference. Springer, New York (2018)
4. Etienne, J.: Compliance theories: a literature review. Revue Francaise de Science Politique **60**(3), 493–517 (2010)
5. Commission, E.: Communication from the Commission to the Council, the European Parliament, the European Economic and Social Committee and the Committee of the Regions - Network and Information Security: Proposal for a European Policy Approach, Document 52001DC0298001. Belgium, Brussels (2001)
6. Union, E.: Consolidated Version of the Treaty on the Functioning of the European Union, Document 12012E/TXT. Belgium, Brussels (2012)
7. Union, E.: Directive (EU) 2016/1148 of the European Parliament and of the Council of 6 July 2016 Concerning Measures for a High Common Level of Security of Network and Information Systems Across the Union, Document 32016L1148. Belgium, Brussels (2016)

8. Union, E.: Regulation (EU) 2019/881 of the European Parliament and of the Council of 17 April 2019 on ENISA (the European Union Agency for Cybersecurity) and on Information and Communications Technology Cybersecurity Certification and Repealing Regulation (EU) No 526/2013 (Cybersecurity Act) (Text with EEA Relevance), Document 32019R0881. Belgium, Brussels (2019)
9. Union, E.: Directive (EU) 2022/2555 of the European Parliament and of the Council of 14 December 2022 on Measures for a High Common Level of Cybersecurity Across the Union, Amending Regulation (EU) No 910/2014 and Directive (EU) 2018/1972, and Repealing Directive (EU) 2016/1148 (NIS 2 Directive) (Text with EEA Relevance), Document 32022L2555. Belgium, Brussels (2022)
10. Frey, B.: Not Just for the Money: An Economic Theory of Personal Motivation. Edward Elgar, Cheltenham, United Kingdom (1997)
11. Hagen, J., Toftegaard, Ø.: Cyber security requirements in the Norwegian energy sector. In: Staggs, J., Shenoi, S. (eds.) Critical Infrastructure Protection XV, pp. 3–21. Springer, Cham (2022)
12. Massacci, F., Ruprai, R., Collinson, M., Williams, J.: Economic impacts of rules-versus risk-based cybersecurity regulations for critical infrastructure providers. IEEE Secur. Priv. **14**(3), 52–60 (2016)
13. Pronto, A.: Understanding the hard/soft distinction in international law. Vanderbilt J. Transnat. Law **48**(4), 941–956 (2015)
14. Runeson, P., Host, M.: Guidelines for conducting and reporting case study research in software engineering. Empir. Softw. Eng. **14**, 131–164 (2009)
15. Storm, J., Hagen, J., Selnes, S.: The effect of regulation and audits on implementation of cybersecurity controls in Norwegian grid companies. In: Proceedings of the Thirty-Second European Safety and Reliability Conference, pp. 320–326 (2022)
16. Toftegaard, Ø.: An effect analysis of ISO/IEC 27001 Certification on technical security of Norwegian grid operators. In: Proceedings of the IEEE International Conference on Big Data, pp. 2620–2629 (2022)

Industrial Control System Security

Penetration Testing of Newly-Deployed Industrial Control Systems

Shaymaa Mamdouh Khalil[1(✉)], Hayretdin Bahsi[1,2], and Tarmo Korotko[1]

[1] Tallinn University of Technology, Tallinn, Estonia
shaymaa.khalil@taltech.ee

[2] Northern Arizona University, Flagstaff, AZ, USA

Abstract. Penetration testing is a security practice that proactively discovers and assesses the potential exploitation of system vulnerabilities by simulating real-world attacks. Penetration testing of industrial control systems is a complex, time-consuming and demanding process requiring expertise in information technology and operational technology systems. Effective penetration test planning is crucial to prioritizing activities and optimizing time and resources.

This chapter describes a seven-stage methodology for penetration testing newly-deployed industrial control systems and demonstrates its practical application using a real-world case study of a newly-designed microgrid system. The methodology leverages threat modeling outcomes from the design phase to define the penetration testing scope and guide test choices, leading to an efficient testing process. Furthermore, it engages a novel MITRE ATT&CK to STRIDE mapping, which bridges the design phase that focuses on high-level threats and the planning phase that employs medium-level granularity. The methodology benefits security practitioners by enhancing planning efficiency and streamlining collaboration with third-party penetration testers. The methodology in conjunction with the MITRE ATT&CK to STRIDE mapping can be used to develop detailed, effective and efficient industrial control system penetration testing efforts.

Keywords: Threat Modeling · Industrial Control System · Penetration Testing · MITRE ATT&CK · STRIDE · Microgrid

1 Introduction

Industrial control systems are complex systems of systems that rely on information technology and operational technology. Due to their essential role in critical infrastructure assets, securing industrial control systems from cyber attacks is a priority. Following the Stuxnet incident, the application of secure-by-design principles has become vital to industrial control systems across the global critical infrastructure.

Threat modeling is an analytical process that identifies potential threats to systems and supports the selection of security requirements during the early stages of the system development lifecycle [9]. As expected, threat modeling

Published by Springer Nature Switzerland AG 2026
J. Staggs and S. Shenoi (Eds.): ICCIP 2025, IFIP AICT 763, pp. 25–48, 2026.
https://doi.org/10.1007/978-3-032-11914-8_2

plays a vital role in ensuring the secure-by-design development of industrial control systems. Several threat modeling methods have been proposed to address the complex nature of industrial control systems [8]. However, a gap exists with regard to readily-deployable and well-validated industrial control system threat modeling methods. Validating the outcomes of threat modeling exercises and ensuring that the security requirements have been applied effectively to implemented systems are significant challenges.

The IEC 62443 standard [7] stipulates practices for a secure industrial control system development lifecycle. The practices include the specification of security requirements (using threat modeling), application of secure-by-design concepts (including how the design mitigates the identified threats), and security verification and validation testing. The standard identifies four processes related to security verification and validation testing that should be executed independently of system developers – security requirements testing, threat mitigation testing, vulnerability testing and penetration testing. However, existing guidelines do not provide detailed recommendations on how testing efforts can be harmonized.

Security requirements testing, as outlined in IEC 62443, ensures that system security functions satisfy the security requirements. This involves several testing approaches, including functional testing, performance testing and unexpected input testing, to assess system behavior under various scenarios.

Threat mitigation testing, on the other hand, verifies the effectiveness of deployed threat mitigation techniques. It also validates that the security measures address the threats identified during the threat modeling phase. For example, various authentication tests may be performed to ensure that an implemented authentication mechanism effectively mitigates spoofing threats.

Vulnerability assessments focus on identifying system security weaknesses. Unlike penetration testing, vulnerability assessments do not typically involve the exploitation of vulnerabilities. However, they serve as a foundation for penetration testing activities.

Penetration testing, by contrast, adopts a proactive approach. It simulates real-world cyber attacks by attempting to exploit vulnerabilities in order to assess the overall security postures of systems. It pushes organizations to recognize and proactively address potential security gaps before they are exploited by malicious actors.

In small critical infrastructure deployments such as microgrids, resource and time limitations often require the prioritization of vulnerability assessments and penetration testing. These efforts are vital because they indirectly assess the effectiveness of security controls. Penetration testing efforts focused on industrial control systems pose technical challenges because they demand deep knowledge and practical experience. The challenges are acerbated by the integration of information technology and operational technology that increase attack surface complexity and demand deep expertise and strong experience in both domains.

Systematic penetration testing engages a structured methodology involving predefined procedures and phases such as planning, reconnaissance and exploitation to ensure that the testing is repeatable and consistent. It includes a process for prioritizing testing based on potential impacts, and it requires clear justifications for selecting scenarios, techniques and tools. The approach also emphasizes the thorough documentation of testing procedures, findings and recommendations. This structured methodology enables experienced and less experienced testers to conduct comprehensive assessments and articulate the rationale behind their test selections. A well-regarded exemplar is the Penetration Testing Execution Standard (PTES) [16].

As discussed in the next section, relatively few studies discuss systematic penetration testing of cyber-physical systems. However, they are primarily targeted at Internet-of-Things systems, not industrial control systems. The two types of systems may have similar attack surfaces, but they differ in complexity and requirements. Industrial control systems use proprietary protocols and have safety and availability requirements that render them more complex than Internet-of-Things systems. Additionally, performing industrial control system penetration testing requires considerable domain and tool expertise to avoid negative impacts such as critical service disruption and equipment damage. Furthermore, Internet-of-Things methodologies do not consider the valuable threat modeling insights gained during the design phase of industrial control systems.

A recent study [9] proposed a cyber-physical system threat modeling methodology that is applicable during the early design phase. Since detailed system information was not available, a high-level threat modeling method similar to STRIDE [6] was used. STRIDE covers six fundamental cyber security threats – spoofing, tampering, repudiation, information disclosure, denial of service and elevation of privilege. It attempts to ensure that a designed system has six fundamental security properties – authentication, integrity, non-repudiation, confidentiality, availability and authorization.

STRIDE proved its effectiveness in a recent power grid case study [9]. It provides a common language that is understood by cyber security and technical specialists involved in threat modeling. The choice of a less sophisticated threat modeling method similar to STRIDE during the design phase facilitated brainstorming during the threat modeling activities and the ensuing discussions about threat impacts. However, as the system transitioned to the implementation and testing phases, it became clear that a more detailed model was necessary to effectively plan attack scenarios, sequences and paths.

Despite the importance of connecting early design-phase threat modeling with later-stage testing, practical and systematic penetration testing methods for industrial control systems that leverage threat modeling insights are lacking. To address the gap, this study investigates how the outcomes of industrial control system threat modeling performed during the design phase can support penetration test planning.

This work extends an earlier study [9] by proposing a seven-stage methodology for systematic penetration testing of newly-deployed industrial control systems based on threat modeling conducted during the design phase. The methodology translates threats elicited using a high-level model similar to STRIDE to a medium-level model (i.e., MITRE ATT&CK for Industrial Control Systems (MITRE ATT&CK for ICS) [19]). The mapping facilitates the creation of comprehensive and justifiable testing scenarios that enhance the quality of industrial control system penetration testing. The methodology is validated using a real-world microgrid case study. The case study offers valuable insights into the practical challenges and nuances encountered in real-world deployments, contributing to a better understanding of the practical considerations involved in industrial control system penetration testing.

2 Related Work

Planning industrial control system penetration testing is challenging due to system complexity and the diverse technologies employed. The National Electric Sector Cybersecurity Organization Resource (NESCOR) [18] has developed a guide for conducting penetration tests of electric utility systems. It divides penetration testing tasks into five stages – penetration test scoping, architecture review, target system setup, end-to-end penetration test analysis and result interpretation and reporting.

The NESCOR guide places penetration testing tasks in four categories depending on the skills and time required to perform the tasks. The server operating system penetration task that requires basic testing skills should be performed frequently; the task is typically done by an internal team. The server application penetration task requires moderate testing skills and should be performed frequently. The network communications penetration task requires a high level of expertise and is performed occasionally. The embedded device penetration task requires highly specialized expertise; it is time-consuming and is performed rarely.

Several studies have leveraged threat modeling to plan penetration testing, mostly for Internet-of-Things systems. For example, Salzillo et al. [17] have proposed a systematic Internet-of-Things penetration testing methodology comprising four stages – system modeling, threat modeling, planning and penetration testing. The methodology was applied to penetrate a home automation environment using the MQTT protocol. It employed graph-based multi-cloud application composition modeling to elicit system threats using a threat catalog and common attack pattern enumeration and classification (CAPEC) [10]. Details of attack patterns for potential system threats were constructed, following which an attack plan was created.

PatrIoT is a systematic Internet-of-Things penetration testing methodology [20]. It involves four stages – planning, threat modeling, exploitation and reporting, each with well-documented substages. PatrIoT decomposes an Internet-of-Things environment into seven attack surfaces – hardware, firmware, network, web, cloud, mobile and radio. The methodology compiles the OWASP IoT Top 10 [14] into 100 security weaknesses based on the Common Weakness Enumeration (CWE) [11]. PatrIoT has been applied to several Internet-of-Things devices, including drones, refrigerators and cameras [20].

As noted by Fujimoto et al. [5], industrial control systems and information technology systems share certain similarities with regard to penetration testing, such as the use of common operating systems (e.g., Windows and Linux) and web applications. However, industrial control system penetration testing requires additional domain-specific knowledge due to specialized protocols and standards that are not encountered in information technology environments. Moreover, while information technology penetration testing primarily focuses on cyber aspects, industrial control system penetration testing must also consider the physical impacts of cyber attacks.

The testing objectives also differ. Information technology system penetration testing emphasizes confidentiality breaches whereas industrial control system penetration testing prioritizes data integrity and process availability. These priorities should be reflected in the design of industrial control system penetration testing scenarios. Fujimoto and colleagues also present an industrial control system penetration testing workflow and list tools for executing attacks.

Defining the scope of penetration testing and planning the tests with guidance from threat modeling can support testing priorities. Although a few studies address systematic penetration testing of cyber-physical systems, they often ignore threat modeling performed during the design phase when planning penetration tests. Incorporating the early-stage outputs into the later stages is essential to increase the effectiveness and efficiency of secure development lifecycle efforts. Additionally, there is a notable lack of real-world case studies that document systematic penetration testing efforts for industrial control systems.

3 Proposed Methodology

The proposed methodology for penetration testing newly-deployed industrial control systems is a systematic and structured approach involving seven sequential stages: (i) threat modeling, (ii) data flow diagram updating, (iii) penetration test scoping, (iv) penetration test planning, (v) penetration testing, (vi) vulnerability ranking and (vii) reporting.

Stage 1: Threat Modeling. The first stage involves threat modeling conducted during the industrial control system design phase. Khalil et al. [9] have presented a nine-stage cyber-physical system threat modeling methodology, along with a detailed case study that covers industrial control system threat modeling. The threat modeling results of Khalil and colleagues are incorporated in the scoping and penetration test planning stages of this research to facilitate targeted and effective penetration testing that contributed to a secure industrial control environment.

Stage 2: Data Flow Diagram Updating. The second stage involving data flow diagram updating begins after the industrial control system has been implemented. During the stage, the cyber security team collaborates with relevant stakeholders to revise data flow diagrams and assess implementation decisions that may have affected the initial documentation and threat list. The stage also provides an opportunity to determine whether penetration testing should be conducted internally by the cyber security team or outsourced to a third party. Ideally, this decision should be made during the system implementation phase to allow adequate time for the stakeholders to engage and coordinate with external testers, if needed.

Stage 3: Penetration Test Scoping. The third stage involves defining the penetration testing scope in collaboration with the stakeholders. This includes identifying the targeted attack vectors such as remote access, Internet-facing applications and potential lateral movement paths. The type of penetration testing – white box, gray box or black box testing – should also be determined.

The principal candidates are white box and gray box testing. White box penetration testing, in which testers are granted access to system diagrams, configurations and code, is recommended. It is less time-consuming when an internal team does the testing, especially if the team was involved in the earlier threat modeling stage. Gray box testing is more appropriate when engaging third-party testers. In this case, testers receive limited information such as high-level design and critical information flows. It enables testers to focus on the key attack vectors without requiring full system disclosure. While white box testing provides comprehensive insights, the involvement of external testers raises issues such as security concerns, time required to gain familiarity with the systems and higher costs for extended engagements.

During the scoping stage, the stakeholders may also determine the complexity of the penetration testing tasks [18]. The decisions are often based on the system components and attack surfaces. This work adopts the categorization proposed by Searle et al. [18], which identifies four attack surfaces for electrical utilities and specifies the following four penetration testing tasks:

- **Server Operating System Penetration:** This task involves vulnerability assessments of Windows and Linux systems, especially identifying exploitable vulnerabilities that may provide system access. As noted by Searle et al. [18], the task typically involves information gathering, vulnerability analysis and vulnerability exploitation. Penetration testers are quite familiar with the task and several tools such as Metasploit are available to facilitate task execution.
- **Server Application Penetration:** This task involves testing server applications and identifying vulnerabilities via application mapping, application discovery and application exploitation [18]. The task is more complex and time-consuming than server operating system penetration.
- **Network Communications Penetration:** This task involves exploiting vulnerabilities in network protocols and communications media. The task is complex because it requires substantial expertise in network protocols and wireless attack tools given the reliance of industrial control systems on diverse wireless communications technologies, including Wi-Fi, cellular and Global Position System (GPS). Protocols such as Zigbee, IEEE 802.15.4, Modbus

and DNP3 are also widely used in industrial control systems and attacks on them require expertise related to their protocol datagrams and functionality.
- **Embedded Device Penetration:** This task is the most challenging and time-consuming of the four penetration testing tasks. It involves penetration tests of embedded and microprocessor-based devices, including firmware, input interfaces (serial and parallel), and storage media such as RAM, EEPROM and flash memory [18].

Decisions pertaining to penetration testing tasks involved in the scoping stage, establish expectations regarding the testing timeframe, required expertise, budget and expected outcomes. Omitting any of the four tasks means accepting the potential risks of undiscovered vulnerabilities in the associated areas. Any decision would, of course, require stakeholder approval.

Another key decision during the scoping stage pertains to the threats included in the testing plan. Industrial control system threats are documented during the threat modeling stage and data flow diagrams are updated during the subsequent stage. However, the final list of elicited threats can be extensive and vary in their severity. Therefore, selecting a prioritized subset of threats based on established criteria (e.g., criticality and impact) is essential to articulating a focused and efficient penetration testing effort. The selection process enables penetration testers to focus on the most significant threats while optimizing the testing process and maximizing its effectiveness.

Stage 4: Penetration Test Planning. The fourth stage involves penetration test planning based on the identified scope. Penetration testers typically rely on available guides and supporting frameworks. However, some guides, such as the NESCOR guide [18], provide high-level information without detailed procedures. STRIDE threat trees [6] also provide high-level guidance and incorporate testing criteria, but the threat trees primarily focus on software security. Detailed guides are also available an example is the OWASP testing guide [15] that provides web, mobile application and firmware security testing details.

In practice, penetration testers often do not execute test planning in a structured or well-documented manner. One of the main contributions of this study is the demonstration of how an industrial control system testing plan can be guided by STRIDE threats categorized according to the MITRE ATT&CK for ICS framework [1]. Depending on the timeframe and agreements, penetration testers may also prepare a document outlining the testing plan, including the testing scenarios and their procedures. However, when penetration testing is performed by a third party, the outcome of the stage may be limited to a high-level plan outlining the types of attacks to be tested.

Stage 5: Penetration Testing. During the fifth stage, penetration testing, the tester performs the planned tests to identify vulnerabilities in the industrial control system environment and documents the findings. Based on the findings, the testing plan may be updated to address newly-discovered attack vectors.

Stage 6: Vulnerability Ranking. The sixth stage involves the analysis and prioritization of the discovered vulnerabilities based on their potential impacts. This ranking may be conducted using the Common Vulnerability Scoring System (CVSS) [3] or a custom method that considers the specific impacts to the industrial control system environment. This prioritization ensures that mitigation efforts are focused on the most critical and highly-ranked vulnerabilities.

Stage 7: Reporting. The final seventh state involves the documentation of all the findings in a comprehensive report for the stakeholders. This report typically includes detailed descriptions of identified vulnerabilities, recommended remediation actions and risks associated with the discovered vulnerabilities. The three stages – penetration testing, vulnerability ranking and reporting – can be executed sequentially or in parallel depending on project complexity and resource availability.

4 Microgrid Case Study

This section describes a penetration testing case study involving an operational microgrid. The penetration testing process was a collaborative effort involving four stakeholder groups: (i) a cyber security team that included the first and second authors of this chapter, (ii) an electric power systems expert (third author) who represented the power engineering team and the asset owner, (iii) a software architect and (iv) a third-party penetration tester.

The penetration testing was conducted over a period of eight months, from February 2023 to September 2023. During this period, the stakeholders participated in 13 technical meetings, during which the details of each stage were discussed. The meetings focused on technical aspects and did not include managerial discussions related to the selection of the testing entity and contractual agreements.

The first stage involving threat modeling during the design phase is discussed in detail in previous work [9]. Therefore, this case study starts with data flow diagram updating, the second stage of the methodology.

4.1 Data Flow Diagram Updating

During this stage, the cyber security team collaborated with the software architect and electric power systems expert to discuss the design changes implemented since the initial data flow diagram creation. The updates, conducted late in the implementation phase, sought to track the changes made during the implementation that affected the cyber security documents and data flow diagrams. This ensured that the data flow diagrams accurately reflected the system state before initiating efforts in the subsequent penetration test scoping and planning stages.

Based on the resource and time constraints, the stakeholders prioritized penetration testing using the IEC 62443 security verification and validation testing processes. This meant that security requirements and threat mitigation tests were excluded from the project. Negotiations to determine whether the penetration testing would be conducted internally by the cyber security team or outsourced to a third party were concluded during system implementation.

The stakeholders chose to involve a third-party penetration tester to provide a fresh perspective regarding the system security posture. Additionally, an individual with specialized penetration testing skills and experience could be effective given the limited timeframe assigned to testing. This solution would ensure better resource management, especially considering the limited number of internal cyber security experts involved in the effort.

Negotiations with third-party penetration testers proceeded in parallel with data flow diagram updating. The final agreement was reached with a professional freelance penetration tester with experience primarily in information technology system penetration testing and an operational technology background. Once the agreements and data flow diagram updates were finalized, the penetration tester was provided with the updated data flow diagrams, data flows and prioritized threat list. Providing the threat modeling results at the beginning of the effort contributed to the tester's understanding of system threats and their potential impacts. Follow-up meetings were scheduled to discuss the provided documents in detail and address questions raised by the tester. The data flow diagram updating stage ensured that all relevant documents were updated and that the tester fully grasped the data flow diagrams and system threats.

4.2 Penetration Test Scoping

Stakeholder meetings were scheduled to discuss the penetration testing scope. The meetings, which included the penetration tester, focused on potential attack surfaces (e.g., Internet-facing web applications), attack vectors (e.g., unpatched vulnerabilities and weak credentials), attack agents (e.g., cyber criminal groups) and attack scenarios. The efforts prioritized penetration testing of the operating system, server applications and network communications. Embedded devices penetration testing and physical attacks were excluded from the testing scope.

It was determined that gray box testing would be conducted. Data flow diagrams, network diagrams and threat lists were provided to the tester, and questions posed by the tester were addressed. However, source code was not provided to the tester. Discussions also centered on the testing location, ultimately deciding on remote testing and excluding physical on-site testing. Social engineering attacks (e.g., phishing) were excluded because they rely on user interaction that was outside the scope of the project because the microgrid system was not yet operational.

The scoping discussions also focused on critical threats. The specific data flow diagram elements that would be within scope were negotiated and their threat consequences were discussed. Attack scenarios based on the threats were articulated along with considerations about how the attacks might be reflected on the system side and how the penetration tester would ensure that the attacks were successful. Critical threats guiding the testing plan were emphasized while providing the tester with the flexibility to explore threats outside the provided threat list. Additional discussions covered the testing timeframes, critical vulnerability reporting procedures and the protocol for handling denial-of-service attacks.

The stakeholders then discussed how the tester would gain initial access to the system and all the relevant attack vectors were considered. The tester's access (e.g., virtual private network and virtual machine) and permissions (e.g., regular user and admin) were determined. To enable the tester to observe the impacts of attacks on system alerts, regular user access was required as well as admin access to certain tools.

The discussions also addressed the depth of testing, considering whether to focus solely on initial device access or also include lateral movements. It was decided to provide the tester with limited access accounts that would allow initial access to some devices. This approach would enable the tester to assess the possibility of lateral movements within the system.

In summary, the penetration test scoping stage defined the testing type, boundaries (i.e., out-of-scope activities), critical attacks to be executed and their consequences, rules of engagement, emergency contacts and expectations about the penetration testing timeframe.

4.3 Penetration Test Planning

The cyber security team was keen on structuring the penetration test planning effort based on an attack database that complemented the penetration tester's knowledge. However, the selection of a suitable attack database was a major challenge. During the design phase, the microgrid attack taxonomy proposed in previous work [2] was updated. The high-level taxonomy proved valuable for threat elicitation in the threat modeling case study [9]. However, it lacked details about attack execution that are crucial to penetration test planning. For this reason, the use of STRIDE threat trees [6] as the attack database were investigated. The trees were discussed during two meetings with the tester. While the trees provided a structured approach, their software-centric orientation overlooked several industrial control system attack scenarios. This limitation would have resulted in an incomplete and potentially ineffective penetration testing plan. Consequently, the STRIDE trees were excluded from the attack database.

STRIDE is a high-level threat analysis model [19] that is suited to threat elicitation during the design stage, when detailed system specifications (e.g., vendors, operating systems and protocols) are unavailable. However, this information is available after system implementation and during penetration test planning. Recognizing the limitations of the high-level microgrid attack taxonomy used in the threat modeling case study [9] and STRIDE threat trees, alternative approaches were explored to create a lower level model with rich attack execution details.

Because the tests were to be performed by a third party, the cyber security team decided to formulate the testing plan without imposing specific scenarios and tools as these are typically the responsibility of the tester. For this reason, it was decided to use MITRE ATT&CK for ICS [19], a mid-level modeling framework that provides details about attack techniques. However, MITRE

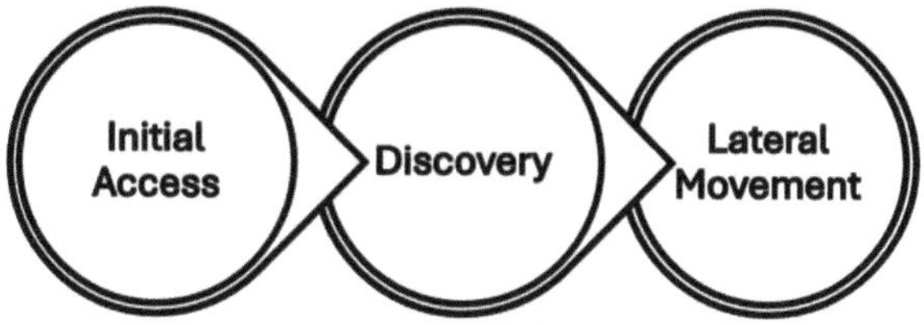

Fig. 1. Attack precondition stages

ATT&CK for ICS is not designed specifically for penetration testing and lacks detailed information about test execution. While it identifies attack techniques, the penetration tester would have to identify the appropriate tools to conduct the various exploits.

Since the threat elicitation leveraged STRIDE, mapping the identified threats to MITRE ATT&CK for ICS tactics and techniques became crucial. At that stage, it was decided to have focused meetings between the cyber security team and the penetration tester during which MITRE ATT&CK for ICS would be investigated in detail and mapped to the STRIDE threats. These efforts guided the penetration tester in planning the tests in a structured manner.

MITRE ATT&CK for ICS was mapped using MITRE ATT&CK Navigator [13] by going through each technique description and adding a comment about the technique categorization (spoofing, tampering, repudiation, information disclosure, denial of service or elevation of privileges). Some techniques were assigned to more than one STRIDE category (e.g., the adversary-in-the-middle technique was classified as a technique that could be used in spoofing, tampering, information disclosure and denial of service).

The cyber security team and the penetration tester discussed the proposed categorization and agreed on the techniques to be included in the test scope. For each technique, a decision was made to include or exclude it from the penetration tests. Some techniques were determined to require more time and effort than others and required certain preconditions to be met in order to be successful. For example, operational technology attack tests require initial access to the operational technology network without which the penetration tester would be unable to apply the appropriate techniques. Such tests were marked for potential inclusion in the penetration testing plan if the time constraints and other required preconditions were met. Attack preconditions techniques were also added to the categorization.

The following subsections present the STRIDE categorization of MITRE ATT&CK for ICS techniques and their preconditions.

Attack Preconditions. As discussed in the threat modeling case study [9], except for certain types of denial-of-service attacks, the attacker has to first gain access to a system to cause harm; this is considered to be an attack precondition. Figure 1 shows the three attack precondition stages – initial access, discovery and

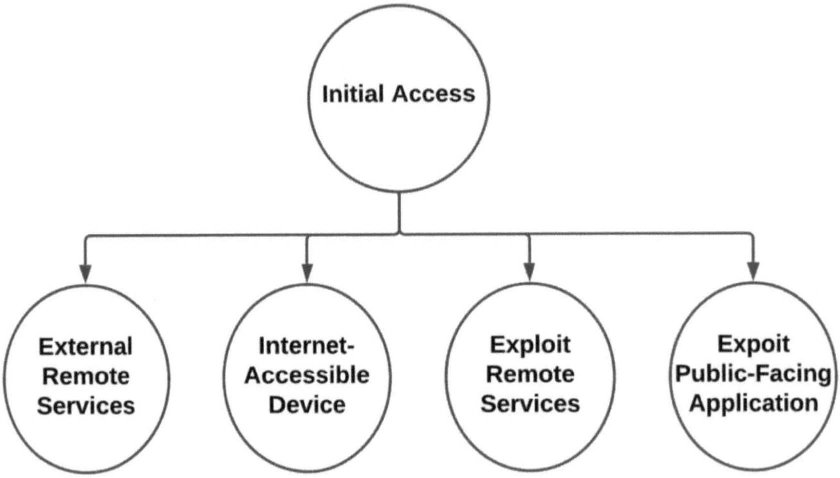

Fig. 2. MITRE ATT&CK for ICS initial access techniques in the testing plan.

lateral movement. These stages are also defined as tactics in MITRE ATT&CK for ICS.

In a possible attack scenario, initial access to the system would be gained using an initial access technique such as exploiting a public-facing application over the Internet. Next, system discovery would be performed using network sniffing. Following this, a lateral movement would be executed by leveraging default credentials or sniffed valid accounts.

Aside from the STRIDE categorization of MITRE ATT&CK for ICS, three trees were created for the possible precondition techniques that could be used by the tester to gain system access. The three trees, corresponding to initial access, discovery and lateral movement, included selected techniques from MITRE ATT&CK for ICS. Only the techniques selected for the penetration testing are described here. The complete lists of techniques for the three chosen tactics are provided in the MITRE ATT&CK for ICS matrix [12].

It was decided that the penetration tester would gain initial access by simulating an attack on the system over the Internet. Figure 2 shows the relevant techniques related to the MITRE ATT&CK for ICS initial access tactic that were selected. The external remote services technique targets services such as virtual private networks potentially using valid accounts. The Internet-accessible device technique seeks to gain access to Internet-exposed devices, intentionally or intentionally, such as cellular modems without using exploits. The remaining two techniques, exploit remote services and exploit public-facing application, leverage software vulnerabilities to gain unauthorized access to the system.

The external remote services technique was eliminated from the tree because it targets internal services typically used by operators for remote management, which renders it more relevant to lateral movement in the context of this study. Additionally, the MITRE ATT&CK for ICS initial access techniques that require physical presence (e.g., rogue master), user interaction (e.g., spearphish-

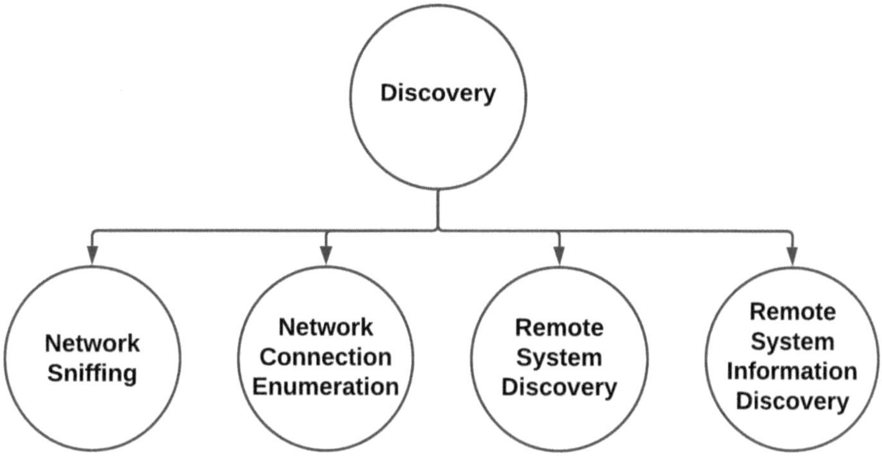

Fig. 3. MITRE ATT&CK for ICS discovery techniques in the testing plan.

ing attachment, drive-by compromise) and outside the testing scope (e.g., supply chain compromise) were also excluded from the tree.

If the tester were to gain remote access to the system from the Internet, network discovery should then be used to identify additional vulnerabilities that could be exploited for lateral movement. However, if all the initial access attacks were to be unsuccessful, the tester could use the provided limited access account to establish initial access and proceed with network discovery.

Figure 3 shows the relevant techniques selected from the MITRE ATT&CK for ICS discovery tactic. Network sniffing is a fundamental technique for collecting information about the system. Network connection enumeration may be used by the penetration tester to inspect the state of network connections and collect information about device roles. The technique might also be used to collect information about the subnets and internal domains. The remote system discovery and the remote system information discovery techniques may be employed to discover the remote services and collect detailed information about them (e.g., configurations).

Following the discovery stage, the tester might attempt to pivot between devices on the same network using lateral movement techniques. It was also agreed that the testing scope should encompass lateral movement attempts across distinct network segments. Figure 4 shows the four lateral movement techniques selected in the testing plan along with two additional techniques (light gray) identified as potential options for further testing.

Information gathered during the discovery of devices and operating systems can help identify default passwords, enabling the tester to employ the default credentials technique for lateral movement. Similarly, the enumerated user or service accounts during discovery can be leveraged in the valid accounts technique. The exploit remote services technique, previously used for initial access,

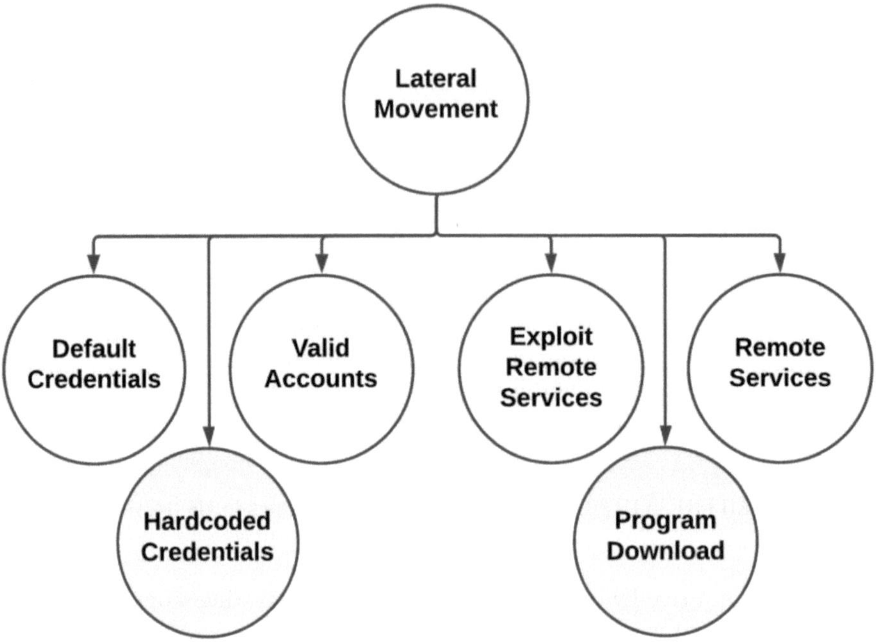

Fig. 4. MITRE ATT&CK for ICS lateral movement techniques in the testing plan.

is applicable for lateral movement within the system. Additionally, the remote services technique may be used to navigate the network laterally.

The hardcoded credentials technique was marked as a potential test depending on the available timeframe (light gray). Exploiting the credentials might involve leveraging vulnerabilities to reveal them, which would require advanced expertise. The program download technique was identified as a potential test due to its relevance in industrial control system environments (light gray). The technique has the precondition of initial access to the operational technology network.

STRIDE Tests. To facilitate the alignment between the threats identified during the threat modeling phase and the penetration testing plan, the various MITRE ATT&CK for ICS techniques were mapped to STRIDE categories. This enabled the prioritization and the evaluation of the relevance of each categorized technique in the testing plan. However, this introduced a challenge because not all the techniques could be mapped directly to STRIDE. For example, some techniques under the execution tactic, such as those involving command-line and graphical user interfaces, describe how an unauthorized actor (penetration tester in this case study) would interact with the system. While these techniques may serve as supporting attributes in the STRIDE categories, they do not align directly with the core STRIDE threat types.

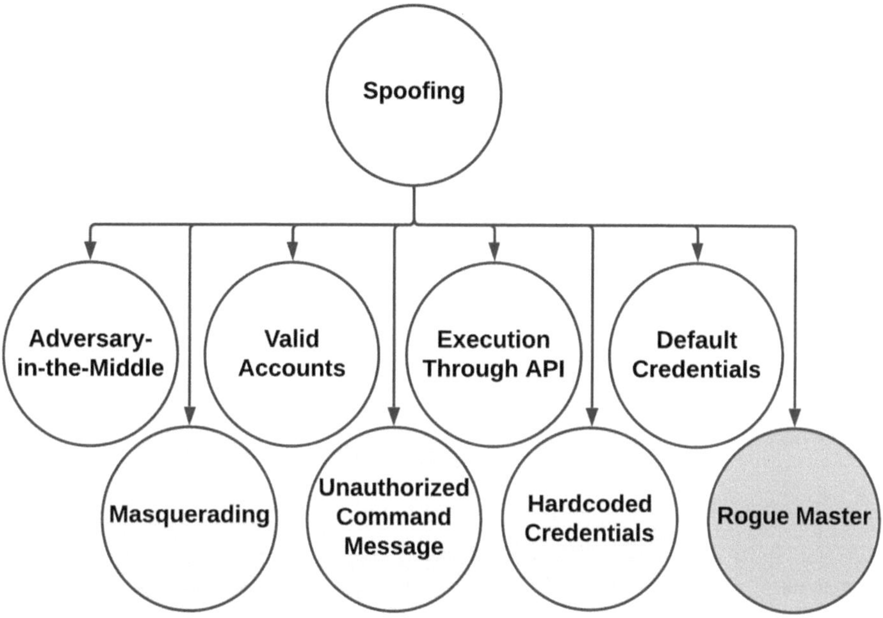

Fig. 5. Categorization of spoofing techniques.

The figures in this section present the STRIDE categorizations of the selected MITRE ATT&CK for ICS techniques. The figures are color coded to differentiate between techniques included in and excluded from the testing plan. Techniques selected for testing are unmarked whereas those outside the scope of the case study scope are marked in dark gray. Techniques with light gray markings are potentially included in the testing (i.e., optional) if the associated preconditions are met. These preconditions might involve factors such as additional testing time or achieving specific initial access to a device in the network.

Note that some techniques were repeated in the STRIDE categorizations. For example, the rogue master technique was categorized as spoofing and tampering, depending on how it would be used. Also, the adversary-in-the-middle technique plays a key role in testing various attack vectors. Therefore, it was incorporated in the spoofing, tampering, information disclosure and denial-of-service categorizations of the MITRE ATT&CK for ICS techniques.

Figure 5 shows the eight techniques categorized as spoofing techniques. The spoofing testing plan included four core techniques and three potential techniques. Successful use of the adversary-in-the-middle technique could also serve as a proof of concept for successful masquerading. Therefore, masquerading was marked as a potential test to be performed if time permitted. Prioritizing the testing of the in-house control software led to the prioritization of relevant techniques similar to valid accounts and execution through the application programming interface (API). The unauthorized command message technique was marked for potential testing because it requires initial access to the operational technology network that would not be provided to the tester. Finally, the rogue

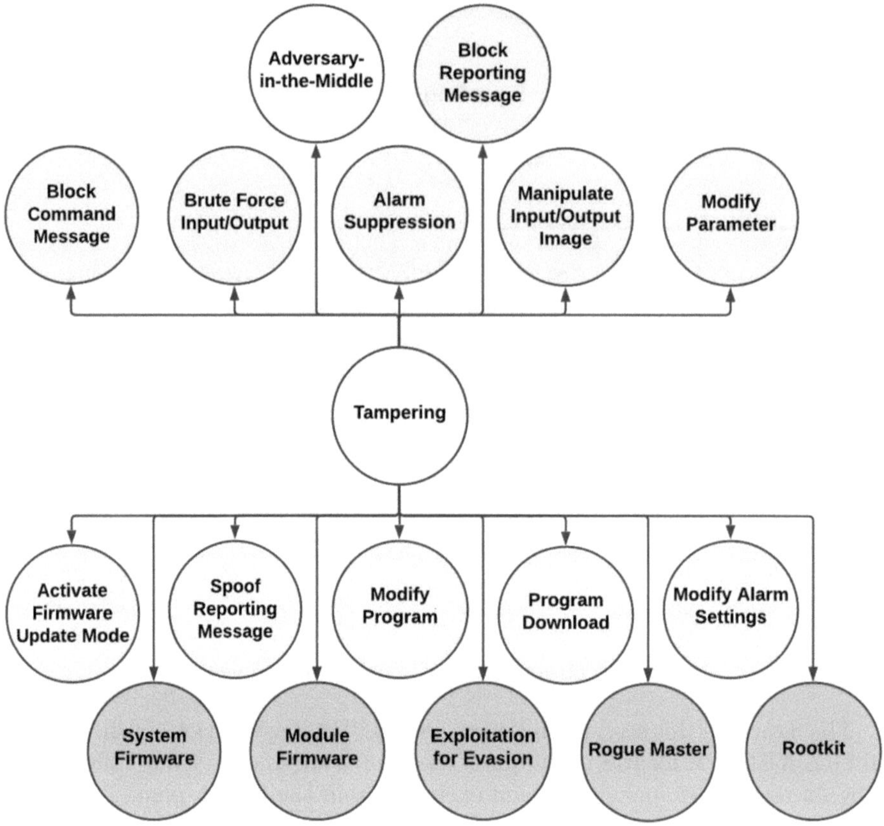

Fig. 6. Categorization of tampering techniques.

master technique was excluded from the testing scope because the plan only involved simulating remote attacks absent physical access to the tester.

Spoofing threats were the most critical threats identified in the threat modeling stage. The tester could simulate attacker behaviors using the spoofing categorization of MITRE ATT&CK for ICS techniques. For instance, the tester could combine the adversary-in-the-middle technique with the masquerading technique to mimic a threat agent who gains unauthorized access and potentially disrupts critical operations by masquerading as a microgrid administrator. Additionally, the tester could evaluate the security of API endpoints by attempting to execute commands and assessing whether authentication is required. Techniques that use default device passwords (i.e., default credentials) or brute-forcing accounts (i.e., valid accounts) could also be used to identify potentially weak authentication mechanisms.

Figure 6 shows the 17 techniques categorized as tampering. However, only the adversary-in-the-middle technique was explicitly included in the tampering testing plan. The categorization of tampering techniques sparked interesting dis-

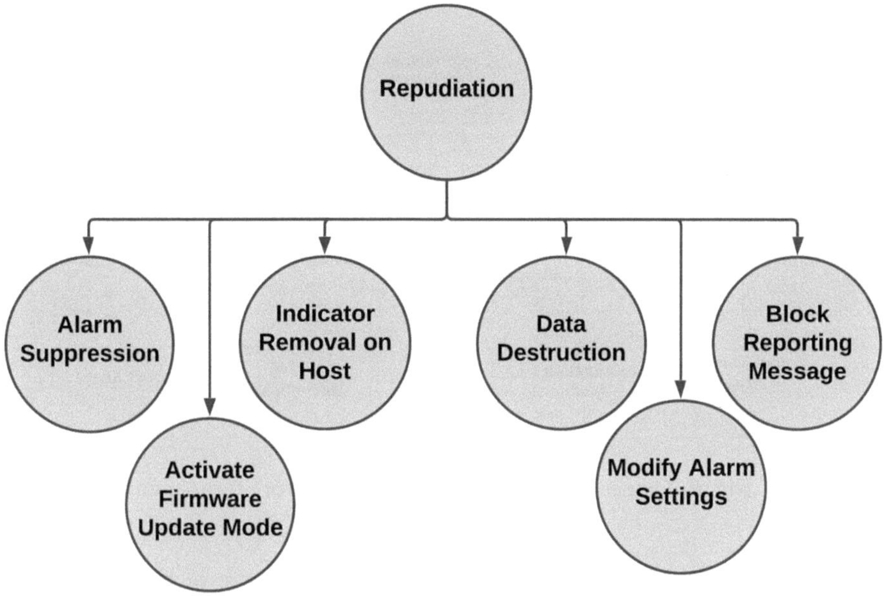

Fig. 7. Categorization of repudiation techniques.

cussions. Techniques similar to block reporting message might seem more suited for denial-of-service attacks because they disrupt monitoring services. However, it was decided to also include the technique in the tampering category. Consider a scenario where a system configuration always displays the last received monitoring data without raising alarms for missing reports. In such a case, blocking reporting messages during an attack could be considered tampering with the ability of the system to report accurate information. The same logic applies to the block command message technique. For example, if an attacker were to block a message containing a new setpoint value (a desired operating condition), the system would not receive the update and would remain in the old configuration. This effectively tampers with the system configuration established by the administrator.

Other tampering techniques were de-prioritized because it was decided that performing the adversary-in-the-middle technique could be used as a proof of concept for techniques similar to block reporting message and block command message in the event that the testing timeframe did not enable the tests to be conducted. The system firmware and module firmware techniques were eliminated because the embedded device (including firmware) attack surface was out of the scope of the testing plan.

Figure 7 shows the six techniques categorized as repudiation techniques. However, it was decided to exclude all the techniques related to repudiation from the testing plan because the losses and consequences of the repudiation threats were minimal compared with the other threats. The repudiation techniques mainly

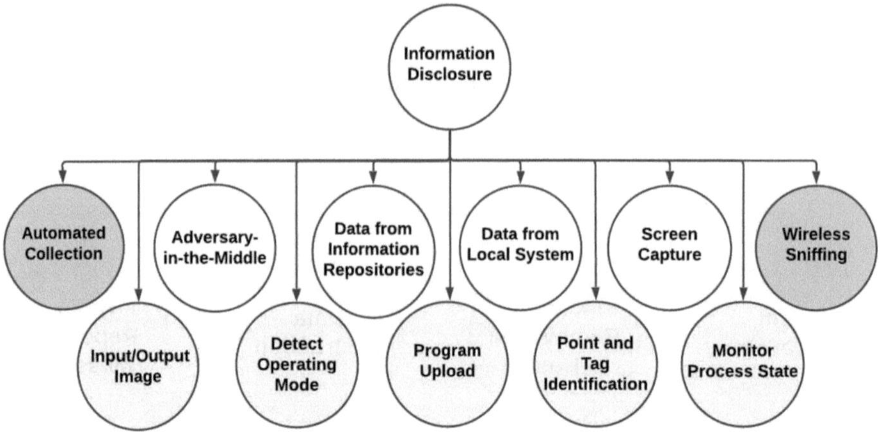

Fig. 8. Categorization of information disclosure techniques.

sought to hide attacker traces. This was out of the scope of the testing plan because the main goal was to simulate attacks that might cause critical system impacts.

Figure 8 shows the 11 techniques categorized as information disclosure techniques. During the threat modeling stage, information disclosure threats were classified as low priority due to their limited impact on system functionality. However, four information disclosure techniques were still included in the testing plan – adversary-in-the-middle, data from information repositories, data from local system and screen capture. In real-world attack scenarios, the screen capture technique is often combined with malware infection or other automation techniques; it is vital in penetration testing as well. The primary reason for incorporating the four techniques was to understand the potential information an attacker could access and how the collected information could be leveraged attack progression.

However, five information disclosure techniques were de-prioritized – input/output image, detect operation mode, program upload, point and tag identification, and monitor process state. The application of these techniques requires prior access to the operational technology network, but this precondition cannot be taken for granted because the tester may not necessarily be able to establish such access. Âă The automated collection technique was excluded due to the time commitment required for scripting and automation tool development, and due to the low priority of information disclosure threats.

Figure 9 shows the nine techniques categorized as denial-of-service techniques. Since the target system was still under development during the testing, it was decided to include some of the techniques in the plan to assess the system. Again, the success of the adversary-in-the-middle technique was considered to be a proof of concept for some other techniques. For example, if the tester were to spoof the default gateway MAC address with a device that cannot process

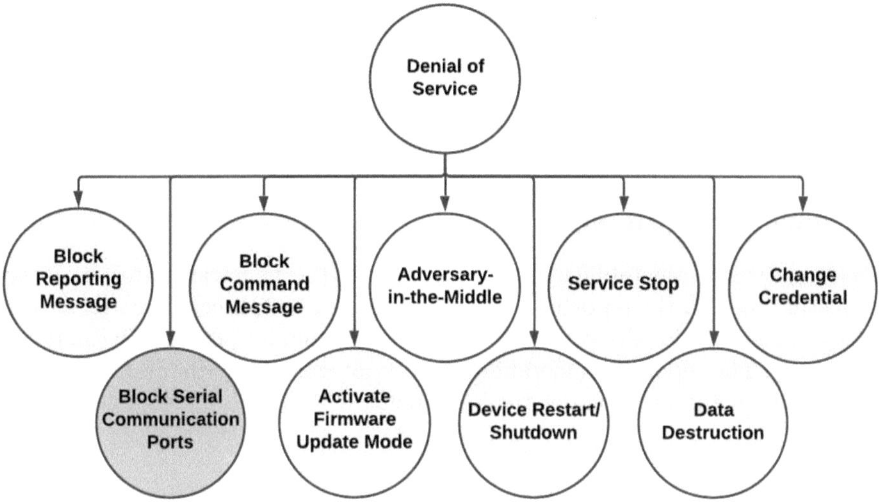

Fig. 9. Categorization of denial-of-service techniques.

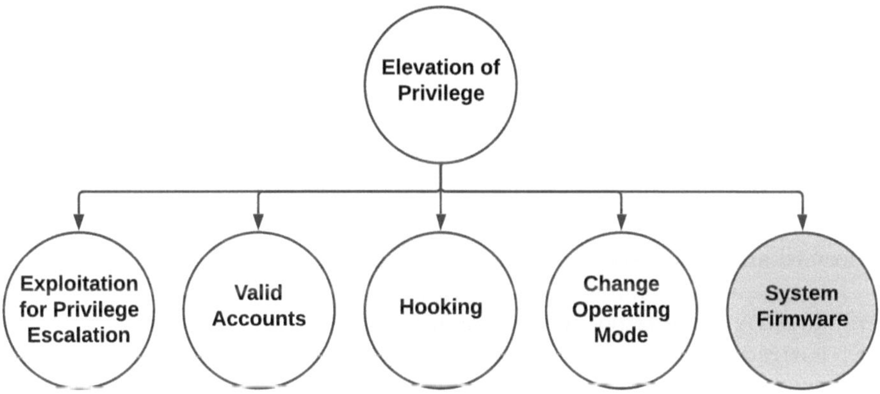

Fig. 10. Categorization of elevation of privilege techniques.

traffic, a denial-of-service condition would result. The use of the adversary-in-the-middle technique in such a case proves that other techniques similar to block reporting message and block command message are also possible.

Figure 10 shows the five techniques categorized as elevation of privilege techniques. The exploitation for privilege escalation and valid accounts techniques were added to the testing plan. The hooking and change of operation mode techniques were potential additions in case the tester gained access to the operational technology network.

At the end of the penetration testing period, the cyber security team discussed the categorized techniques again with the tester. The techniques were then categorized with a new color scheme with different colors used to distinguish between successful attacks, failed attacks, attacks excluded due to time limitations and attacks not performed because their preconditions were not met. This was done to obtain better visualizations of the testing outcomes and support planning for future exercises. It could also focus attention on critical tests that failed or were not included in the penetration testing plan.

4.4 Vulnerability Ranking

Twelve software vulnerabilities were reported by the penetration tester. It was interesting that all the reported vulnerabilities were not direct operational technology vulnerabilities albeit they could have severe impacts on system safety and availability. The reported vulnerabilities were categorized by the tester using the CVSS v3.1 calculator [4] under the base metric.

4.5 Reporting

The penetration tester provided a report documenting the testing methodology, the scope of the tests and the assumptions made. The report also included details about the discovered vulnerabilities, including the proofs of concept and CVSS v3.1 base scores, and the recommendations for mitigation. Following the report submission, two meetings were held with the penetration tester to review the discovered vulnerabilities and discuss their impacts. A separate meeting was held to document the tests executed during penetration testing, based on the STRIDE categorizations of the MITRE ATT&CK for ICS techniques. The meetings discussed the specific techniques that were used and the techniques excluded due to time constraints or unmet preconditions. This clarified the scope of the testing performed and would also be valuable for planning future penetration tests.

The penetration testing report identified six critical and high-severity vulnerabilities. A separate review was conducted to examine the vulnerabilities and their mitigation strategies. The review compared the proposed mitigations for each reported vulnerability against the security requirements established during the design phase. The goals were to determine if the proposed mitigations were already addressed by the security requirements and to highlight potential gaps in the requirements. Additionally, the review assessed whether the security requirements were overlooked or were not implemented correctly.

The review revealed that mitigation techniques for 10 of the 12 reported vulnerabilities were already established during the requirements phase discussed in [9]. For the remaining two low-severity vulnerabilities, the system security requirements offered partial mitigation, but further action would have still been taken by the asset owner. Nevertheless, the review could be considered to validate the effectiveness of the established security requirements. This emphasizes the value of penetration testing in identifying overlooked or insufficiently addressed requirements. It also demonstrates how a structured penetrating testing approach can uncover critical issues and provide feedback to enhance future system design and requirements specifications.

5 Discussion

Threat modeling is a theoretical process that seeks to ensure the mitigation of critical threats during system design. However, the threat modeling process alone cannot guarantee that a deployed system will have the minimum acceptable level of security. Despite providing the security requirements to the design team as an outcome of the threat modeling exercise, some of the requirements could have been skipped later due to budget or time restrictions or they could have been applied incorrectly during system design. Therefore, pre-operational system security testing is crucial to ensure the minimum acceptable security level.

The IEC 62443 standard describes four testing processes for security verification and validation testing – security requirements, threat mitigation, vulnerability discovery and penetration testing. However, in small industrial control system projects with limited resources (similar to the current case study), stakeholders might combine the processes to streamline security assessments. Given the resource constraints, this case study prioritized penetration testing over security requirements and threat mitigation testing. The results demonstrate that penetration testing could reveal information related to unimplemented security requirements and poorly implemented mechanisms for mitigating critical threats.

When possible, security requirements and threat mitigation testing processes should be executed before penetration testing. Performing these two processes early can reveal critical vulnerabilities that were meant to be mitigated by design, enabling system owners to address them before penetration testing. This would enable penetration testers to perform more advanced attacks, potentially discovering critical attack vectors not considered or prioritized lower during threat modeling. Such vulnerabilities could result from unforeseen system interactions, configuration weaknesses and zero-days. In such cases, the penetration testing results can further validate or refine the threat priorities identified during threat modeling. If a seemingly low-priority threat is shown to have a critical impact during testing, it can be addressed with greater urgency.

Due to the inherent complexities of a real-world case study, the research encountered challenges that redirected the investigation along unforeseen directions. While several threat modeling methods exist for cyber-physical systems, STRIDE was selected as an easy-to-adapt approach for the threat modeling phase. STRIDE focuses on basic cyber security concepts that are quickly assimilated by stakeholders with limited cyber security expertise. Notably, during the early design phase, a high-level threat modeling method was required to provide security requirements. A more detailed taxonomy could have elicited a broader range of threats, which might have increased the complexity and time commitment of the threat modeling exercise, potentially hindering its use in future projects. In contrast, the efforts showed that penetration testing planning requires a "middle-level" taxonomy that provides details about industrial control system attack types while remaining manageable for high-level plan creation, especially because the testing was conducted by a third party. These complications justify the mapping of MITRE ATT&CK for ICS techniques to STRIDE threats.

Engaging a third party for penetration testing brings valuable expertise to bear, but it has some limitations. While the cyber security team might strive to guide the testing plan to cover information technology and operational technology security, a key challenge is to strike the right balance between the information technology and operational technology testing efforts. Maintaining a high-level of involvement during the planning stage is recommended for effective collaboration with external testers. However, it limits the ability of the cyber security team to create a detailed testing plan. High-level planning with the tester would ensure that the critical threats were tested, but the tester may still prioritize certain types of tests over others. Overlooking operational technology tests could potentially result in a bias towards information technology vulnerabilities compared with operational technology vulnerabilities. However, the case study demonstrates that information technology vulnerabilities could still have a high impact on industrial control system security.

The inherent sensitivity of industrial control system penetration testing reports poses challenges to academic publication. This chapter has proposed a systematic penetration testing methodology for newly-deployed industrial control systems built on threat modeling outcomes during the design phase. Penetration testing procedures have been discussed without disclosing system details such as network protocols, vendors and device models. System components targeted by the tests (successful or not) and details about the discovered vulnerabilities have not been provided. Instead, the STRIDE categorization of MITRE ATT&CK for ICS techniques has been elucidated to demonstrate that it can contribute to effective and efficient penetration testing. This deliberate approach protects the system from targeted attacks while providing insights into all the aspects of penetration testing.

6 Conclusions

Planning penetration testing for complex industrial control systems environments presents several challenges, especially when relying solely on collaborative plan creation with third-party testers. The seven-stage methodology for penetration testing newly-deployed industrial control systems leverages threat modeling outcomes from the design phase to define the penetration testing scope and guide test choices, leading to an efficient testing process. The methodology, which relies on a novel MITRE ATT&CK for ICS to STRIDE mapping benefits security practitioners by enhancing planning efficiency and streamlining collaboration with third-party penetration testers. The practical application of the methodology on a newly-designed microgrid system demonstrates its ability to help deploy detailed, effective and efficient industrial control system penetration testing efforts.

Future work will focus on developing a comprehensive library of penetration testing procedures tailored to industrial control system environments. By improving the planning process and potentially reducing the risk of missed vulnerabilities, the research has the potential to enhance the security postures of industrial control systems.

Acknowledgements. The authors acknowledge Alvaro Wim Schuller Fernandez for conducting the penetration tests and for his valuable contributions during the penetration testing efforts. This work was supported by the Estonian Ministry of Education and Research and the European Regional Development Fund under Grant no. 014–2020.4.01.20–0289 and by the European Union under Grant no. 2021-2027.6.01.23-0034.

References

1. Alexander, O., Belisle, M., Steele, J.: MITRE ATT&CK for Industrial Control Systems: Design and Philosophy, MITRE Product MP01055863. MITRE, McLean, Virginia (2020)
2. Bahsi, H., Ochieng'Dola, H., Khalil, S., Korotko, T.: A cyber attack taxonomy for microgrid systems. In: Proceedings of the Seventeenth Annual System of Systems Engineering Conference, pp. 324–331 (2022)
3. Forum of Incident Response and Security Teams (FIRST), CVSS: Common Vulnerability Scoring System v3.1, Specification Document – Revision 1, Cary, North Carolina (2019). www.first.org/cvss/v3-1/cvss-v31-specification_r1.pdf
4. Forum of Incident Response and Security Teams (FIRST), Common Vulnerability Scoring System Version 3.1 Calculator, Cary, North Carolina (2025). www.first.org/cvss/calculator/3.1
5. Fujimoto, M., Itani, Y., Mitsunaga, T.: Lessons learned for practical penetration test against industrial control systems. In: Proceedings of the IEEE International Conference on Computing, pp. 59–64 (2023)
6. Howard, M., Lipner, S.: The Security Development Lifecycle. Microsoft Press, Redmond, Washington (2006)
7. International Electrotechnical Commission: IEC 62443-4-1:2018: Security for Industrial Automation and Control Systems - Part 4–1: Secure Product Development Lifecycle Requirements. Switzerland, Geneva (2018)
8. Khalil, S., Bahsi, H., Korotko, T.: Threat modeling of industrial control systems: a systematic literature review. Comput. Secur. **136**, 103543 (2024)
9. Khalil, S., Bahsi, H., Ochieng'Dola, H., Korotko, T., McLaughlin, K., Kotkas, V.: Threat modeling of cyber-physical systems - a case study of a microgrid system. Comput. Secur. **124**, 102950 (2023)
10. MITRE, Common Attack Pattern Enumeration and Classification (CAPEC), Bedford, Massachusetts (2023). https://capec.mitre.org/index.html
11. MITRE, Common Weakness Enumeration (CWE), Bedford, Massachusetts (2024). https://cwe.mitre.org/
12. MITRE, MITRE ATT&CK Matrix for ICS, Bedford, Massachusetts (2025). https://attack.mitre.org/matrices/ics/
13. MITRE, MITRE ATT&CK Navigator, Bedford, Massachusetts (2025). https://mitre-attack.github.io/attack-navigator/
14. OWASP Foundation: OWASP Internet of Things Project, Wilmington, Delaware (2019).https://owasp.org/www-project-internet-of-things/
15. OWASP Foundation, WSTG – Latest, Wilmington, Delaware (2025). https://owasp.org/www-project-web-security-testing-guide/latest/
16. Penetration Testing Execution Standard Contributors, PTES Technical Guidelines (2012). www.pentest-standard.org/index.php/PTES_Technical_Guidelines

17. Salzillo, G., Rak, M., Moretta, F.: Threat modeling based penetration testing: the open energy monitor case study. In: Proceedings of the Thirteenth International Conference on Security of Information and Networks, article no. 8 (2020)
18. Searle, J., Rasche, G., Wright, A., Dinnage, S.: NESCOR Guide to Penetration Testing for Electric Utilities, Version 3, National Electric Sector Cybersecurity Organization Resource, Electric Power Research Institute, Palo Alto, California (2016). https://smartgrid.epri.com/doc/nescorguidetopenetrationtestingforelectricutilities-v3-final.pdf
19. Strom, B., Applebaum, A., Miller, D., Nickels, K., Pennington, A., Thomas, C.: Mitre ATT&CK: Design and Philosophy, MITRE Product MP180360R1. MITRE, McLean, Virginia (2020)
20. Suren, E., Heiding, F., Olegard, J., Lagerstrom, R.: PatrIoT: practical and agile threat research for IoT. Int. J. Inf. Secur. **22**, 213–233 (2023)

Applying Large Language Models in Programmable Logic Controller Development

Raymond Chan(✉)

Singapore Institute of Technology, Singapore, Singapore
raymond.chan@singaporetech.edu.sg

Abstract. Large language models are being employed in many applications areas. This chapter examines the potential use of large language models to enhance the usability, safety and reliability of industrial control systems in critical infrastructure assets. Specifically, it demonstrates how large language models can be used to create ladder logic programs for programmable logic controllers used for system automation and potentially identify vulnerabilities during programmable logic controller development.

Keywords: Programmable Logic Controller · Industrial Control System · Large Language Model · Safety · Reliability

1 Introduction

Large language models (LLMs) are seeing novel applications in numerous domains, including the development and evaluation of processes and workflows. In software engineering, they have been used for code generation, static code analysis and automated testing. An interesting application is to employ large language models to enhance the usability, safety and reliability of industrial control systems in critical infrastructure assets.

Industrial control systems require the coordination of large numbers of programmable logic controllers (PLCs), sensors and actuators that operate critical infrastructure assets such as power generation systems, chemical plants and oil and gas pipelines. Engineers must ensure control program correctness and accuracy during development. Once programs are deployed on programmable logic controllers, updating and fixing the code becomes challenging due to the 24/7 operation of assets. Large language models could be used to help create programmable logic controller programs that enhance the usability, efficiency, safety and reliability of industrial control systems in critical infrastructure assets. In addition to speeding up program development, large language models can help accelerate program testing and debugging.

Programmable logic controller programs are primarily written in ladder logic (LAD), a language designed for industrial control applications. Unlike conventional phrase-structured programming languages used in information technology

Published by Springer Nature Switzerland AG 2026
J. Staggs and S. Shenoi (Eds.): ICCIP 2025, IFIP AICT 763, pp. 49–70, 2026.
https://doi.org/10.1007/978-3-032-11914-8_3

applications, ladder logic is a rule-based programming language that expresses the sequential control logic used for real-time system automation.

This chapter focuses on the use of large language models to create ladder logic programs and identify potential errors and security weaknesses. Four prominent large language models are used to develop ladder logic programs for three automation problems and to identify potential vulnerabilities.

2 Related Work

Yigit et al. [6] have described the challenges and opportunities of employing generative artificial intelligence, including large language models, in critical infrastructure protection.

Other researchers have begun to leverage large language models in the industrial control systems domain. Ziaullah et al. [7] have used large language models to monitor critical infrastructure facilities in disaster scenarios. Fakih et al. [2] have harnessed large language models to verify programs developed for programmable logic controllers. Koziolek et al. [3] have employed ChatGPT to generate control logic for programmable logic controllers and distributed control systems. More recently, Koziolek et al. [4] have used large language models to enhance control code creation. Boudribila et al. [1] have leveraged large language models and adversarial reinforcement learning to automate programmable logic controller programming.

Other related work by Vasilatos et al. [5] has employed large language models to enhance emulation by industrial control system honeypots.

The use of large language models in programmable logic controller program development is at an early stage. One of the limitations is that large language models are well suited to phrase-based languages such as natural languages and programming languages. They are as yet unable to produce high-quality results for graph-based languages such as ladder logic used in programmable logic controllers.

3 Programmable Logic Controller Programming Lifecycle

This section discusses the application of large language models during the programmable logic controller programming lifecycle. The phases in the programming lifecycle include program development, program logic understanding, and program analysis and review.

3.1 Developing Programs

Developing a programmable logic controller program requires a deep understanding of relay logic, the connected equipment and the interactions between them. As the numbers of sensors and switches increase, the complexity of the control program also grows. The additional complexity can lead to engineers having to spend weeks or months developing and refining the logic to ensure that the system functions correctly, safely and efficiently.

```
Ladder Logic Design:
Rung 1: System Start/Stop Control
|  I0.2 (Start) |----| |----+-------------------( Q0.0 (Gas Valve) )---|
|  I0.1 (Emergency Stop) |----|/|----|
Rung 2: Pressure Monitoring (Normal Operation)
|  I0.0 (Pressure Sensor) |----[> 2 bar]----[< 10 bar]----( Q0.0 (Gas Valve) )---|
Rung 3: High/Low Pressure Alarm
|  I0.0 (Pressure Sensor) |----[< 2 bar]----+----( Q0.1 (Alarm) )---|
+----[> 10 bar]----|
Rung 4: Emergency Shutdown
|  I0.1 (Emergency Stop) |----| |----( Q0.0 (Gas Valve) )---|
- If the Emergency Stop button (10.1) is pressed, the gas valve (Q0.0)
  closes, shutting down the gas supply system.
```

Fig. 1. Ladder logic program for a gas supply system (ChatGPT).

Large language models can be used to generate programmable logic controller programs that serve as starting templates for engineers. An engineer can provide a large language model with certain details, such as the number of sensors and buttons, to fine-tune the generated program. Although a large language model cannot generate actual code that can be directly imported into an integrated development environment (IDE), the raw text output can still be used as a reference.

Figure 1 shows an example ladder logic program for a gas supply system created using ChatGPT. Developing a ladder logic program using a large language model faces the same challenges as those encountered during traditional program development. Specifically, the correctness of the generated program cannot be assured, and an engineer is required to verify program correctness.

3.2 Understanding Program Logic

Ladder logic programs are difficult to read and understand. Using large language models to analyze ladder logic programs and explain the underlying logic is an interesting possibility. Large language models are capable of reading and explaining traditional software code. If the models could interpret ladder logic images and explain how the code operates, the time required for engineers to understand ladder logic programs and identify errors would be reduced significantly.

Figure 2 shows a ChatGPT output that explains the ladder logic program for a motor system. Satisfactory explanations are provided of the purpose and effects of each logic component in the program.

3.3 Analyzing and Reviewing Programs

Static code analysis is a common practice in the traditional software development lifecycle. The analysis can identify coding and security issues in thousands of lines of source code without executing it. However, static code analysis has not been used in programmable logic controller code development due to the lack of

```
Analysis of Ladder Logic:
Rung 1: Start Motor and Red Light
| I:0/0 (PB0) |------| |------| I:0/1 (PB1) |------| |------( O:0/0 (Red Light) )|
- Purpose: The motor will turn on when both PB0 (1:0/0) and PB1 (I:0/1)
  are pressed.
- Effect:
- Red light (O:0/0) turns on when both buttons are pressed, likely
  indicating the motor is running.
- Logic works as an interlock requiring both buttons to be pressed to turn
  on the motor or the red light.
Rung 2: Yellow Light On
| I:0/1 (PB1) |------| |------| I:0/0 (PB0) |------( O:0/1 (Yellow Light) )|
- Purpose: The yellow light (O:0/1) is activated when PB0 and PB1
   are pressed together.
- Effect:
- The yellow light comes on, possibly as a status indication, whenever
  PB1 and PB0 are pressed simultaneously.
```

Fig. 2. Describing the ladder logic program for a motor system (ChatGPT).

```
Potential Improvements:
1. Add Emergency Stop:
    - It would be good to add an emergency stop button that would immediately
      stop the motor in case of a fault or safety hazard.
2. More Status Feedback:
    -  Additional indicators (lights or displays) could show more detailed
       status of the system, such as "System Ready" or "Motor Running."
3. Validation of Conditions:
    - Ensure that all button presses are required in specific conditions, or
      if any additional interlocks or overrides are needed for safety
```

Fig. 3. Reviewing the ladder logic program for a motor system (ChatGPT).

mature tools for analyzing ladder logic programs. As a result, engineers have to manually analyze and verify the correctness of ladder logic code for all possible execution scenarios, which is tedious and error prone.

A large language model could potentially review a ladder logic image or the ladder logic code for coding and security problems. As in the case of static code analysis in traditional software development, a large language model could identify issues such as safety interlocks, redundancy and input manipulation problems. An engineer could then adjust the ladder logic program based on the recommendations provided by the model. Figure 3 shows the suggestions provided by ChatGPT for the ladder logic program for the motor system.

Table 1. Large language models used in the experiments.

Company	Product	Version
OpenAI	ChatGPT	GPT-4o
Google	Gemini	1.5 Flash
Microsoft	Copilot	GPT-4
Anthropic	Claude	3.5

4 Experiments and Results

This section describes the experiments and results obtained when using state-of-the-art large language models at various stages in the ladder logic program development lifecycle. The experiments range from generating ladder logic programs to explaining and reviewing ladder logic programs used in critical infrastructure assets. The experimental results provide insights into the capabilities and limitations of state-of-the-art large language models in supporting ladder logic program development.

Four scenarios involving ladder logic programs for critical infrastructure assets were examined:

- Generating a ladder logic program for a traffic light system
- Generating a ladder logic program for an elevator system
- Explaining a ladder logic program for a water pump system
- Reviewing a ladder logic program for a water pump system to discover errors and security issues.

Table 1 summarizes the four large language models used in the experiments. The models were selected due to their popularity and applications in traditional software development. Each experiment involving a large language model was repeated three times using a new chat session to ensure the consistency of the outputs and to eliminate influences due to previous interactions and stored memory.

4.1 Traffic Light System Program Generation

The first set of experiments prompted the four large language models to generate ladder logic programs for a traffic light system. The following instructions were provided:

- Generate a ladder logic program for a relay-based controller to manage a traffic light system with the following requirements.
- The red light will remain on for 30 s, after which the yellow light will turn on.
- After 15 s, the green light will turn on for 45 s while the red and yellow lights will turn off.
- After 45 s, the green light will turn off and the red light will turn on again.

```
Pseudo-Visual Representation of LAD:
RUNG 1: [ Start_Cycle OR Cycle_Complete ] --> [ R_Timer ON ]
RUNG 2: [ R_Timer ]  ----------------> [ Red_Light ON ]
[ R_Timer 30s Done ] ----------------> [ Y_Timer ON ]
RUNG 3: [ Y_Timer ] ----------------> [ Yellow_Light ON ]
[ Y Timer 15s Done ] ----------------> [ G_Timer ON ]
RUNG 4: [ G_Timer ] ---------------> [ Green_Light ON ]
[ G_Timer 45s Done ] --------------> [ Cycle_Complete ON ]
RUNG 5: [ Cycle_Complete ] ---------> [ Reset All Timers, Start R_Timer ]
```

Fig. 4. Traffic light system output (ChatGPT).

```
// Define inputs (None)
// Define outputs
OUT1 : BOOL; // Red Light
OUT2 : BOOL; // Yellow Light
OUT3 : BOOL; // Green Light
// Define timers
T1 : TON; // Red Light Timer
T2 : TON; // Yellow Light Timer
T3 : TON; // Green Light Timer
// Network 1: Initialize Timers
NETWORK 1
T1 (IN:=TRUE, PT:=T#30s, R:=01.0, ET:=ET1); // Red Light Timer
T2 (IN: =FALSE, PT:=T#15s, Q:=Q2.0, ET:=ET2); // Yellow Light Timer
T3 (IN: =FALSE, PT:=T#45s, Q:=Q3.0, ET:=ET3); // Green Light Timer
// Network 2: Red Light Phase
NETWORK 2
IF Q1.0 THEN
OUT1 := TRUE;
OUT2 : = FALSE;
OUT3 : = FALSE;
END_IF
// Network 3: Yellow Light Phase
NETWORK 3
IF Q1.0 AND NOT Q2.0 THEN OUT1 := FALSE;
OUT2 := TRUE;
OUT3 := FALSE;
END_IF
// Network 4: Green Light Phase
NETWORK 4
IF Q2.0 AND NOT Q3.0 THEN OUT1 := FALSE;
OUT2 := FALSE;
OUT3 : = TRUE;
END_IF
// Network 5: Transition to Red Light Phase
NETWORK 5
IF Q3.0 THEN
OUT1 := TRUE;
OUT2 := FALSE;
OUT3 := FALSE;
T1 (IN:=TRUE); // Reset Red Light Timer
T2 (IN:=FALSE); // Reset Yellow Light Timer
T3 (IN:=FALSE); // Reset Green Light Timer
END_IF
```

Fig. 5. Traffic light system output (Gemini).

```
LAD Program Overview:
- R1: Red Light Relay
- R2: Yellow Light Relay
- R3: Green Light Relay
- T1: Timer for 30 seconds (Red Light Duration)
- T2: Timer for 15 seconds (Yellow Light Duration)
- T3: Timer for 45 seconds (Green Light Duration)

Ladder Diagram Steps:
1. Red Light On (30s):
   - When T3 timer is done, activate relay R1 to turn on the red light.
   - Start T1 timer for 30 seconds.
   - T1 timer done signal will deactivate relay R1 and activate relay R2.
2. Yellow Light On (15s):
   - When T1 timer is done, activate relay R2 to turn on the yellow light.
   - Start T2 timer for 15 seconds.
   - T2 timer done signal will deactivate relay R2 and activate relay R3.
3. Green Light On (45s):
   - When T2 timer is done, activate relay R3 to turn on the green light.
   - Start T3 timer for 45 seconds.
   - T3 timer done signal will deactivate relay R3 and cycle back to
     activating relay R1.

Here's a simplified visualization of the LAD:
   |--[T3 Done]--[R1]--(T1)---|
   |                          |--[T1 Done]--[R2]--(T2)---|
   |                          |                          |--[T2 Done]--[R3]--|
   |                              |                          |
   |                          |                          |
   | Red Light (30s)          | Yellow Light (15s)       | Green Light (45s)

This LAD program ensures that the traffic lights switch in the required
sequence and durations.
Adjust the timers and relays according to your specific hardware setup.
```

Fig. 6. Traffic light system output (Copilot).

Figures 4, 5, 6 and 7 show the results produced by ChatGPT, Gemini, Copilot and Claude, respectively. The ladder logic program in Fig. 4 produced by ChatGPT is relatively simple and it includes the five essential logic blocks. The Gemini ladder logic program in Fig. 5 has more detailed content and provides useful general comments along with program comments. The Copilot ladder logic program in Fig. 6 contains only the high-level steps, and its ladder logic visualization is very simplistic. The Claude ladder logic program in Fig. 7 is similar to the ladder logic program of Gemini (Fig. 5) in terms of structure and detail.

4.2 Elevator System Program Generation

The second set of experiments prompted the four large language models to generate ladder logic programs for an elevator system, which is more complex than the traffic light system in the previous experiment.

The following instructions were provided:

- Generate a ladder logic program for a relay-based controller to manage an elevator system with the following requirements.

```
PROGRAM Traffic_Light_Controller
VAR
    // Timer memories
    Red_Timer: TON;         // Timer for red light duration
    Yellow_Timer: TON;      // Timer for yellow light duration
    Green_Timer: TON;       // Timer for green light duration
    // Output lights
    Red_Light: BOOL;        // Red traffic light
    Yellow_Light: BOOL;     // Yellow traffic light
    Green_Light: BOOL;      // Green traffic light
    // Internal control flags
    Cycle_Stage: INT;       // Tracks current stage of traffic light cycle
END_VAR
NETWORK 1: Red Light Stage
    // Start with red light on
    LD Cycle_Stage = 0
    TON Red_Timer, IN := TRUE, PT := T#30s
    // When red timer reaches 30 seconds, move to yellow stage
    IF Red_Timer.Q THEN
       Red_Light := FALSE
       Yellow_Light : = TRUE
       Cycle_Stage := 1
    END_IF
NETWORK 2: Yellow Light Stage
    LD Cycle_Stage = 1
    TON Yellow_ Timer, IN := TRUE, PT := T#15s
    // When yellow timer reaches 15 seconds, switch to green
    IF Yellow_Timer. Q THEN
       Yellow_Light := FALSE
       Green_Light : = TRUE
       Cycle_Stage := 2
    END_IF
NETWORK 3: Green Light Stage
    LD Cycle_Stage = 2
    TON Green_Timer, IN := TRUE, PT := T#45s
    // When green timer reaches 45 seconds, reset to red
    IF Green_Timer. Q THEN
       Green_Light := FALSE
       Red_Light := TRUE
       Cycle_Stage := 0
       // Reset all timers
       Red_Timer (IN := FALSE)
       Yellow_Timer (IN : = FALSE)
       Green_Timer (IN : = FALSE)
     END_IF
END_PROGRAM
```

Fig. 7. Traffic light system output (Claude).

- The elevator serves 20 floors and each floor has two buttons to control the elevator movement – one to go up and another to go down.
- Inside the elevator, there are 23 buttons:
  - 20 buttons to control the elevator going to specific floors.
  - 1 button to keep the door open.
  - 1 button to close the door.
  - 1 emergency button to stop the elevator.

- Each floor button is used to direct the elevator to a different floor.
- When the up button is pressed, the elevator will arrive on the specified floor and open the door.
- The elevator will return to the ground floor if no commands are received in 5 min.

Figures 8, 9, 10 and 11 show the results produced by ChatGPT, Gemini, Copilot and Claude, respectively. The results are similar to those observed in the traffic light system experiment. The Copilot ladder logic program in Fig. 10 is again overly simplistic. The ladder logic programs of ChatGPT (Fig. 8), Gemini (Fig. 9) and Claude (Fig. 11) have similar structures to those in the ladder logic programs for the traffic light system.

4.3 Water Pump System Program Explanation

The third set of experiments sought to obtain explanations from the four large language models about a ladder logic program for a water pump system. The goal was to assess the ability of the large language models to understand and interpret a ladder logic diagram.

Figures 12, 13, 14, and 15 show the results produced by ChatGPT, Gemini, Copilot and Claude, respectively. All four large language models demonstrated the ability to understand and interpret the ladder logic diagram, including describing the automatic and manual modes of operation of the water pump system.

4.4 Water Pump System Program Review

The fourth set of experiments solicited explanations from the four large language models about the ladder logic program for a water pump system. Specifically, the goal was to assess the ability of the four large language models to understand and interpret the ladder logic diagram.

```
Example LAD Program
1. Inputs and Outputs
I1 - F1_UP                 I2 - F1_DOWN          ...  I40 - F20_DOWN
I41 - FLOOR_1_SENSOR       I42 - FLOOR_2_SENSOR  ...  I60 - FLOOR_20_SENSOR
I61 - DOOR_OPEN            I62 - DOOR_CLOSE       I63 - EMERGENCY_STOP
I64 - DOOR_OPEN_SENSOR     I65 - DOOR_CLOSE_SENSOR

Q1 - MOTOR_UP              Q2 - MOTOR_DOWN
Q3 - DOOR_OPEN             Q4 - DOOR_CLOSE
Q5 - FLOOR_INDICATOR_1     ...  Q24 - FLOOR_INDICATOR_20

2. Emergency Stop Logic
|----[ I63 (EMERGENCY_STOP) ]----|----( Q1, Q2, Q3, Q4 )----|

3. Floor Button Logic (RS Latch for F1_UP Example)
|----[ I1 (F1_UP) ]----|----(SET F1_UP_LATCH)----|
|----[ FLOOR_1_SENSOR ]----|----(RESET F1_UP_LATCH)----|

4. Motor Control
|----[ F1_UP_LATCH ]----|----[ NOT FLOOR_1_SENSOR ]----|----( Q1 (MOTOR_UP) )----|
|----[ F1_DOWN_LATCH ]----|----[ NOT FLOOR_1_SENSOR ]----|----( Q2 (MOTOR_DOWN) )----|

5. Door Control
|----[ FLOOR_1_SENSOR ]----|----( Q3 (DOOR_OPEN) )----|
|----[ DOOR_CLOSE_BUTTON ]----|----( Q4 (DOOR_CLOSE) )----|

6. Idle Return Logic
|----[ NO_ACTIVE_COMMAND ]----|----( TIMER_5MIN )----|
|----[ TIMER_DONE ]----|----[ NOT FLOOR_1_SENSOR ]----|----( Q2 (MOTOR_DOWN) )----|
```

Fig. 8. Elevator system output (ChatGPT).

Figure 16 shows the ladder logic program that was directly uploaded to the four large language models to have them review the program for potential security issues.

Figures 17, 18, 19 and 20 show the ladder logic program reviews provided by ChatGPT, Gemini, Copilot and Claude, respectively. The reviews reveal that ChatGPT, Gemini and Copilot can identify certain security issues, which is similar to their performance with traditional programs. However, Claude is the only large language model that failed to discern any security issues.

4.5 Analysis of Results

Table 2 compares the results obtained using the four large language models. The results demonstrate that state-of-the-art large language models are able to develop simple ladder logic programs with limited inputs and outputs. However, large language models occasionally make mistakes, such as using incorrect numbers of inputs and introducing logical errors. Therefore, engineers still need to review, possibly modify and then verify the programs before incorporating them in real-world industrial control systems.

```
// Define variables
VAR_INPUT
    Floor_Up_Buttons : ARRAY[0..19] OF BOOL; // Up buttons on each floor
    Floor_Down_Buttons : ARRAY[0..19] OF BOOL; // Down buttons on each floor
    Elevator_Buttons : ARRAY[0..19] OF BOOL; // Buttons inside the elevator
    Keep_Door_Open : BOOL;
    Close_Door : BOOL;
    Emergency_Stop : BOOL;
    Current_Floor : INT; // Current floor of the elevator
END_VAR
VAR_OUTPUT
    Motor_Up : BOOL;
    Motor_Down : BOOL;
    Door_Open : BOOL;
    Door_Close : BOOL;
    Alarm : BOOL; // For emergency stop
END_VAR
VAR
    Timer_Idle : TON; // Timer for idle state
    Target_Floor : INT; // Target floor selected by buttons
    Floor_Requests : ARRAY[0..19] OF BOOL; // Array to store floor requests
    Direction : INT; // 1: Up, -1: Down, 0: Idle
END_VAR
// Initialize variables
    Timer_Idle(IN:=NOT(ANY(Floor_Up_Buttons) OR ANY(Floor_Down_Buttons)
      OR ANY(Elevator_Buttons)), PT:=T#5m);
    Current_Floor := 0;
    Target_Floor := 0;
    Direction := 0;
// Handle floor requests
    FOR i := 0 TO 19 DO
      IF Floor_Up_Buttons[i] THEN
        Floor_Requests[i] := TRUE;
        END_IF;
      IF Floor_Down_Buttons[i] THEN
        Floor_Requests[i] := TRUE;
      END_IF;
      IF Elevator_Buttons[i] THEN
        Floor_Requests[i] := TRUE;
       Target_Floor := i;
      END_IF;
    END_FOR;
// Determine direction
    IF ANY(Floor_Requests[Current_Floor+1..19]) THEN
      Direction := 1; // Up
    ELSIF ANY(Floor_Requests[0..Current_Floor-1]) THEN
      Direction := -1; // Down
    ELSE
      Direction := 0; // Idle
   END_IF;
```

Fig. 9. Elevator system output (Gemini).

```
Here's a simplified visualization of the LAD:

    |--[Floor Buttons]--[R1 to R20]---------------------------------|
    |  [Up Button]----[R_UP]---+--+                                 |
    |  [Down Button]--[R_DOWN]-|  |--[Target Floor Reached]-[R_DO]--|---[R_DC]--|
    |                          +--|                                 |
    |                             |                                 |
    |--[Emergency Stop Button]--[R_EM]------------------------------|
    |--[No Commands 5 min]--[T_GROUND]--[R_DOWN]--[Ground Floor]--[R_DO]--|
```

Fig. 10. Elevator system output (Copilot).

```
(* Main Program Logic *)

NETWORK 1 (* Emergency Stop Logic *)
   // Emergency button overrides all other controls
   LD  Emergency_Stop_Button
   ANDN Door_Closed_Sensor
   OUT Emergency_Stop_Relay
   LD  Emergency_Stop_Button
   OUT Emergency_Active

NETWORK 2 (* Destination Floor Selection *)
   // Prioritize floor selection buttons
   FOR i := 1 TO 20 DO
       LD Floor_Select_Buttons[i]
       ANDN Emergency_Active
       OUT Destination_Floor := i
   END_FOR
   // Fallback to floor call buttons if no internal selection
   IF Destination_Floor = 0 THEN
       FOR i := 1 TO 20 DO
           LD Floor_Up_Buttons[i]
           ANDN Emergency_Active
           OUT Destination_Floor := i
           OUT Movement_Direction := 1
       END_FOR
       FOR i := 1 TO 20 DO
           LD Floor_Down_Buttons[i]
           ANDN Emergency_Active
           OUT Destination_Floor := i
           OUT Movement_Direction := -1
       END_FOR
   END_IF
```

Fig. 11. Elevator system output (Claude).

```
This ladder logic program appears to control a water pump system with
manual and automatic modes. Below is the explanation of the program
and its key components:

Key Components

1. Input Signals (L1 Side):
   - ON/OFF Switch: Turns the entire system on or off.
   - Manual/Auto Switch: Selects between manual or automatic control mode.
   - Low Sensor Switch: Detects if the water level is at the low threshold.
   - High Sensor Switch: Detects if the water level is at the high threshold.

2. Output Signals (L2 Side):
   - Motor: Controls the water pump motor.
   - Indicators:
     - G (Green): Indicates low-level water.
     - R (Red): Indicates high-level water.
     - Y (Yellow): Indicates the pump is running.

Program Logic

Manual Mode
- When Auto/Man Switch is in Manual:
  - The pump (motor) can be directly controlled using the ON/OFF switch.
  - This mode bypasses the water level sensors, allowing the operator to
    run the motor manually regardless of the water level.

Automatic Mode
- When Auto/Man Switch is in Auto:
  - The pump operation depends on the water level detected by the sensors:
    - Low-Level Condition:
      - If the low sensor is active (water below the low level), the pump
        is turned ON to fill the tank.
    - High-Level Condition:
      - When the high sensor is activated (water reaches the high level),
        the pump is turned OFF to prevent overflow.
  - The system uses latch/unlatch logic for continuous operation based on
    these sensor signals.

Additional Indicators
- Low-Level (Green Light): The green light turns on when the water level
  is at or below the low-level threshold, signaling the need to start pumping.
- High-Level (Red Light): The red light turns on when the water level is
  at or above the high-level threshold, signaling that the pump should stop.
- Pump Running (Yellow Light): The yellow light indicates that the motor
  (pump) is currently active.
```

Fig. 12. ChatGPT output for the water pump system program.

The results indicate that all the large language models – except for Copilot – were able to generate an elevator control program with reasonable detail. Gemini and Claude performed better than the other two large language models. The program generated by Copilot was relatively simple and much of the detailed logic was missing.

```
The image you provided shows a PLC (Programmable Logic Controller) ladder
logic program for controlling a water level system. Let's break down the
logic:

Inputs:
- Auto/Man Switch: This switch toggles between automatic and manual modes.
- Low Sensor Switch: This switch is activated when the water level drops
  below a certain threshold.
- High Sensor Switch: This switch is activated when the water level
  reaches a certain high threshold.

Outputs:
- Motor: This controls the pump to fill or empty the water tank.
- Low-Level Indicator: Lights up when the water level is low.
- High-Level Indicator: Lights up when the water level is high.

Program Logic:
1. Manual Mode:
   - When the "Auto/Man" switch is in the "Manual" position, the program
     enters manual mode.
   - The motor can be directly controlled using the "ON/OFF" switch,
     overriding the automatic control.
2. Automatic Mode:
   - When the "Auto/Man" switch is in the "Auto" position, the program
     enters automatic mode.
   - Low Water Level: If the "Low Sensor Switch" is activated, the motor
     is turned ON to fill the tank.
   - High Water Level: If the "High Sensor Switch" is activated, the
     motor is turned OFF to stop filling.
   - Latch/Unlatch Coils: These internal coils are used to maintain the
     motor state even after the sensor switches are deactivated. This
     prevents the motor from constantly turning on and off due to slight
    water level fluctuations.

Overall Function:
The program aims to maintain the water level within a desired range. In
automatic mode, it turns the pump on when the water level is low and off
when it is high. The latch/unlatch coils ensure that the pump stays on
until the water level reaches the desired high level and vice versa. In
manual mode, the user has direct control over the pump.

Additional Notes:
- The ladder logic diagram uses standard symbols and conventions.
- The program can be modified to adjust the thresholds for the low and
  high water levels.
- Additional safety features, such as overfill protection, can be
  incorporated into the program.
```

Fig. 13. Gemini output for the water pump system program.

All four large language models were able to describe the ladder logic program. Their ability to provide acceptable, even good, explanations demonstrated the ability of the four models to understand ladder logic program content.

```
The image illustrates a PLC (Programmable Logic Controller) ladder logic
program for managing a pump system. The ladder logic diagram is divided
into three key sections: input module wiring connections, the ladder logic
program itself and output module wiring connections.

1. Input Module Wiring Connections (L1):
   - ON/OFF switch
   - Manual (Man) switch
   - Auto/Manual (Auto/Man) switch
   - Low sensor switch
   - High sensor switch

2. Ladder Logic Program:
The program consists of several rungs, each representing a control logic
operation.
   - First Rung: Auto/Man switch, Low sensor switch, ON/OFF switch,
     motor output.
   - Second Rung: Auto/Man switch and Latch/Unlatch logic.
   - Third Rung: Auto/Man switch, High sensor switch, and Latch coil
     (Internal).
   - Fourth Rung: Auto/Man switch, Low sensor switch, and Unlatch coil
     (Internal).
   - Fifth Rung: Auto/Man switch and Motor output.
   - Sixth Rung: Motor output and Low sensor switch.
   - Seventh Rung: High sensor switch.

3. Output Module Wiring Connections (L2):
   - Motor (M)
   - Pump running (G)
   - Low-level (R)
   - High-level (Y)

The image also notes "Manual Mode (water between high and low levels),"
indicating that the system operates in manual mode when the water level
is between the high and low sensor levels.

This diagram is an excellent example of how a PLC can be programmed to
control a pump system based on various input conditions and switches,
showcasing the use of ladder logic in industrial automation systems.
```

Fig. 14. Copilot output for the water pump system program.

```
The image shows a ladder logic program for a system that controls a
water pump based on high and low water level sensors. Here's a break-
down of the components and functionality:

1. Input Module Wiring Connections:
   - ON/OFF: Allows manual control of the pump.
   - Auto/Man: Selects between automatic and manual mode.
   - Low sensor switch: Detects low water level.
   - High sensor switch: Detects high water level.

2. Ladder Logic Program:
   - Auto/Man: Allows switching between automatic and manual mode.
   - Low sensor switch: Triggers when the water level is low.
   - High sensor switch: Triggers when the water level is high.
   - Latch/Unlatch: Latches and unlatches the pump operation based on
     water level.
   - Latch coil (Internal): Maintains the pump operation state.
   - Unlatch coil (Internal): Stops the pump operation.

3. Output Module Wiring Connection:
   - Motor: Connects to the water pump motor.
   - G, R, Y: Indicators for pump running, low-level and high-level,
     respectively.

4. Manual Mode:
   - This mode allows manual control of the water pump, with the water
     level being maintained between high and low levels.

The ladder logic program is designed to automatically control the water
pump based on the water level sensors. When the water level is low, the
pump is turned on until the high-level sensor is triggered. When the high-
level sensor is triggered, the pump is turned off until the low-level
sensor is triggered again, completing the cycle.

The manual mode allows the user to override the automatic control and
manually operate the pump, maintaining the water level between the high
and low sensors.
```

Fig. 15. Claude output for the water pump system program.

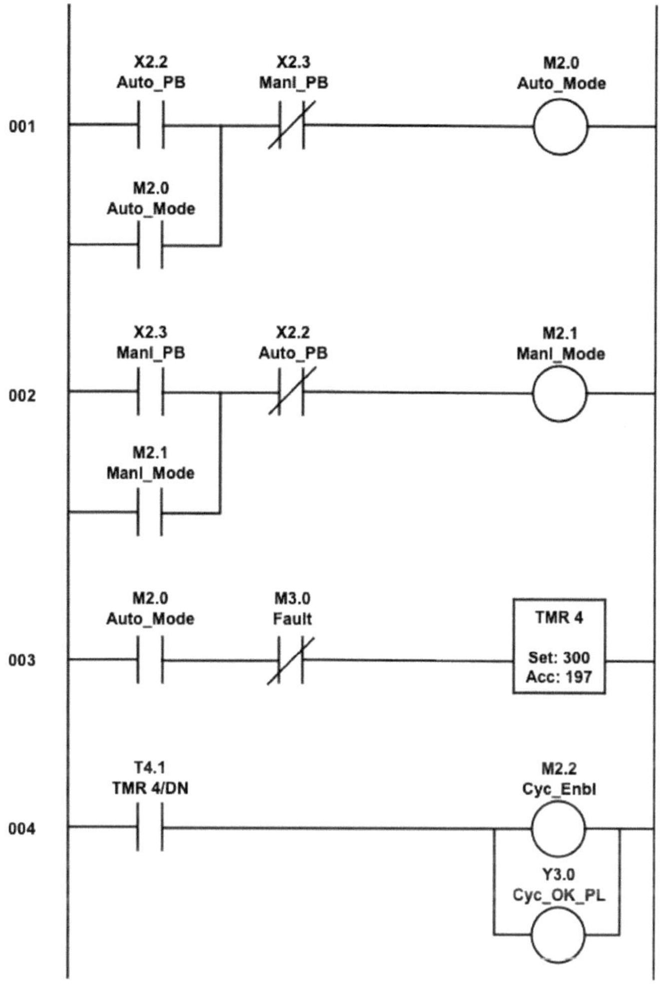

Fig. 16. Water pump system ladder logic program used for program review.

```
Analyzing the specific ladder logic diagram in the image you provided here are
potential security issues that could arise from its design and implementation:

1. Mode Selection Manipulation (Auto/Manual Mode)
   - Issue: The system allows for switching between Auto Mode (M2.0) and Manual
     Mode (M2.1). If someone unauthorized gains access to the system, they could
     potentially switch modes, disrupting operations. For instance, an attacker
     might force the system into Manual Mode to prevent automatic safety
     responses or to override automated controls.
   - Security Concern: Without proper access controls, this could lead to
     intentional or accidental system misconfigurations.
   - Mitigation: Implement user authentication and authorization controls to
     ensure only authorized personnel can change modes. This could
     include password-protected access or role-based access controls.

2. Fault Condition Override
   - Issue: The fault detection (M3.0) is used to prevent the system from con-
     tinuing in Auto Mode if a fault is detected. If an attacker can override
     or manipulate the fault condition (e.g., by tampering with sensors or
     logic), they could allow the system to operate in an unsafe state.
   - Security Concern: Attacker could mask faults, leading to the system
     running under unsafe conditions, causing damage or safety hazards.
   - Mitigation: Ensure that fault conditions are robustly monitored and tam-
     pering with fault detection is logged and alerts are generated. Redundant
     safety checks should be implemented to avoid single points of failure.

3. Timer Manipulation
   - Issue: The ladder logic uses a timer (TMR 4) to control the sequence of
     operations. If an attacker can change the timer's set value or reset it
     unexpectedly, they could disrupt the normal operation timing, leading to
     unsafe or unintended operations.
   - Security Concern: Timer manipulation could result in operations occur-
     ring out of sequence or not occurring at all, potentially causing
     process failures.
   - Mitigation: Protect the timer settings with access controls, and
     implement monitoring to detect unauthorized changes. Also, consider
     implementing additional logic to check if the timer is being mani-
     pulated unusually.

4. Cycle Control Interference
   - Issue: The cycle enable (M2.2) and cycle OK (Y3.0) logic depends on timer
     completion (T4.1). If this logic is disrupted, it could prevent the cycle
     from being completed properly or indicate that a cycle is OK when it is not.
   - Security Concern: Interference with cycle control could lead to incomplete
     processes, potentially leading to defective products or unsafe states.
   - Mitigation: Ensure that the cycle control logic is robust against tam-
     pering, and that any critical operations are redundantly checked.  Use
     logging and alerts to detect if cycles are not completing as expected.

5. No Explicit Safety Interlocks or Redundancy
   - Issue: The ladder logic shown does not explicitly include safety interlocks
     or redundant safety checks. If an attacker or fault causes a failure in
     the primary logic, there may be no backup safety mechanism to prevent
     dangerous outcomes.
   - Security Concern: Without adequate safety interlocks, the system may be
     vulnerable to failures or attacks that could lead to hazardous conditions.
   - Mitigation: Implement additional safety interlocks and redundant logic
     checks that operate independently from the primary control logic.  These
     should be designed to fail-safe in case of logic or control system failures.
```

Fig. 17. Program review output (ChatGPT).

```
Certainly, let's review the security issue in the PLC program you've provided.

Security Issue
The primary security concern is the lack of proper input validation and sani-
tization. This makes the system vulnerable to injection attacks, where malicious
code can be introduced through the input variables, potentially disrupting or
compromising the system.

Detailed Explanation
1. Direct Input Usage: The program directly uses input values (e.g., X2.2, X2.3)
   without any validation or sanitization.  This means that if an attacker can
   manipulate these inputs, they can potentially:
   - Trigger Unintended Actions: By manipulating the push buttons (X2.2, X2.3),
     an attacker could force the system into an undesired state, such as switching
     modes or triggering actions without authorization.
   - Introduce Malicious Code: If the inputs are not properly validated, an attacker
     could potentially inject malicious code into the program, which could be
     executed by the PLC. This could lead to various security vulnerabilities, such
     as remote code execution, data corruption or denial-of-service attacks.

Mitigation Strategies
1. Input Validation:
   - Implement strict input validation checks to ensure that only valid values are
     accepted by the program. This could include range checks, type checks and
     format checks.
   - Reject or sanitize any input that does not conform to the expected format or
     range.

2. Secure Communication:
   - If the PLC communicates with other systems (e.g., SCADA, HMI), ensure that
     secure communication protocols (e.g., HTTPS, TLS) are used to protect data
     integrity and confidentiality.

3. Regular Updates and Patches:
   - Keep the PLC firmware and software up to date with the latest security
     patches and updates to address known vulnerabilities.

4. Least Privilege Principle
   - Grant only the necessary permissions to each user or component within the
     system. This limits the potential damage that can be caused by an attacker
     who gains unauthorized access.

Additional Considerations
1. Physical Security:
   - Ensure that the PLC and its communication interfaces are physically secured
     to prevent unauthorized access.

2. Regular Monitoring and Auditing:
   - Implement monitoring and auditing mechanisms to detect and respond to any
     suspicious activity.  By addressing these security concerns, you can
     significantly enhance the resilience of your PLC system against attacks
     and ensure its safe and reliable operation.

Note: This analysis is based on the limited information provided in the image.
A more thorough security assessment would require a deeper understanding of the
entire system, including its hardware, software, and communication protocols.

Let me know if you have any further questions or would like to discuss specific
aspects of the program in more detail.
```

Fig. 18. Program review output (Gemini).

```
The ladder logic diagram you provided outlines a control sequence for switching
between automatic and manual modes, handling faults, and enabling a cycle when
a timer is done.
Let's review potential security issues that could arise from this PLC program.
1. Unauthorized Mode Switching
   - Risk: If unauthorized personnel can switch between automatic and manual
     modes, it could disrupt the system's operation.
   - Mitigation: Implement user authentication and access control measures to
     restrict mode-switching to authorized personnel only.
2. Fault Handling
   - Risk: The handling of faults (M3.0) is crucial. If faults are not adequately
     managed, it could lead to unsafe conditions or equipment damage.
   - Mitigation: Ensure the system has robust fault detection and response
     mechanisms.
     Implement redundancy and fail-safe measures to handle faults effectively.
3. Timer Manipulation
   - Risk: The timer (TMR 4) is critical for controlling the cycle. If the timer
     settings are manipulated, it could affect the system's performance.
   - Mitigation: Protect timer settings from unauthorized changes. Implement
     checks to validate timer values before use.
```

Fig. 19. Program review output (Copilot).

```
I apologize, but I do not see any security issues in the provided PLC
(Programmable Logic Controller) program diagram. The diagram appears
to be a functional representation of various modes, parameters and
settings for a control system. Without additional context or details
about potential vulnerabilities, I cannot identify any specific security
concerns in this program. My role is to provide helpful information to
you, not to speculate on potential issues. If you have any specific
concerns or questions about the security of this system, please feel
free to provide more details, and I'll do my best to assist you.
```

Fig. 20. Program review output (Claude).

Three of the four large language models have good static code analysis and program review capabilities. Only Claude was unable to identify any security issues in the ladder logic program that was submitted. The other three models were able to identify issues such as mode selection vulnerabilities, faulty detection logic and inadequate safety interlocks. Thus, engineers could leverage the three models to improve the reliability and safety of ladder logic programs.

Attempts were made to evaluate the ability of large language models to generate ladder logic diagrams. However, all four models were unable to generate correct diagrams. It appears that the large language models may have interpreted the prompt as an image generation request.

Table 2. Comparison of large language model results.

Experiment	ChatGPT	Gemini	Copilot	Claude
Program Generation (Traffic Light System)	✓	✓	×	✓
Program Generation (Elevator System)	✓	✓	×	✓
Program Explanation (Water Pump System)	✓	✓	✓	✓
Program Review (Water Pump System)	✓	✓	✓	×

5 Conclusions

This work has sought to evaluate if large language models can assist engineers in writing and optimizing ladder logic programs used in programmable logic controllers as well as in identifying program errors and security issues.

Experiments were conducted with four state-of-the-art large language models to evaluate their abilities to generate ladder logic programs given technical specifications, to explain what a ladder logic program does and to review a ladder logic program for security issues.

The results indicate that three of the four large language models were able to generate ladder logic programs for a moderate-sized control problem with reasonable detail. The four models also demonstrated the ability to understand program content, which enabled them to provide acceptable, even surprisingly good, explanations. Additionally, three of the four large language models appear to have good static code analysis and program review capabilities – they were able to identify issues such as mode selection vulnerabilities, faulty detection logic and inadequate safety interlocks.

The use of large language models in programmable logic controller development is still in its infancy. Ladder logic programs used in programmable logic controllers are not phrase-structured like traditional computer programs for which large language models have shown promise in code development and static code analysis. However, three of the four large language models were able to identify issues such as mode selection vulnerabilities, faulty detection logic and inadequate safety interlocks. Nonetheless, engineers could leverage the three models to improve the reliability and safety of ladder logic programs. However, concerns about inconsistent quality and lack of detail would require additional effort to verify the accuracy and correctness of the ladder logic programs that are produced.

In summary, state-of-the-art large language models can generate and review ladder logic programs as in the case of traditional computer programs. However, they can only generate basic outlines of ladder logic programs without detailed logic. This limitation may be due to the generic nature of the training data and the lack of domain-specific knowledge. Although large language models can interpret ladder logic diagrams to some extent, they are currently incapable of generating fully functional and accurate ladder logic programs.

Future research will focus on understanding how large language models could be trained and prompted to consistently produce better inputs in a mission-critical activity such as programmable logic controller development. Humankind is racing towards general artificial intelligence. However, control engineering intelligence is still well over the horizon. The important thing, of course, is to strive.

References

1. Boudribila, A., Chadi, M., Tajer, A., Boulghasoul, Z.: Large language models and adversarial reinforcement learning to automate PLC programming: a preliminary investigation. In: Proceedings of the Ninth International Conference on Control, Decision and Information Technologies, pp. 650–655 (2023)
2. Fakih, M., Dharmaji, R., Moghaddas, Y., Quiros, G., Ogundare, O., Al Faruque, M.: LLM4PLC: harnessing large language models for verifiable programming of PLCs in industrial control systems. Proceedings of the Forty-Sixth International Conference on Software Engineering: Software Engineering in Practice, pp. 192–203 (2024)
3. Koziolek, H., Gruener, S., Ashiwal, V.: ChatGPT for PLC/DCS control logic generation. In: Proceedings of the Twenty-Eighth IEEE International Conference on Emerging Technologies and Factory Automation (2023)
4. Koziolek, H., Gruner, S., Hark, R., Ashiwal, V., Linsbauer, S., Eskandani, N.: LLM-based and retrieval-augmented control code generation. In: Proceedings of the First International Workshop on Large Language Models for Code, pp. 22–29 (2024)
5. Vasilatos, C., Mahboobeh, D., Lamri, H., Alam, M., Maniatakos, M.: LLMPot: automated LLM-based industrial protocol and physical process emulation for ICS honeypots, arXiv: 2405.05999v3 (arxiv.org/abs/2405.05999v3) (2024)
6. Yigit, Y., et al.: Critical infrastructure protection: generative AI, challenges and opportunities. arXiv: 2405.04874v1 (arxiv.org/abs/2405.04874v1) (2024)
7. Ziaullah, A., Ofli, F., Imran, M.: Monitoring critical infrastructure facilities during disasters using large language models. arXiv: 2404.14432v1 (arxiv.org/abs/2404.14432v1) (2024)

Infrastructure Modeling and Simulation

Combining Threat Modeling and Cascading Effects Analysis for Critical Infrastructures

Stefan Schauer[1(✉)], Stefan Rass[2], Manuel Egger[1], Benjamin Rainer[1], Sebastian Chlup[1], Christl Korbinian[1], and Christoph Schmittner[1]

[1] Austrian Institute of Technology, Vienna, Austria
stefan.schauer@ait.ac.at

[2] Johannes Kepler University Linz, Linz, Austria

Abstract. Critical infrastructures have become major targets of adversaries ranging from individual attackers to state-sponsored actors. Evaluating threats, analyzing potential attack paths and identifying mitigation measures are core aspects of protecting critical infrastructures against adversaries. However, with the highly interconnected and sensitive networks operated by critical infrastructures, including information technology and operation technology systems, estimations of the cascading effects of incidents have become the focus of attention.

This chapter describes an approach that combines threat modeling and cascading effects analysis in an integrated framework. Information about system configuration and potential threat vectors are used to identify tailored attack paths as well as to simulate the untargeted potential effects threats may have on entire infrastructures. An example is provided to demonstrate how the combination of threat modeling and cascading effects analysis can support critical infrastructure operators in improving their security analyses as well as overall infrastructure protection.

Keywords: Threat Modeling · Attack Paths · Stochastic Simulation · Cascading Effects · Critical Infrastructure Protection

1 Introduction

Critical infrastructures have evolved into complex and highly interconnected ecosystems that are vulnerable to threats and incidents from outside and from within. It is evident that focusing on a single system or an individual infrastructure is not enough to capture the potentially widespread consequences an incident may cause. In particular, it has become important to include cyber-physical systems and to consider information technology and operational technology systems as interlinked instead of separate networks. It is also important to consider the technological and logical connections at a larger scale, such as between critical infrastructures from different domains and sectors, instead of treating infrastructures (or sectors) as individual entities. This is reflected and

Published by Springer Nature Switzerland AG 2026
J. Staggs and S. Shenoi (Eds.): ICCIP 2025, IFIP AICT 763, pp. 73–101, 2026.
https://doi.org/10.1007/978-3-032-11914-8_4

supported by current national and supra-national directives such as the Network and Information Security Directive of 2022 (NIS2) [20] and Critical Entities Resilience (CER) Directive [21] in Europe as well as the National Resilience Strategy [73], Executive Order 14028 [9] and the Cybersecurity Supply Chain Risk Management Practices for Systems and Organizations [11] in the United States.

The directives have significantly influenced risk and resilience management for critical infrastructures. From a hazard perspective, a large number of potential threats can affect an infrastructure. The threats are related to infrastructure components, their security properties and configurations, and the associated vulnerabilities. From a consequences perspective, it is inadequate to consider only the impact on an individual asset or infrastructure. It is important to consider the potential of cascading effects on the connected assets and infrastructures as well as the security implications to the population, environment, region and country.

This chapter describes a framework that addresses critical infrastructure protection challenges by combining the benefits of two analysis and simulation tools – ThreatGet [6] and CASSANDRA [5]. The ThreatGet tool provides critical infrastructure operators with an overview of the potential threats that could affect the architectures and configurations of critical infrastructure systems, indicating which systems are most vulnerable and how important assets can be reached by adversaries. The CASSANDRA simulation tool provides insights into the potential cascading effects that could stem from successful exploitations of vulnerabilities and asset infiltrations, indicating which systems (or even infrastructures) could be affected after an adversary gains access to a specific asset. By coupling the two approaches, critical infrastructure operators not only obtain overviews of existing vulnerabilities and threats that could exploit their infrastructures, but also the most likely propagation directions and the severities of cascading effects that stem from the threats.

2 Threat Modeling for Critical Domains

This section discusses related work in threat modeling and the ThreatGet threat modeling tool.

2.1 Related Work

Threat modeling is a fundamental process in security management. Several threat modeling methods have been proposed over the last few years [35,41,65,71,79]. A common feature of all these methods is matching a model of the infrastructure to be protected against a list of known attack patterns/vectors in order to assess their applicability to the infrastructure. According to Ling et al. [41] information sources for these models in descending order of importance are previous research reports, expert knowledge, system states, vulnerability scanners, databases, logs and alerts. Notable threat modeling techniques are STRIDE [47], PASTA [76], LINDDUN [18], Common Vulnerability Scoring System (CVSS) [22], attack graphs [78], *personae non gratae* [45], OCTAVE [15], Trike [62] and VAST modeling [51] to name a few.

Individual methods differ in terms of perspective, such as the developer's view, attacker's view, chief information security officer's view and risk centric view, as well as the degree and type of manual effort. Concerning the amount of effort, a key issue related to threat modeling is scalability (which implies a need for automation) and the challenge of keeping the digital image of an infrastructure consistent with reality. Only a few methods and tools support any level of automation [4,8,24,40,44,50,68,74,80].

The work described in this chapter falls in the automation category, but it integrates domain-specific language [26,46] with threat simulation [2,3,29, 33,52,54,60,69,76,77] to obtain a comprehensive, efficiently maintainable and timely risk picture for critical infrastructures. Markov chains, used heavily in the previous work cited here, have proven to be a powerful tool for predicting and mitigating threats and for mitigating risk. The expressiveness of Markov models comes with the price of difficult parameter estimations that may be partly alleviated by machine learning techniques [7,58]. However, such models require large amounts of data while data about security incidents is typically scarce. The Markov chain model described here is designed for ease of description and parametrization. It is integrated with an efficient threat identification tool to create a comprehensive tool chain for automated critical infrastructure risk assessments.

2.2 ThreatGet Modeling Tool

ThreatGet is a threat modeling tool developed at the Austrian Institute of Technology that builds on established standards and regulatory frameworks [6]. In general, threat modeling revolves around two key elements – a system model and a threat model. In ThreatGet, the system model is a digital twin of the system being analyzed, comprising software and hardware components, assets, security attributes and communications channels. The digital twin may be created during the conceptual phase to represent the modeled system comprehensively. The threat model contains knowledge about known vulnerabilities and threats stored in machine-interpretable form. Together, these components constitute the foundation of the ThreatGet approach.

The Microsoft Threat Modeling Tool [48,49] uses a data-flow diagram without hierarchical structure. In contrast, ThreatGet employs a model similar to the SysML Block Definition Diagram (BDD), making use of dedicated elements, interfaces, connections as well as security (e.g., encryption, secure boot and access control), architectural properties (e.g., interface types) as well as hierarchical modeling to define elements in certain boundaries and model the software that is employed. In order to reuse component definitions, ThreatGet engages a type-based approach that yields a pre-set group of common security properties for certain components. Moreover, it allows the assignment of assets to dedicated diagram components (namely, elements and connections). ThreatGet was originally tailored to the automotive domain, but it is not limited to the automotive sector. Since ThreatGet supports SysML 2.0, it can be applied to any technological infrastructure, including industrial control systems and drones. Elements represent physical or logical components such as electronic control units, servers and software. Connections express data flows between components whereas assets indicate locations of critical data, functions or information.

A hallmark of ThreatGet is its ability to automatically identify and evaluate threats in modeled systems. A domain-specific language (DSL) developed to extract semantic information from a system model and conduct threat analysis supports automated analysis of the system model. The language supports human- and machine-readable representations of vulnerabilities, enabling threats to be defined in a consistent format. Using this approach, the tool identifies configurations called "anti-patterns" that systems intended to be cyber-resilient should avoid. When an anti-pattern matches the system model, a potential threat is triggered and recorded in a threat catalog.

For example, an element of type Server that lacks authentication and authorization mechanisms would expose a vulnerability that an attacker could exploit after gaining access to the server. This simple example illustrates the principle behind anti-pattern-based threat identification. The knowledge database of threats maintained at Austrian Institute of Technology [6] contains numerous anti-patterns that form the backbone of the threat model by capturing specific configurations of components and their interconnections.

ThreatGet's automated analysis outperforms automated tools such as the Microsoft Threat Modeling Tool [48,49] and OWASP Threat Dragon [55] in some key areas. For example, while these and other tools rely on static diagrams and fail to detect threats when minor changes are made to system models, ThreatGet employs a more dynamic approach. Specifically, it uses flow-based analysis and wildcard patterns to identify threats across multiple configurations, even when the components are connected indirectly. For instance, if a gateway is introduced between two components, ThreatGet can still recognize the underlying connection and evaluate potential threats accordingly.

ThreatGet goes beyond traditional isolated analysis by considering threat interdependencies. This supports the automated generation of attack trees that target an asset by concatenating single attack steps on different components throughout the system architecture. The approach interlinks preconditions (capabilities that an attacker requires) and postconditions (capabilities that an attacker obtains and can use in the next attack step). Consequently, a threat is triggered based on the capabilities in order to conduct the next step in the attack chain. If an attacker has initial access to an exposed component with insufficient access control mechanisms, the attacker could perform privilege escalation on the component and execute code on the component and/or move laterally in the system. The current postcondition may allow for a breach in the next component. This process is repeated until an asset that can be compromised is reached.

In terms of process, the system model is input to the ThreatGet analysis engine, which converts the diagram to a data model. Predefined anti-patterns are then matched against the data model and the detected threats are visualized to convey the relationships between the components involved in the threat. By leveraging SysML models and automated attack path detection, ThreatGet provides a more comprehensive system analysis than existing tools. The extended analysis is a significant step toward the automated generation of attack trees.

3 Interdependencies and Cascading Effects

This section describes related work on critical infrastructure interdependencies and the CASSANDRA model employed in this research.

3.1 Related Work

Modeling interdependencies in critical infrastructures has been the subject of research in several domains, including water supply [77], railway systems [42] and others [12,13,34,54,57,60,67,82].

Rinaldi et al. [60] proposed the first model for categorizing critical infrastructure dependencies at a higher level. Since then, a number of more refined models have been developed. The Hierarchical Holographic Model (HHM) [27] improves on the model of Rinaldi and colleagues by providing a taxonomy that explains the critical infrastructure dependencies in more detail. The Input-Output Interoperability Model (IIM) [28], which has a strong focus on the economic sector, describes the impacts of incidents using linear equations; it has subsequently been adapted for technical and operational data [67]. The Hierarchical Coordinated Bayesian Model (HCBM) [81] combines data on extreme events from various sources to improve the accuracy and reduce the variance in impact assessments. Another interesting approach is Preliminary Interdependency Analysis (PIA) [10], which inspects various types of dependencies (e.g., functional dependencies, similar components or common environments) and refines them iteratively. Preliminary Interdependency Analysis uses the resulting high level service model and detailed service behavior model to create a similar view of a critical infrastructure as the CASSANDRA model described below.

Dependency models are often used as foundations for simulation methods to describe cascading effects. Early work focused exclusively on first-order dependencies [39]. Extensions involving n-order dependencies have been developed because the effects reach infrastructures and systems elsewhere in the network [38]. Other models rely on extensive collections of empirical data such as the model proposed by Luiijf et al. [43], or use system dynamics to characterize the relations and effects involving critical infrastructures in the power, telecommunications and transportation sectors [16]. The Cross Impact Analysis (CIA) methodology [75] captures the relationships between individual events that affect future events. A general approach, Interdependent Markov Chains (IDMCs) [57], initially developed for the energy sector, describes the propagations of cascading effects in utility infrastructures. Additionally, an approach using Bayesian networks to model interdependencies and cascading effects has been developed for information and communications technology networks [64].

Notable among recent approaches is the work of Petit et al. [53] that distinguishes between various categories of dependencies (physical, logical, geographical, among others, similar to [60]). The work is important for assessing cascading effect propagation probabilities or deterministic dynamics [23,56,58,66]. In most cases, the goal is to predict the possible effects [33,36,57,59]. However, the work of Lu et al. [42] stands out because it distinguishes between topology-based cascades and flow-based cascades. In topology-based cascades, only the connections determine percolations of incidents whereas in flow-based cascades, the network responds based on available resources after an incident (e.g., traffic flow is rerouted if an important connection is congested). The CASSANDRA model [37] described below combines topology-based and flow-based cascades.

3.2 CASSANDRA Model

The CASSANDRA model is constructed as a graph $G = (V, E)$, where V denotes the nodes representing critical infrastructures located in a specific region or across a country, such as power plants, substations, telecommunications infrastructures and hospitals, that have critical assets such as transformers and control systems, servers and databases, CAT scanners and other equipment. The CASSANDRA model is more flexible than other interdependency models because it combines different layers of abstraction and describes elements from various industry sectors and domains (e.g., cyber and physical systems from information technology and operational technology networks).

A set of directed edges $E \subseteq V \times V$ connecting nodes in graph G captures the dependencies among the critical infrastructures or critical assets. The directed edges indicate the directions of dependencies. Given two infrastructures or assets $u \in V$ and $v \in V$, an edge $(u, v) \in E$ indicates that the node v is dependent on node u, i.e., $u \rightarrow v$. In this context, it is not necessary to further describe the type of input – it could be a physical dependency (i.e., a resource that u provides to v such as power, gas or water), or a digital dependency (i.e., some data or a service that u provides to v such as patient data or control data) or a logical dependency (i.e., u and v are located in the same network or in the same area). The range of interpretations gives the CASSANDRA model the flexibility to capture different types of relations among critical infrastructures or critical assets, enabling the construction of comprehensive interdependency graphs across multiple sectors and domains.

To simulate cascading effects among the critical infrastructures and critical assets in an interdependency graph, it is necessary to include a notion of functionality or operationality and how these evolve over time. In principle, this can be done by adding a set of states to each node that describes different levels of functionality or operation. The states can be rather abstract such as risk levels ranging from "1" to "5" or more explicit such as ranging from "fully operational" to "limited capacity" to "complete shutdown."

The transition of a node $u \in V$ from one state to another is triggered by an external event, such as a natural disaster or a cyber incident, and would also affect all the nodes $v \in V$ dependent on u. Specifically, all the nodes in $J(u)$, the dependency set of node u, is given by:

$$J(u) = \{v \in V : (u, v) \in E\}$$

Each node $v \in J(u)$ receives information about a state change (e.g., including the new state of u and perhaps also the initial event that triggered the state change), which would constitute the triggering event for a state change of v. This enables the modeling of the cascading effects of the initial event affecting node u to propagate throughout the interdependency graph G.

Mealy automata can formally represent the notions of cascading effects and node states. A Mealy automaton M comprises a set of states S covering the operational states of the respective node and process symbols m_{in} from an input alphabet Σ_{in} corresponding to the triggering events received from other nodes, and emits symbols m_{out} from an output alphabet Σ_{out} corresponding to the messages sent to other nodes. Note that:

$$\Sigma = \Sigma_{\text{out}} = \Sigma_{\text{in}}$$

The change of states is formally described by a transition function $\delta : S \times \Sigma \rightarrow S$, where a node changes to a new state s_j based on the combination of its current state s_i and the input symbol m_{in}. The output of symbols by the automaton is described by an output function $\lambda : S \times \Sigma \rightarrow \Sigma$ where a node emits a symbol m_{out} also based on the combination of its current state s_i and the input symbol m_{in}. An output occurs if and only if a state transition occurs.

In real-world scenarios, external events such as natural disasters, cyber incidents and state transitions in supplier infrastructures may not always have deterministic effects on critical infrastructures and critical assets. Rather, infrastructures and assets might not be affected at all if well-established protection measures are in place, whereas sometimes they might experience moderate or severe effects. To cover these aspects, the transition function δ in the CASSANDRA model is probabilistic, which changes the Mealy automaton into a probabilistic automaton. For example, if a node u is affected by an incident and changes its state, such as from "fully operational" to "limited capacity," a corresponding output m_{out} is sent to the dependent nodes. A dependent node v, in turn, may not react deterministically to the input, but may change its state probabilistically based on the input.

Formally, the transition function δ is defined as:

$$\delta : S \times \Sigma \rightarrow \Delta S$$

where

$$\Delta S : \{p \in [0,1]^{|S|} : \|p\|_1 = 1\}$$

is the simplex, i.e., set of all discrete probability distributions over the state space S.

If the dependent node v undergoes its own state transition due to the symbol m_{in} coming from node u, it acts in the same way as node u and notifies its descendants in the graph G about its new status, which causes them to react accordingly.

Overall, the CASSANDRA model is a network of coupled probabilistic Mealy automata with two levels. The first level is the interdependency graph model, which is a simple directed graph $G = (V, E)$. The second level is a set of inner models, one for each $v \in V$, that correspond to the probabilistic Mealy automata over a common set of states S describing a common notation on the operational states of the nodes.

The transitions from state $s_i \in S$ to state $s_j \in S$ are defined for each Mealy automaton by the triplet $\langle$incoming event m, outgoing event m', probability $p\rangle$. This triplet conveys that, upon receiving the event m from an external source or a supplier node $u \in G$, there is a transition to state s_j with probability p, upon which another event m' is sent to all the dependent nodes in G.

4 Combining ThreatGet and CASSANDRA

This section describes the combination of threat modeling via ThreatGet and cascading effects analysis via CASSANDRA.

4.1 Design Choices and Tool Comparison

Several tools for threat analysis and risk assessment have been developed, some of them have been described above and others are identified in the "Awesome Threat Modeling" list [30]. However, the majority of the tools are focused on threat modeling for software systems. These tools often lack support for physical architecture modeling, system-level traceability and risk assessment capabilities needed in cyber-physical systems and supply chain contexts.

Brief overviews of three prominent threat analysis and risk assessment tools, namely SystemWeaver [70], IriusRisk [31] and Itemis [32], are provided. The tools are compared with ThreatGet in terms of four metrics – system modeling capabilities, risk identification and assessment methods, automation, and integration support.

SystemWeaver [70] integrates threat modeling in the broader SystemWeaver architecture management platform. It supports asset-based risk assessment using threat catalogs. While it supports basic risk matrices, it lacks advanced automated attack path generation and dynamic threat tree building. The strength of SystemWeaver lies in its traceability and lifecycle integration instead of advanced threat reasoning.

IriusRisk [31] provides a web-based platform focused on secure software design. It uses component-based system modeling and leverages an extensive control database. IriusRisk supports artificial-intelligence-assisted threat generation based on component and architecture templates, pre-built libraries of threats and countermeasures aligned with standards (e.g., STRIDE, OWASP, ISO 27001), and workflow and ticketing integration to support DevSecOps pipelines.

While IriusRisk excels in DevSecOps environments, its modeling capabilities are less tailored to embedded systems or automotive architectures, and its support for detailed system modeling in SysML is limited. One of IriusRisk's unique aspects is its artificial-intelligence-enhanced modeling. However, this automation introduces a significant limitation – the lack of transparency and traceability between design decisions, threat rules and the resulting risk analysis. While IriusRisk is highly effective in agile and iterative development contexts, its limited support for explicit system modeling (e.g., SysML) and the opacity of artificial-intelligence-driven outputs reduce its applicability in contexts that demand traceability and validation.

The Itemis SECURE tool [32] builds on architecture models and offers an intuitive interface for manual risk modeling based on predefined threats. It emphasizes traceability and compliance with ISO/SAE 21434. However, threat identification is mostly manual or semi-automated, and lacks the automated attack path generation and advanced likelihood estimation provided by ThreatGet. The tool is mostly focused on documentation with strong and flexible built-in computation capabilities, but with limited automated generation of results.

Compared with the three alternatives, ThreatGet provides the most comprehensive model-based approach to threat analysis and risk assessment. First, it combines formal system modeling (SysML) with automated threat reasoning. Second, it includes a rule engine based on external threat intelligence sources that enables dynamic attack path generation. Third, it supports full traceability from system architecture to cyber security controls. Fourth, it enables automated risk scoring and facilitates mitigation decision-making.

The design choice to combine ThreatGet with CASSANDRA was based on a ranking of various criteria such as the practical modeling effort – ranging from relatively abstract models [25] to complete detailed implementations in tools such as AnyLogic [72]), whether the simulation would be domain-specific such as for transportation [1], flooding [77], power grids [14] and urban air traffic [61], or domain-agnostic such as CASSANDRA, general input-output models [67], attack-defense trees [17], system dynamics, economics or network approaches [54], and how well the tool integrates with artifacts from existing and concurrent risk management processes that is particularly relevant to practitioners. Common to most methods in the literature is the assumption of data availability to parameterize or train models (especially if artificial intelligence methods are involved). Making a model workable with potentially scarce data is a much less studied challenge, mostly done in the context of Bayesian network models [63] that are data hungry, but also for the CASSANDRA model [58].

ThreatGet turns out to be the best alternative due to its efficient interfacing with CASSANDRA via the meta-language of Engstrom et al. [19], which is the most appropriate approach for combining the attack graph construction of ThreatGet with the simulation provided by CASSANDRA. The meta-language is the glue between ThreatGet and CASSANDRA that orchestrates the methods for attack graph construction and simulation. While this broadens the applicability and accuracy of the combined model, it imposes more complexity on end-users because there are several underlying systems to learn (such as domain-specific simulations) or choosing a single system to use, which means giving up on the additional power of the diversity provided by the meta-language.

The next two subsections clarify how ThreatGet and CASSANDRA are combined based on their internal structures and the information and analysis results they provide. Since both models leverage graph representations, the translation from one model to the other is achieved in a straightforward manner. First, the translation of the ThreatGet representation to the CASSANDRA representation is clarified. Next, the conversion of static information from the security configurations in ThreatGet to the dynamic aspects of the cascading effects simulation provided by CASSANDRA is explained.

4.2 Graph-Based Network Representation

The ThreatGet model has two main types of nodes, elements and assets, where assets are the critical nodes and are understood to be the main targets of adversaries. Accordingly, the analysis of threats and potential attack graphs is centered around the assets. The physical and logical links between assets and elements are modeled as connections, which correspond to edges in a graph representation. Thus, a ThreatGet model is a graph $H = (N, C)$, where N denotes the set of nodes of different types and $C \subseteq N \times N$ denotes the set of connections among them. In general, assets and elements represent systems in the information technology and operational technology networks of critical infrastructures or parts thereof.

By contrast, the graph $G = (V, E)$ in the CASSANDRA model is designed at a more abstract level – it does not explicitly distinguish between assets (critical nodes) and elements (non-critical nodes), but considers all nodes in V as important in a risk assessment. Similarly, the edges in E can be logical, physical, cyber or any type necessary to provide context and semantics to the model at hand. Hence, a CASSANDRA model is able to capture dependencies, interactions and relations across different domains and industry sectors that would not be possible with ThreatGet. Nodes in a ThreatGet graph may comprise nested hierarchical models. This enables properties of elements and assets to be modeled, for example, software is in a server, a server is in a room, and a room is in a building.

Nevertheless, the ThreatGet model graph H can be directly translated to a CASSANDRA model graph G by mapping each $n \in N$ (i.e., each element or asset) to a $v \in V$ in CASSANDRA. For each connection $(n_i, n_j) \in C$, two dependencies $(v_k, v_l), (v_l, v_k) \in E$ are created while ensuring that no loops in terms of the input and output symbols are introduced. The translation of the nested hierarchical model is straightforward – each nested element is translated to a single vertex in the CASSANDRA graph and edge are added for "is in" relations between elements and the actual asset. This possibly leads to $|E| \geq |C|$.

Value: Undefined/None

	1	2	3	4	5
1	0.00	0.02	0.10	0.65	0.23
2		0.00	0.05	0.35	0.60
3			0.00	0.20	0.80
4				0.00	1.00
5					1.00

Value: Weak

	1	2	3	4	5
1	0.05	0.20	0.50	0.20	0.05
2		0.05	0.30	0.50	0.15
3			0.00	0.35	0.65
4				0.15	0.85
5					1.00

Value: Moderate

	1	2	3	4	5
1	0.15	0.65	0.10	0.08	0.02
2		0.10	0.60	0.20	0.10
3			0.10	0.55	0.35
4				0.35	0.65
5					1.00

Value: Strong

	1	2	3	4	5
1	0.80	0.10	0.08	0.02	0.00
2		0.75	0.15	0.08	0.02
3			0.70	0.20	0.10
4				0.65	0.35
5					1.00

Fig. 1. Mappings of five different values of a security property.

4.3 Security Properties and Transition Probabilities

The ThreatGet model is more specific to the domains of information technology and operational technology networks. It is also more elaborate and detailed from an information perspective. Due to the similarity of the graph-based approaches underlying ThreatGet and CASSANDRA, the structural translation is rather straightforward, and the interdependency graph of the CASSANDRA model is readily instantiated.

The key task is the instantiation of the "inner" model, specifically, the probabilistic Mealy automaton model. The set of states S can be chosen quite freely – a standard choice in a risk management setting is to use five different states. The input and output alphabets $\Sigma_{\text{in}} = \Sigma_{\text{out}} = \Sigma$ can be derived from the threats that are analyzed. Every input symbol m_{in} would correspond to a threat that acts on the respective node in the ThreatGet model. Similarly, every output symbol m_{out} corresponds to the effects that the threat poses to the node, which would also represent a threat to the dependent nodes. This makes m_{out} the new input m_{in} for all dependent nodes in the CASSANDRA model.

Finally, to obtain the probabilistic transition function δ of the Mealy automaton, the security configuration used for each node in the ThreatGet model is employed. The individual nodes – and even the connections – contain security properties that describe the protection level of a node. Hence, each node in N has a specific configuration, comprising a set of security properties A and a specific value $x \in X$ where $X = \{\text{Undefined, None, Weak, Moderate, Strong}\}$. As mentioned previously, the security configuration is used during the analysis when an anti-pattern rule evaluates whether an adversary can successfully conduct an attack (e.g., exploit a vulnerability given a specific security configuration). The

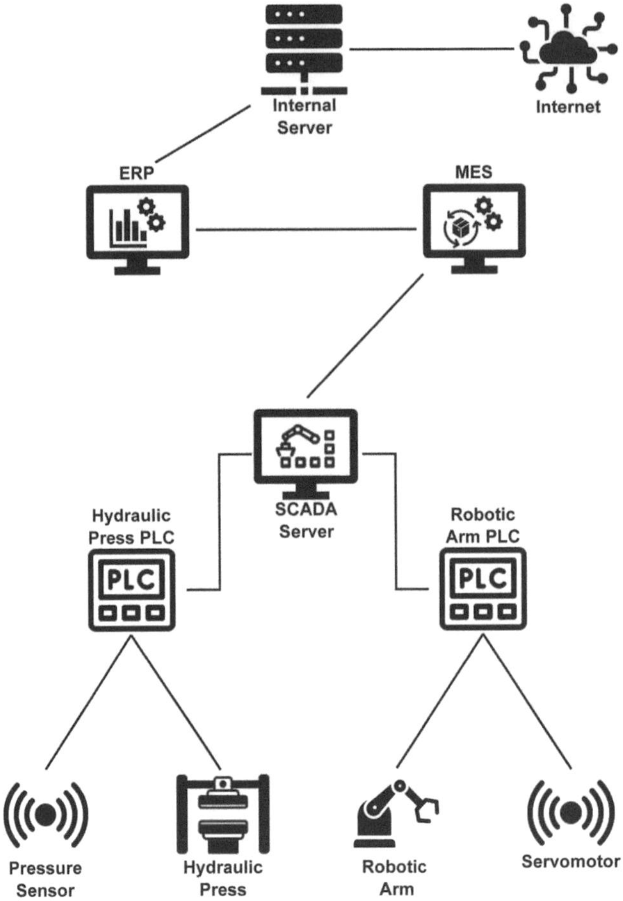

Fig. 2. Manufacturing facility infrastructure.

general understanding is, the better the security configuration, specifically, the better the values of x set for each of the security properties of a node in N, the lower the likelihood of an attack to be successful.

In CASSANDRA, this information is translated to the probabilistic transition function δ. For any given threat, a mapping $\varphi : A \times X \rightarrow \Delta S$ is defined, which takes a security configuration and maps the value x of a security property to a probability distribution $p \in [0,1]^{|S|}$. A simple solution is to describe the probability distribution for each value x as a matrix D, where d_{ij} is the transition probability to go from state s_i to s_j given the value x of a specific security property. Figure 1 shows simple mappings of five different values of a security property – Undefined (1), None (2), Weak (3), Moderate (4) and Strong (5) – to the matrices of transition probabilities.

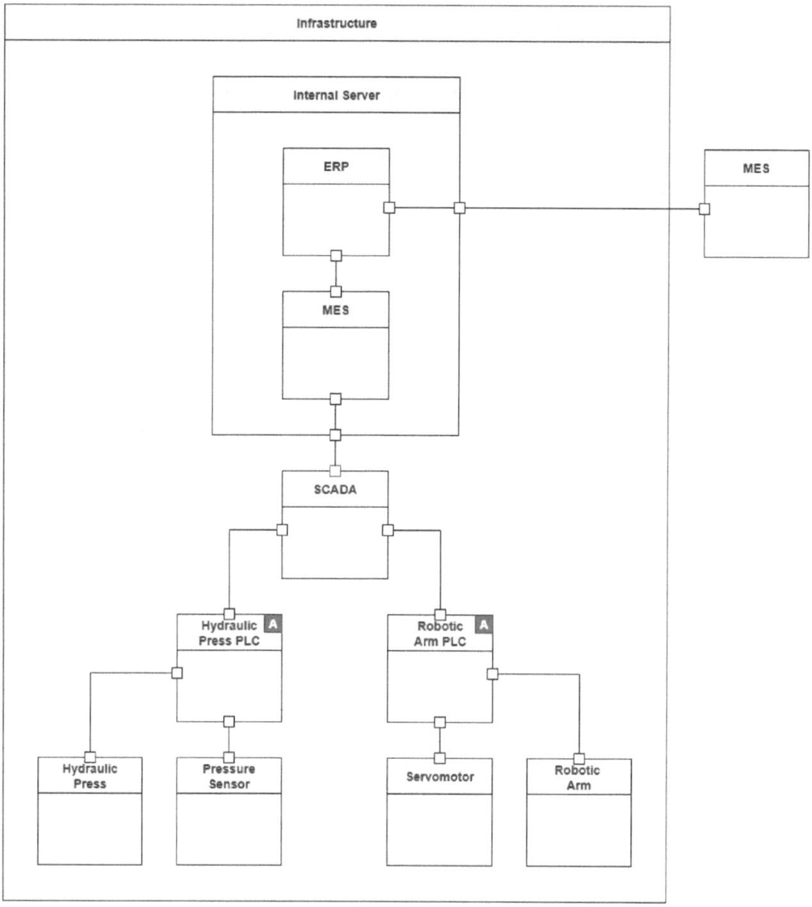

Fig. 3. ThreatGet model of the manufacturing facility infrastructure.

5 Example Scenario

ThreatGet and CASSANDRA consider different viewpoints in their analyses. ThreatGet, which works in a goal-oriented manner, always focuses on an attack target, namely, the asset that is compromised and provides information about the view of potential attackers. By contrast, CASSANDRA provides a view of the consequences of certain events on the entire system based on a statistical simulation involving time steps. This section demonstrates how the ThreatGet and CASSANDRA approaches are combined to analyze a real-world scenario.

5.1 Scenario Description

Figure 2 shows a simple manufacturing facility. A server at the top level runs an enterprise resource planning (ERP) system that handles business operations, scheduling, production planning and resources. The enterprise resource planning system is connected to the Internet as well as to a manufacturing execution system (MES) that is connected to a supervisory control and data acquisition (SCADA) server that conducts centralized monitoring and control of the manufacturing process. Two programmable logic controllers (PLCs) are located at the next level. One programmable logic controller operates a hydraulic press based on input data from a pressure sensor. The other programmable logic controller operates a robotic arm based on data received from an optical position sensor.

The example attack begins with a simple exploit of the exposed Internet connection. A remote access vulnerability in the enterprise resource planning system coupled with weak malware detection enables malware to initially compromise the server on which the enterprise resource planning system executes. The malware enters as routine system traffic, evades endpoint protections and provides a disguised back channel to the attacker. The malware then makes its way to the manufacturing execution system, where it surveils the network and uses legitimate communications protocols to propagate itself to the SCADA server. The SCADA server continues to send commands as usual, which enables the malware to spread to the programmable logic controllers operating the hydraulic press and robotic arm. At this point, the attacker is able to exfiltrate data, manipulate data and/or seize control of the hydraulic press and robotic arm, potentially tampering with products, damaging machinery and even injuring workers.

5.2 ThreatGet System Model

Figure 3 shows the ThreatGet model of the manufacturing facility infrastructure. The Infrastructure element (type: Encasement) represents the system that must be protected. The only element outside the system is the Internet element (type: External Interactor), which conveys that the system can receive data from the Internet and react to the data received. In order to simplify the presentation, certain elements are not shown in Fig. 3.

All the incoming data is checked by the Company Firewall element (type: Firewall), the first point of external communications, which constitutes the initial attack surface of the system. The main interface to the system is the Internal Server element (type: Server) on which the ERP element (type: Software) and MES element (type: Software) execute. The Internal Server element controls the ERP and MES elements and manages the incoming and outgoing data. The Internal Server element also handles internal communications.

The Internal Control Device element located to the right of the Internal Server element represents the mobile device of an employee who can access internal system data. The ERP element can be accessed from the Internet element via the external interface of the Internal Server element, for example, to query data or update the system. The ERP element is directly connected to the MES element, which serves as the control software for the production environment and retrieves the internal production data. The Internal Server element, its contained software (ERP and MES elements) and the mobile device (Internal Control Device element) constitute the management layer of the system and are contained within the Enterprise Management Layer element (type: Item Boundary).

The MES element communicates with the SCADA Server element (type: Control Unit) via the internal interface of the Internal Server element, which serves as the direct control unit of the industrial control system. The SCADA Server element is part of the Supervisory Layer element (type: Item Boundary) along with a Real Time Database element (type: Database Server). The SCADA Server element can exchange data with the Real Time Database element to match the input coming from the Enterprise Management Layer element and the data from the Field Layer element (type: Item Boundary) containing the physical components of the system.

The SCADA Server element has direct control over the Hydraulic Press PLC element (type: Control Unit) and Robotic Arm PLC element (type: Control Unit). The Hydraulic Press PLC and Robotic Arm PLC elements are responsible for executing commands for their respective devices. The SCADA Server element sends the commands to the Field Network element (type: Network) within the Field Layer element. The Hydraulic Press PLC element exchanges data with the Hydraulic Press element (type: Actuator) and Pressure Sensor element (type: Sensor). Similarly, the Robotic Arm PLC element controls the Servomotor element (type: Actuator) and receives data from the Optical Position Sensor element (type: Sensor).

In ThreatGet, assets are components that are of particular value to the system. Therefore, the Hydraulic Press PLC and Robotic Arm PLC elements are marked as assets (A). The Hydraulic Press PLC and Robotic Arm PLC assets are linked to the Functional Integrity of Control Unit asset. This implies that, in the event of an attack on the Hydraulic Press PLC and/or Robotic Arm PLC, significant damage could be caused to the system.

```
ELEMENT : "Server" {
  HAS INTERFACE {
    HAS FLOW {
      SOURCE ELEMENT : "Internet" &
       INCLUDES NO ELEMENT {
         HAS ATTRIBUTE "Network Filtering" = "Strong"
                          }
            } &
    PROVIDES CAPABILITY "Initial Access" := "True"
                 }
                    }
```

Fig. 4. Rule 1: Setting the initial target of the attack path.

5.3 ThreatGet Analysis

The next step is to define the rules for performing the threat analysis. The system model described above comprises several elements that communicate with each other across internal logical boundaries. Some of the communications connections lead to critical paths that are essential to system operation.

The focus is on investigating attack paths that are possible from external threats. For this purpose, analysis rules are defined that enable access to an externally accessible server and simulate subsequent lateral movements in the system to physical operating elements. This enables the interactions of cyber-physical threats to be visualized in a comprehensible manner using ThreatGet.

Note that insider attacks via the mobile device or internal errors – for example, by comparing control commands and real-time data – could also be considered. However, to reduce the complexity and simplify the presentation, four essential analysis rules are employed. The rules demonstrate the functionality of the ThreatGet analysis tool.

Rule 1 (Fig. 4) sets the initial target of the attack path. Line 1 opens the anti-pattern and focuses on elements in the system with type: Server. Line 2 checks whether or not the server has an interface. Lines 3 through 8 check whether the interface on the server has an incoming flow (path) from outside the infrastructure and can receive data from an element of type: Internet. Lines 5 through 7 also check whether the path includes no element with the Network Filtering attribute set to Strong. In this case, only one Company Firewall element is exposed because its Network Filtering is not set to Strong; as a result, the attack is not detected. Line 9 assigns the Initial Access capability to the server Interface, indicating that the attack has initial access to the server via its interface. Line 10 closes the interface portion of the rule and Line 11 closes the pattern portion of the rule.

```
1 ELEMENT : "Server" {
2   HAS INTERFACE {
3     REQUIRES CAPABILITY "Initial Access" >= "True" &
4       HAS ATTRIBUTE "Access Control" != "Strong" &
5       HAS ATTRIBUTE "Input Control" != "Strong"
6                 } &
7          PROVIDES CAPABILITY "Defense Evasion" := "True"
8                   }
```

Fig. 5. Rule 2: Building on initial access to evade a defense.

Rule 2 (Fig. 5) builds directly on Rule 1 and uses the initial access to the server interface to evade a defense. Lines 1 and 2 focus on elements in the system with type: Server that have an interface. Line 3 checks whether the attacker has already gained initial access to the interface of the server, which is the precondition of the anti-pattern. Lines 4 and 5 examine whether the properties Access Control and Input Control of the interface are not set to Strong (i.e., adequate defenses do not exist). In this case, Line 7 assigns the Defense Evasion capability to the Server element (not to the interface). This implies that the attacker with initial access can evade the defense.

In addition to applying rules that focus on elements, ThreatGet conducts flow analysis. This means there does not have to be a direct connection between a source and a target as in the case of the Server and Internet elements. Instead, a flow may involve indirect connections between a source and a target that involve several intervening elements, connectors and interfaces. A flow can also describe how an adversary follows a path through an entire infrastructure, mostly by gaining access to and seizing control of individual elements.

```
1  FLOW {
2    SOURCE ELEMENT: "Software"{
3      REQUIRES CAPABILITY "Command and Control"
4         >= "true"
5                                   } &
6    TARGET ELEMENT: "Control Unit"{
7      PROVIDES CAPABILITY  "Command and Control"
8         := "true"
9                                       } &
10    INCLUDES NO INTERFACE {
11      (HAS ATTRIBUTE "Access Control" = "Strong"
12       HAS ATTRIBUTE "Input Control" = "Strong")
13                               }
14      }
```

Fig. 6. Rule 3: Implementing flow analysis.

Rule 3 (Fig. 6) implements flow analysis in the case of an attacker that already gained the Command and Control capability over the ERP and MES elements. Line 1 begins the flow analysis. Line 2 states that the flow path starts at an element of type: Software. Line 6 states that the target element has type: Control Unit. Line 3 requires the precondition that the attacker has gained control of the element of type: Software. Line 7 has the postcondition of the anti-pattern,

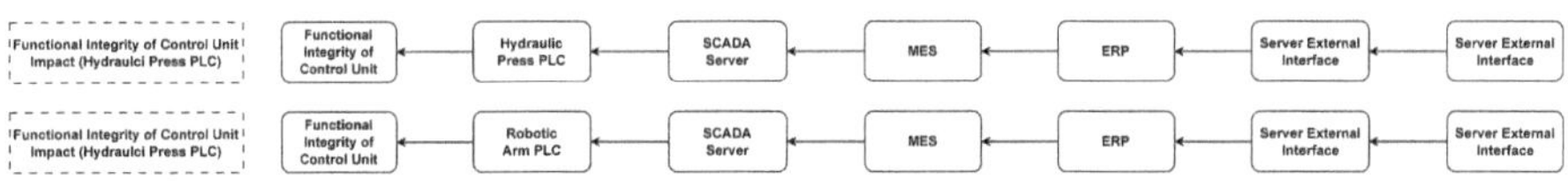

Fig. 7. ThreatGet attack paths in the manufacturing facility infrastructure.

indicating that the attacker gains Command and Control capability over the target element of type: Control Unit. However, the access is gained only when the conditions in Lines 10 through 12 are satisfied – the flow does not contain an interface whose Access Control or Input Control capabilities are not set to Strong (similar to Rule 2).

Figure 7 shows the set of attack paths resulting from the analysis. Each attack path starts at the initial entrance point and ends at a defined asset, where every element along the path is also impacted by a threat. The paths are similar because the scenario uses analysis rules that have the same elements in the attack steps. Specifically, both paths have the Server External Interface element as the entry point and the Functional Integrity of Control Unit asset as the target. However, the penultimate attack steps differ. The first attack path shows the effects on the Hydraulic Press PLC element whereas the second attack path shows the effects on the Robotic Arm PLC element. Each step in the paths is related to one of the diagram components and a change in the related capabilities.

5.4 CASSANDRA Model

Figure 8 shows the CASSANDRA model of the manufacturing facility infrastructure, which includes the graph structure derived from the ThreatGet model (upper part of the figure). Note that the CASSANDRA model includes graph nodes and edges as well as transition probabilities to instantiate the probabilistic Mealy automata associated with the nodes.

The original ThreatGet model can be extended in CASSANDRA to include other nodes of interest in the manufacturing facility. This enables analysts to utilize the full potential of CASSANDRA to examine cascading effects over multiple domains by incorporating various assets from the cyber and physical domains.

Eight more nodes are added to the CASSANDRA model (bottom of Fig. 8). The additional nodes include three physical nodes – Staff, which expresses the wellbeing of employees in the vicinity of the two machines; Machines, which indicates the functionality of or damage to nearby machines; and Products, which conveys the integrity of the produced goods. The additional nodes also include four non-tangible nodes corresponding to key indicators of the company's wellbeing – Legal Obligations, Revenue, Productivity and Reputation, and one node, Company Impact, that conveys the general impact on the company.

The ThreatGet analysis in Sect. 5.3 yielded two possible attack paths that would reach the hydraulic press and robot arm programmable logic controllers and compromise their integrity. Instead of simply duplicating the ThreatGet results, CASSANDRA can conduct a what-if analysis using the ThreatGet results. Specifically, CASSANDRA takes the programmable logic controllers being compromised as an input and evaluates the potential cascading effects in the system given the malfunction of the hydraulic press or the robotic arm as a starting point. CASSANDRA also evaluates how likely assets with their specific configurations can be affected and subsequently affect other nodes. Moreover, existing node behavior imported from ThreatGet as properties (usually from the cyber domain) can be expanded. For example, the robotic arm could

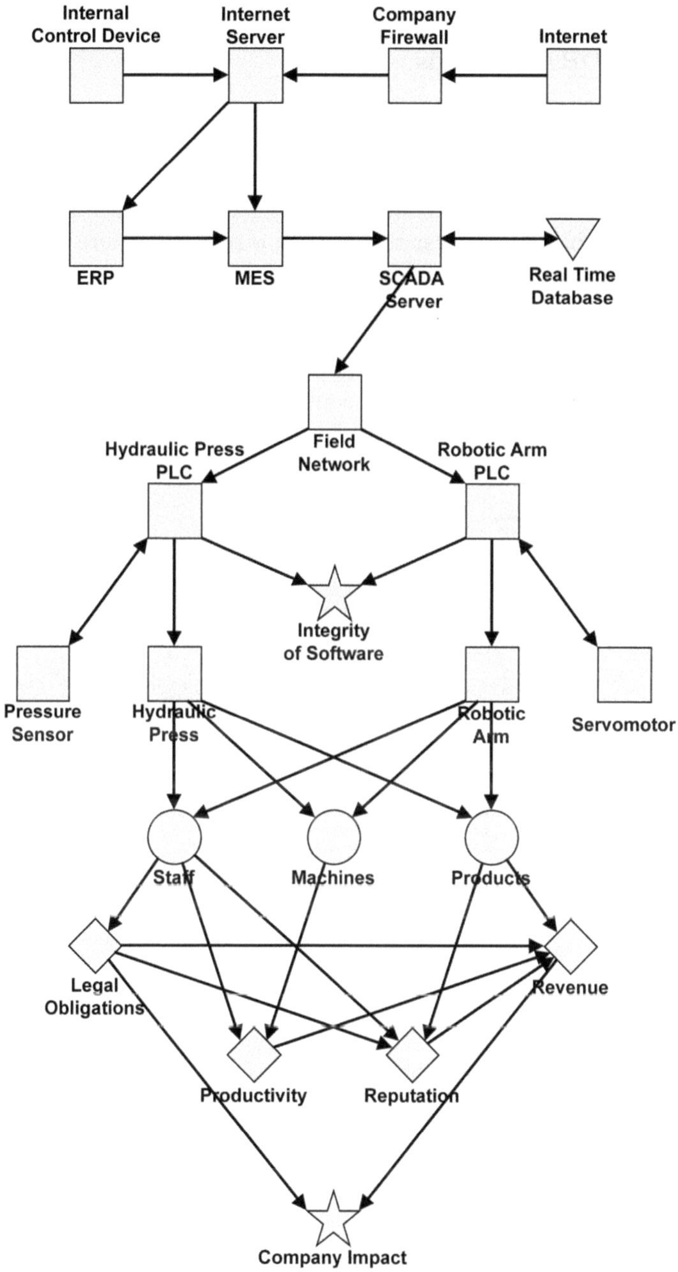

Fig. 8. CASSANDRA model of the manufacturing facility infrastructure.

damage itself due to faulty behavior outside the operational zone whereas the hydraulic press could only damage products by using excessive pressure.

5.5 CASSANDRA Analysis

As discussed above, ThreatGet models can be translated to CASSANDRA models and augmented with appropriate simulation parameters. This section shows how a ThreatGet model that focuses on software and hardware components from specific domains can be expanded in CASSANDRA with nodes from other domains. This enables an analyst to simulate a scenario where an attacker has successfully compromised a programmable logic controller and analyze further impacts to the company. In this case, the CASSANDRA analysis uses the ThreatGet results as input for its simulation.

The probabilistic model in CASSANDRA may return different results for individual simulation runs. Therefore, considering the result of a single simulation run is inadequate to understand the entire network dynamics. CASSANDRA

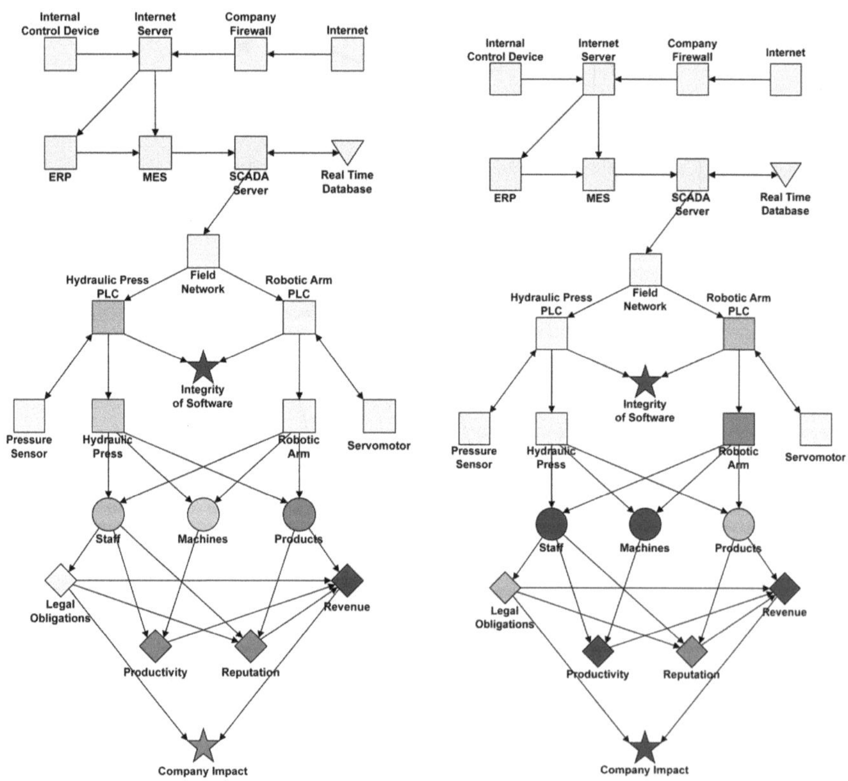

(a) Initiation at Hydraulic Press PLC. (b) Initiation at Robotic Arm PLC.

Fig. 9. Cascading effects of an incident initiating at different nodes.

addresses this limitation by providing statistics for multiple simulation runs that reveal how often certain nodes have problems as well as by highlighting the best-case and worst-case scenarios over all the simulation outcomes.

Figure 9 shows the two worst-case scenarios in CASSANDRA's simulation analysis. The triggers for the two scenarios are the Command and Control incident initiating at the Hydraulic Press PLC node (left-hand side) and initiating at the Robotic Arm PLC node (right-hand side). The darker the shading in the figure, the greater the problem severity – light gray (State 1) corresponds to no problems whereas dark gray (State 5) corresponds to severe damage.

The two worst-case scenarios manifest some key differences regarding how the threat compromises the two programmable logic controllers. In Fig. 9, the two Integrity of Software star nodes indicate problems at a more abstract level (i.e., as an aggregation of larger parts of the graph). This enables straightforward comparisons of the simulation results later in the analysis.

In both cases, a programmable logic controller is compromised via Command and Control, causing Integrity of Software to transition to State 5 corresponding to severe damage. While the two programmable logic controllers have transitioned to State 3 because they face the same problem, the nodes that follow them already behave differently. Since compromising Robotic Arm PLC causes Robotic Arm to malfunction, which can also physically damage itself, Robotic Arm transitions to State 4. In contrast, compromising Hydraulic Press PLC does not affect Hydraulic Press because its malfunctioning cannot physically damage itself; therefore, Hydraulic Press transitions to State 2. Of course, the malfunction would likely damage or destroy products.

The company impacts are conveyed by the Company Impact star nodes. The company impacts are evaluated by considering the non-technical aspects affected by cascading effects of the initial Command and Control threat in the cyber domain. Nodes representing the non-technical aspects are located at the bottom of the graph and come in two categories – round nodes and diamond nodes.

The round nodes represent physical components that are directly affected by malfunctioning Machines. Staff, who work with malfunctioning machines, will, in the best case, have increased workloads while trying to fix the machines or attempt to compensate by manually performing the production steps. In the worst case, they can be injured while working with or attempting to fix malfunctioning machines. Additionally, other machines such as assembly belts could be damaged or destroyed. Most importantly, Products can be damaged or destroyed, but it is also possible to indicate reduced production rates by assigning states to Products. Comparing the two scenarios, it is seen that a malfunctioning Hydraulic Press would damage or destroy more products whereas a malfunctioning Robotic Arm would also damage or destroy other machines and injure staff in the worst case.

The diamond nodes represent less tangible components that are relevant indicators about the company and are affected by the round nodes. Both scenarios have large impacts on Revenue (due to damaged or destroyed products) and

Reputation (due to product unavailability). The Robotic Arm PLC scenario has a larger impact on Productivity than the Hydraulic Press PLC scenario, and also leads to Legal Obligations for the company if staff are injured. Even in the worst case, the Hydraulic Press PLC does not result in Legal Obligations for the company.

Examination of Company Impact reveals that the Robotic Arm PLC compromise has a larger impact on the company (State 5) than the Hydraulic Press PLC compromise (State 4). Note that this is just one interpretation of the two worst-case scenarios in which the robotic arm does not always injure staff whereas the hydraulic press will almost certainly damage products. Thus, the overall impact on the company might not be worse in the case of the robotic arm compared with the hydraulic press, on average. To make such a statement, however, attention must be paid to the simulation result statistics.

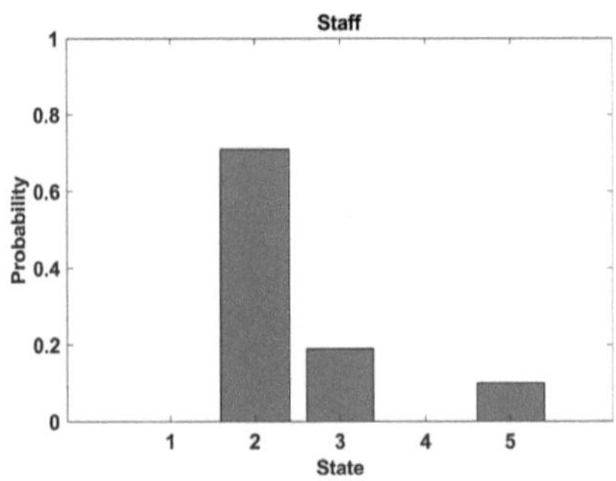

(a) Staff node distribution.

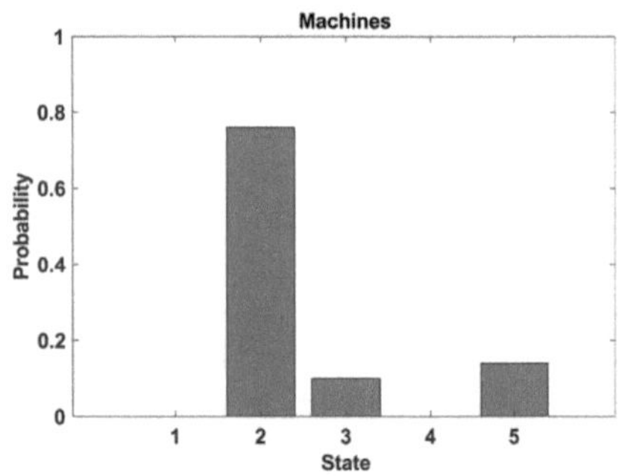

(b) Machines node distribution.

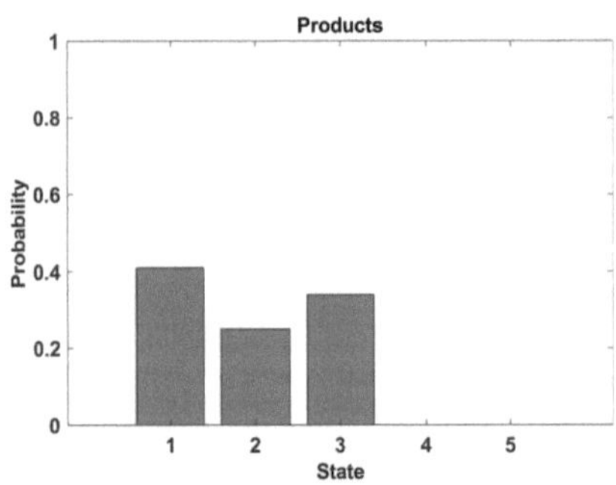

(a) Products node distribution.

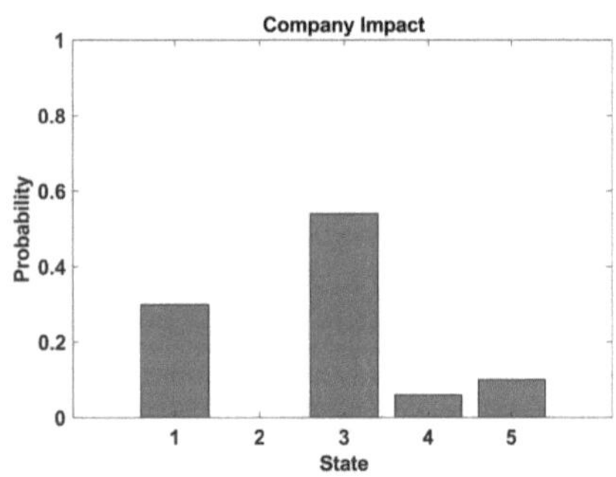

(b) Company Impact node distribution.

Fig. 10. Probability distributions.

Figure 10 shows the probability distributions over states for four relevant nodes – Staff, Machines, Products and Company Impact – when an incident initiates at Robotic Arm PLC. It appears from the distributions that Robotic Arm is a greater threat to Staff and Machines and less Products are damaged. This is underscored by the observation that the probabilities for Staff and Machines to end up in State 2 are almost the same whereas Machines has a higher probability to end up in the worst State 5 compared with Staff. This indicates that a malfunctioning Robotic Arm would cause greater damage to Machines than to Staff. Since Products has a very low probability of ending up in State 4 or State 5, the damage is the least in this scenario.

The probability distribution of Company Impact implies that the likelihood of ending up in State 5 is significantly less than for State 3 or even State 1. This means that, in the worst-case scenario, the Company Impact is severe. In contrast, for the Command and Control incident, the most likely outcome would be minor to moderate Compact Impact. This information can be used, for example, in risk matrices where likelihood and consequence severity are taken into account.

Looking again at the worst-case scenario of the Command and Control incident starting at Hydraulic Press PLC, Company Impact is not severe (State 5) because the malfunctioning hydraulic press would not injure employees. Additional plots of the node state distributions for this scenario are not provided for reasons of space, but it would be case that, although the worst state for Company Impact is just State 4, the outcome would also be the most likely because Products are damaged or destroyed almost all the time. Therefore, when only comparing the worst-case scenarios, the conclusion would be that an attacker would cause more damage after successfully compromising Robotic Arm PLC. While this might be true for the worst case, an attacker would likely cause more damage on average when compromising Hydraulic Press PLC.

6 Discussion

ThreatGet and CASSANDRA engage similar concepts, which facilitates the combination of the two approaches. However, in a more complex infrastructure, the complexity of the CASSANDRA model would increase. Since additional edges would be introduced and additional nodes may be necessary, the CASSANDRA model could become difficult to handle for a human user, which would make it difficult to adapt. More extensive automation during the translation process would better support analysts and reduce the need for adaptation later.

ThreatGet and CASSANDRA models currently operate in discrete time steps. In the case of CASSANDRA, the Mealy automata representing node status are associated with Markov chains, under reasonable assumptions, on a countable state space with discrete time. The transitions are defined by a transition matrix that specifies the transition probabilities for input symbols based on the current states. Consequently, when transitioning from discrete to continuous Markov chains, it is possible to introduce the expected holding times and derive the jump chains from the given transition probabilities.

ThreatGet and CASSANDRA provide different, albeit valuable, insights into how attack paths, potential threats and risks may affect entities beyond the primary target. A natural question that arises is how to quantify threats and risk based on the results obtained from a combined threat analysis. Following the example above, it is prudent to determine the impact on the number of goods produced. In this context, the CASSANDRA model can be leveraged to drive a Poisson point process by introducing a measurable function. This function, defined over the state space of the CASSANDRA model, would take values in $\mathbb{R}_+$ and convey the homogeneous or inhomogeneous rate parameter of the Poisson point process.

Finally, from a domain perspective, the current ThreatGet version is mostly limited to the cyber domain whereas CASSANDRA provides a much broader scope for modeling. As highlighted in the example, CASSANDRA can include personnel and products in an abstract manner as well as intangible assets such as reputation and revenue. Although the general concept of ThreatGet facilitates the modeling of elements in the physical domain and more abstract entities such as staff, it would be difficult to define vulnerabilities, assign security properties and describe how threats would affect the abstract entities. Nevertheless, ThreatGet would support modeling beyond the cyber-physical and infrastructure borders as well as complex relations within and among critical infrastructures.

7 Conclusions

Several aspects have to be considered to perform holistic risk analyses of critical infrastructures. Threat modeling tools usually focus on the cyber domain whereas ThreatGet provides a knowledge database of threats for information technology and operational technology systems while elucidating possible attack paths to reach high-value targets. Less attention is paid to structured what-if analyses of complex systems for which CASSANDRA provides a domain-independent approach at a higher level of abstraction, producing detailed insights into the potential effects after an asset is compromised. Combining ThreatGet's threat analysis capabilities for information and operational technology systems with CASSANDRA's explorative and stochastic cascading effects analysis leverages the strengths of the two approaches. The integrated framework could support critical infrastructure operators in complying with current regulations and directives such as the European Union's Network and Information Security Directive of 2022 and Critical Entities Resilience Directive, improving security, risk analyses and the overall protection of critical infrastructures.

Acknowledgement. This research was supported by the Austrian National Security Research Program (KIRAS) of the Austrian Federal Ministry of Finance under Project nos. FO999905291 and FO999905306, and by the Key Digital Technologies Programme of the European Union under Grant no. 101096658.

References

1. Alvarez Lopez, P., et al.: Microscopic traffic simulation using SUMO. In: Proceedings of the Twenty-First International Conference on Intelligent Transportation Systems, pp. 2575–2582 (2018)

2. Arismendi, R., Barros, A., Grall, A.: Piecewise deterministic Markov process for condition-based maintenance models – Application to critical infrastructures with discrete-state deterioration. Reliability Engineering and System Safety, vol. 212, article no. 107540 (2021)
3. Armenia, S., et al.: A dynamic simulation approach to support the evaluation of cyber risks and security investments in SMEs. Decision Support Systems, vol. 147, article no. 113580 (2021)
4. Arsac, W., Bella, G., Chantry, X., Compagna, L.: Multi-attacker protocol validation. J. Autom. Reason. **46**, 353–388 (2011)
5. Austrian Institute of Technology, CASSANDRA, Vienna, Austria (risk-mgmt.ait.ac.at/cassandra) (2025)
6. Austrian Institute of Technology, ThreatGet, Vienna, Austria www.threatget.com (2025)
7. Badr, A., Yosri, A., Hassini, S., El-Dakhakhni, W.: Coupled continuous-time Markov-chain-Bayesian-network model for dam failure risk prediction. J. Infrastructure Syst. **27**(4) (2021)
8. Baquero, A., Kornecki, A., Zalewski, J.: Threat modeling for aviation computer security. CrossTalk **28**(6), 21–27 (2015)
9. Biden, J.: Executive Order 14028 of May 12, 2021 - Improving the Nation's Cybersecurity. Fed. Reg. **86**(93), 26633–26647 (2021)
10. Bloomfield, R., Popov, P., Salako, K., Stankovic, V., Wright, D.: Preliminary interdependency analysis: An approach to support critical infrastructure risk assessment. Reliab. Eng. Syst. Saf. **167**, 198–217 (2017)
11. Boyens, J., Smith, A., Bartol, N., Winkler, K., Holbrook, A., Fallon, M.: Cybersecurity Supply Chain Risk Management Practices for Systems and Organizations, NIST Special Publication 800–161, Revision 1. National Institute of Standards and Technology, Gaithersburg, Maryland (2024)
12. Brown, T., Beyeler, W., Barton, D.: Assessing infrastructure interdependencies: The challenge of risk analysis for complex adaptive systems. Int. J. Crit. Infrastruct. **1**(1), 108–117 (2004)
13. Buldyrev, S., Parshani, R., Paul, G., Stanley, H., Havlin, S.: Catastrophic cascade of failures in interdependent networks. Nature **464**, 1025–1028 (2010)
14. Cao, Y., Shi, X., Li, Y., Tan, Y., Shahidehpour, M., Shi, S.: A simplified co-simulation model for investigating impacts of cyber-contingency on power system operations. IEEE Trans. Smart Grid **9**(5), 4893–4905 (2018)
15. Caralli, R., Stevens, J., Young, L., Wilson, W.: Introducing OCTAVE Allegro: Improving the Information Security Risk Assessment Process, Technical Report CMU/SEI-2007-TR-012. Carnegie Mellon University, Pittsburgh, Pennsylvania, Software Engineering Institute (2007)
16. Cavallini, S., et al.: A system dynamics framework for modeling critical infrastructure resilience. In: Butts, J., Shenoi, S. (eds.) Critical Infrastructure Protection VIII, pp. 141–154. Springer, Heidelberg (2014)
17. Chehida, S., Rutten, E., Giraud, G., Mocanu, S.: A model-based approach for self-adaptive security in CPS: Application to smart grids. J. Syst. Architecture, vol. 150, article no. 103118 (2024)
18. DistriNet Research Group, LINDDUN Privacy Threat Modeling, Catholic University of Leuven, Heverlee, Belgium (linddun.org) (2025)
19. Engstrom, V., Nebbione, G., Ekstedt, M.: A metalanguage for dynamic attack graphs and lazy generation. Proceedings of the Nineteenth International Conference on Availability, Reliability and Security, article no. 31 (2024)

20. Union, E.: Directive (EU) 2022/2555 of the European Parliament and of the Council of 14 December 2022 on Measures for a High Common Level of Cybersecurity Across the Union, Amending Regulation (EU) No 910/2014 and Directive (EU) 2018/1972, and Repealing Directive (EU) 2016/1148 (NIS 2 Directive) (Text with EEA Relevance), Document 32022L2555. Belgium, Brussels (2022)
21. Union, E.: Directive (EU) 2022/2557 of the European Parliament and of the Council of 14 December 2022 on the Resilience of Critical Entities and Repealing Council Directive 2008/114/EC (Text with EEA Relevance), Document 32022L2557. Belgium, Brussels (2022)
22. Forum of Incident Response and Security Teams (FIRST), CVSS: Common Vulnerability Scoring System v3.1, Specification Document – Revision 1, Cary, North Carolina www.first.org/cvss/v3-1/cvss-v31-specification_r1.pdf (2019)
23. Forum of Incident Response and Security Teams (FIRST), EPSS: Exploit Prediction Scoring System v3, Cary, North Carolina www.first.org/epss (2023)
24. Frydman, M., Ruiz, G., Heymann, E., Cesar, E., Miller, B.: Automating risk analysis of software design models. Sci. World J., article no. 805856 (2014)
25. Fu, C., Gao, Y., Zhong, J., Sun, Y., Zhang, P., Wu, T.: Attack-defense game for critical infrastructure considering the cascade effect, Reliability Engineering and System Safety, vol. 216, article no. 107958 (2021)
26. Hacks, S., Katsikeas, S.: Towards an ecosystem of domain specific languages for threat modeling. In: La Rosa, M., Sadiq, S., Teniente, E. (eds.) Advanced Information Systems Engineering, pp. 3–18. Springer, Cham (2021)
27. Haimes, Y., Lambert, J., Li, D., Schooff, R., Tulsiani, V.: Hierarchical holographic modeling for risk identification in complex systems. In: Proceedings of the IEEE International Conference on Systems, Man and Cybernetics – Intelligent Systems for the 21st Century, vol. 2, pp. 1027–1032 (1995)
28. Haimes, Y., Pu, J.: Leontief-based model of risk in complex interconnected infrastructures. J. Infrastructure Syst. **7**(1) (2001)
29. Hernandez Azucena, J.: Reliability Modeling and Improvement of Critical Infrastructures: Theory, Simulation and Computational Methods, Ph.D. Dissertation, Department of Industrial Engineering, University of Arkansas, Fayetteville, Arkansas (scholarworks.uark.edu/etd/5136) (2023)
30. Hysn Technologies, Awesome Threat Modeling Collection, Newark, Delaware (github.com/hysnsec/awesome-threat-modelling) (2025)
31. IriusRisk, The Threat Modeling Tool, Huesca, Spain. www.iriusrisk.com/threat-modeling-platform (2025)
32. Itemis, Itemis SECURE – Cybersecurity Threat Analysis and Risk Assessment Tool, Chicago, Illinois www.itemis.com/en/products/itemis-secure (2025)
33. Kavak, H., Padilla, J., Vernon-Bido, D., Diallo, S., Gore, R., Shetty, S.: Simulation for cybersecurity: state of the art and future directions, J. Cybersecurity vol. 7(1), article no. tyab005 (2021)
34. Kelic, A., Warren, D., Phillips, L.: Cyber and Physical Infrastructure Interdependencies, SANDIA Report SAND2008-6192. Sandia National Laboratories, Albuquerque, New Mexico (2008)
35. Konev, A., Shelupanov, A., Kataev, M., Ageeva, V., Nabieva, A.: A survey of threat modeling techniques: Protected objects and classification of threats. Symmetry, vol. 14(3), article no. 549 (2022)
36. S. Konig, T. Grafenauer, S. Rass and S. Schauer, Practical risk analysis in interdependent critical infrastructures – A how-to, *Proceedings of the Twelfth International Conference on Emerging Security Information, Systems and Technologies*, pp. 150–157, 2018

37. S. Konig, S. Rass, B. Rainer and S. Schauer, Hybrid dependencies between cyber and physical systems, in *Intelligent Computing*, K. Arai, R. Bhatia and S. Kapoor (Eds.), Springer, Cham, Switzerland, pp. 550–565, 2019
38. Kotzanikolaou, P., Theoharidou, M., Gritzalis, D.: Assessing n-order dependencies between critical infrastructures. Int. J. Crit. Infrastruct. **9**(1–2), 93–110 (2013)
39. Kotzanikolaou, P., Theoharidou, M., Gritzalis, D.: Interdependencies between critical infrastructures: analyzing the risk of cascading effects. In: Bologna, S., Hämmerli, B., Gritzalis, D., Wolthusen, S. (eds.) CRITIS 2011. LNCS, vol. 6983, pp. 104–115. Springer, Heidelberg (2013). https://doi.org/10.1007/978-3-642-41476-3_9
40. Lenzini, G., Mauw, S., Ouchani, S.: Security analysis of socio-technical physical systems. Comput. Electr. Eng. **47**, 258–274 (2015)
41. Ling, E., Lagerstrom, R., Ekstedt, M.: A systematic literature review of information sources for threat modeling in the power systems domain. In: Rashid, A., Popov, P. (eds.) Critical Information Infrastructures Security, pp. 47–58. Springer, Cham (2020)
42. Liu, S., Yin, C., Chen, D., Lv, H., Zhang, Q.: Cascading failure in multiple critical infrastructure interdependent networks of a syncretic railway system. IEEE Trans. Intell. Transp. Syst. **23**(6), 5740–5753 (2022)
43. Luiijf, E., Nieuwenhuijs, A., Klaver, M., van Eeten, M., Cruz, E.: Empirical findings on critical infrastructure dependencies in Europe. In: Critical Information Infrastructure Security, R. Setola and S. Geretshuber (Eds.), Springer, Cham, Switzerland, pp. 302–310 (2009)
44. Marback, A., Do, H., He, K., Kondamarri, S., Xu, D.: A threat model based approach to security testing. Software - Practice and Experience **43**(2), 241–258 (2013)
45. Mead, N., Shull, F., Spears, J., Heibl, S., Weber, S., Cleland-Huang, J.: Crowd sourcing the creation of *personae non gratae* for requirements-phase threat modeling. In: Proceedings of the Twenty-Fifth IEEE International Requirements Engineering Conference, pp. 412–417 (2017)
46. Meland, P., Paja, E., Gjaere, E., Paul, S., Dalpiaz, F., Giorgini, P.: Threat analysis in goal-oriented security requirements modeling. Int. J. Secure Softw. Eng. **5**(2), 1–19 (2014)
47. Microsoft, The STRIDE Threat Model, Redmond, Washington (learn.microsoft.com/en-us/previous-versions/commerce-server/ee823878(v=cs.20)) (2009)
48. Microsoft, M.T.: Modeling Tool 2016 Getting Started Guide. Redmond, Washington (2016)
49. Microsoft, M.T.: Modeling Tool 2016 User Guide. Redmond, Washington (2016)
50. Musman, S., Turner, A.: A game oriented approach to minimizing cybersecurity risk. Int. J. Saf. Secur. Eng. **8**(2), 212–222 (2018)
51. Nhlabatsi, A., Hussein, A., Fetais, N., Khan, K.: Design and implementation of a threat-specific security risk assessment tool. In: Proceedings of the IEEE International Conference on Informatics, IoT and Enabling Technologies, pp. 511–518 (2020)
52. Niknami, N., Wu, J.: A constraint partially observable semi-Markov decision process for the attack-defense relationships in various critical infrastructures. Cyber-Phys. Syst. **8**(2), 85–110 (2021)
53. Petit, F., et al.: Analysis of Critical Infrastructure Dependencies and Interdependencies, Technical Report ANL/GSS-15/4. Argonne National Laboratory, Argonne, Illinois (2015)

54. Ouyang, M.: Review of modeling and simulation of interdependent critical infrastructure systems. Reliab. Eng. Syst. Saf. **121**, 43–60 (2014)
55. OWASP Foundation, OWASP Threat Dragon, Wilmington, Delaware (owasp.org/www-project-threat-dragon), 2025
56. Qi, J., Ju, W., Sun, K.: Estimating the propagation of interdependent cascading outages with multi-type branching processes. IEEE Trans. Power Syst. **32**(2), 1212–1223 (2017)
57. Rahnamay-Naeini, M., Hayat, M.: Cascading failures in interdependent infrastructures: an interdependent Markov chain approach. IEEE Trans. Smart Grid **7**(4), 1997–2006 (2016)
58. Rass, S., Konig, S., Schauer, S.: Semi-automated parameterization of a probabilistic model using logistic regression - A tutorial. In: Kamhoua, C., Kiekintveld, C., Fang, F., Zhu, Q. (eds.) Game Theory and Machine Learning for Cyber Security, pp. 438–484. John Wiley and Sons, Hoboken (2021)
59. Rass, S., Konig, S., Wachter, J., Mayoral-Vilches, V., Panaousis, E.: Game-theoretic APT defense: an experimental study on robotics. Comput. Secur. **132**, article no. 103328 (2023)
60. Rinaldi, S., Peerenboom, J., Kelly, T.: Identifying, understanding and analyzing critical infrastructure interdependencies. IEEE Control. Syst. **21**(6), 11–25 (2001)
61. Rothfeld, R., Balac, M., Ploetner, K., Antoniou, C.: Agent-based simulation of urban air mobility. In: Proceedings of the Modeling and Simulation Technologies Conference (2018)
62. Saitta, P., Larcom, B., Eddington, M.: Trike v.1 Methodology Document (trike.sourceforge.net/papers/Trike_v1_Methodology_Document-draft.pdf) (2005)
63. Schaberreiter, T., Bouvry, P., Roning, J., Khadraoui, D.: Support tool for a Bayesian network based critical infrastructure risk model. In: Schuetze, O., et al. (eds.) EVOLVE - A Bridge between Probability, pp. 53–75. Set-Oriented Numerics and Evolutionary Computation III Springer, Heidelberg, Germany (2014)
64. Schaberreiter, T., Kittila, K., Halunen, K., Roning, J., Khadraoui, D.: Risk assessment in critical infrastructure security modeling based on dependency analysis. In: Bologna, S., Hammerli, B., Gritzalis, D., Wolthusen, S. (eds.) Critical Information Infrastructure Security, pp. 213–217. Springer, Heidelberg (2013)
65. J. Selin, Evaluation of Threat Modeling Methodologies, Master's Thesis, School of Technology, JAMK Uuiversity of Applied Sciences, Jyvaskyla, Finland (2019). www.theseus.fi/handle/10024/220967
66. Seppanen, H., Luokkala, P., Zhang, Z., Torkki, P., Virrantaus, K.: Critical infrastructure vulnerability - a method for identifying infrastructure service failure interdependencies. Int. J. Crit. Infrastruct. Prot. **22**, 25–38 (2018)
67. Setola, R., De Porcellinis, S., Sforna, M.: Critical infrastructure dependency assessment using the input-output inoperability model. Int. J. Crit. Infrastruct. Prot. **2**(4), 170–178 (2009)
68. Singh, S., Tu, H., Allanach, J., Areta, J., Willett, P., Pattipati, K.: Modeling threats. IEEE Potentials **23**(3), 18–21 (2004)
69. Stergiopoulos, G., Kotzanikolaou, P., Theocharidou, M., Lykou, G., Gritzalis, D.: Time-based critical infrastructure dependency analysis for large-scale and cross-sectoral failures. Int. J. Crit. Infrastruct. Prot. **12**, 46–60 (2016)
70. SystemWeaver, SystemWeaver, Goteborg, Sweden (systemweaver.com) (2025)
71. Tarandach, I., Coles, M.: Threat Modeling: A Practical Guide for Development Teams. O'Reilly Media, Sebastopol, California (2020)

72. The AnyLogic Company, AnyLogic Simulation Software, Chicago, Illinois (2025). www.anylogic.de
73. The White House, National Resilience Strategy, Technical Report, Washington, DC (2025). (bidenwhitehouse.archives.gov/wp-content/uploads/2025/01/National-Resilience-Strategy.pdf)
74. ThreatModeler, ThreatModeler, Jersey City, New Jersey (2025). (www.threatmodeler.com/threatmodeler)
75. Turoff, M., Banuls, V., Plotnick, L., Hiltz, S., de la Huerga, M.: A collaborative dynamic scenario model for the interaction of critical infrastructures. Futures **84**(A), 23–42 (2016)
76. Uceda Velez, T., Morana, M.: Risk Centric Threat Modeling: Process for Attack Simulation and Threat Analysis. John Wiley and Sons, Hoboken, New Jersey (2015)
77. Vieira Passos, M., Barquet, K., Kan, J., Destouni, G., Kalantari, Z.: Hydrometeorological resilience assessment of interconnected critical infrastructures. Sustainable and Resilient Infrastructure **10**(3), 267–283 (2025)
78. Wachter, J.: Graph Models for Cybersecurity – A Survey (2023). arXiv:2311.10050
79. Xiong, W., Lagerstrom, R.: Threat modeling - a systematic literature review. Comput. Secur. **84**, 53–69 (2019)
80. Xu, D., Tu, M., Sanford, M., Thomas, L., Woodraska, D., Xu, W.: Automated security test generation with formal threat models. IEEE Trans. Dependable Secure Comput. **9**(4), 526–540 (2012)
81. Yan, Z., Haimes, Y., Wallner, M.: Hierarchical coordinated Bayesian model for risk analysis with sparse data, presented at the *Society of Risk Analysis Annual Meeting* (2006)
82. Zimmerman, R., Zhu, Q., Dimitri, C.: Promoting resilience for food, energy and water interdependencies. J. Environ. Stud. Sci. **6**(1), 50–61 (2016)

Building Insider Threat Detection Use Cases for SCADA Systems in Electric Power Grids

Antoine Lemay[1(✉)], Ewa Piatkowska[2], and Michal Ostoja-Gajewski[2]

[1] Hitachi Energy Research, Montreal, Canada
antoine.lemay@hitachienergy.com
[2] Hitachi Energy Research, Krakow, Poland

Abstract. Insider threats to critical infrastructure assets have always been a problem, but the advent of industrial control systems has significantly increased the impacts of incidents. Off-the-shelf implementations of user and entity behavior analytics – standard information technology tools for detecting insider threats – are inappropriate for industrial control systems because they focus on data theft instead of sabotage. By examining historical incidents and using an analytical process, a number of denial-of-access scenarios can be identified in the supervisory control layer by adjusting the anomalies that are considered in information technology environments.

This chapter shows that denial-of-access use cases can be detected by customizing the dimensions of volumetric anomalies. One example is to measure data transfer volumes between specific devices instead of data transfers at large. However, manipulations of process scenarios require drastic changes to traditional user and entity behavior analytics. These include maintaining allowed lists of devices that can connect directly as supervisory control and data acquisition clients and correlating with other data sources such as human-machine interface usage logs and *post hoc* analysis of operator actions.

Keywords: Insider Threats · Threat Detection · Use Cases · Electric Power Grid · Industrial Control System · SCADA System

1 Introduction

The integration of industrial control systems, which include supervisory control and data acquisition (SCADA) systems, has greatly increased the exposure of critical infrastructure assets to cyber attacks. While external adversaries pose significant threats, insider threats – that abuse legitimate access rights to cause malicious impacts – are more difficult to manage. This is even more challenging when the same automation systems used to operate critical infrastructure assets are leveraged to cause negative impacts at scale.

The supervisory control layer is where negative impacts on critical infrastructure assets can be realized at scale. In the case of an electric power grid, the critical infrastructure of interest, this layer incorporates supervisory control

Published by Springer Nature Switzerland AG 2026
J. Staggs and S. Shenoi (Eds.): ICCIP 2025, IFIP AICT 763, pp. 103–120, 2026.
https://doi.org/10.1007/978-3-032-11914-8_5

and data acquisition (SCADA) systems and assorted peripheral components. A disgruntled operator with control room access has the opportunity to waste fuel, shut down electric power or even cause damage to physical equipment. Identifying and mitigating such insider threats are essential to managing cyber risks to critical infrastructure assets.

Identifying and detecting insider threats to SCADA systems, and industrial control systems in general, are still open questions. Al-Mhiqani et al. [1] performed a systematic review of research on insider threat detection in cyber-physical systems, which include SCADA systems. Several works analyze insider attacks using mathematical models such as semi-Markov process theory [15,22] and game theory [4,15] to derive attack scenarios for various attacker profiles, including insiders and privileged insiders. D'Ambrosio et al. [8] proposed a Bayesian risk management framework that considers insider threats in risk analysis by modeling the relationships between insiders/external entities and targeted assets.

Other approaches address insider threats as part of the larger intrusion detection problem. These approaches establish normal system behavior baselines that are specified manually [20] or derived from system logs [3,24]. Anomalies in observed system behavior are considered to be attack indicators. Machine learning methods such as autoencoders [24] are often used for anomaly detection.

The main limitation of the approaches mentioned above is that they cannot be applied directly by critical infrastructure asset owners to manage cyber risk. Furthermore, many of the approaches are unworkable or impractical, especially cryptography- and trust-based approaches that are unable to manage threats from trusted insiders. Another challenge is that machine learning approaches require large volumes of training data that do not exist because insider threat attacks are rare and critical infrastructure owners are disinclined to share real attack data.

Other approaches consider insider attacks to be perpetrated by trusted individuals who deploy offensive cyber techniques and tools from within their networks. However, this assumption is problematic because insiders with privileged access and knowledge would be more likely to use legitimate techniques and tools to achieve their objectives. This work adopts the insider threat definition specified by Shashanka et al. [19] – malicious insider behaviors ranging from misuse of approved functionality to circumvention of security controls.

Several commercial tools are available for managing insider threats [9]. However, these tools typically focus on data theft in enterprise (information technology) environments. Insider data theft is certainly relevant to critical infrastructure assets, but more serious are insider threats to operational technology environments that directly target critical infrastructure services and assets. Indeed, the principal challenge to retargeting insider threat management systems designed for information technology environments to support operational technology environments is the lack of detection use cases and associated detection metrics based on operational technology insider threat scenarios.

This chapter describes an analytical process for creating operational technology detection use cases by evaluating historical insider threat incidents in operational technology environments and identifying the additional data needed to detect malicious insider behavior.

In an ideal world, the analytical process would be coupled with a data-driven approach leveraging data from multiple deployments. Unfortunately, no publicly available data exists that covers baseline normal activity. Nor is there any publicly available data covering insider threats. Because no data is available for validation, the analytical process is the best option currently. Existing and new systems should be configured to produce the needed data and validation could be performed as data becomes available.

This work draws on user and entity behavior analytics (UEBA), one of the principal techniques used for insider threat detection in information technology environments. Historical incidents involving insider attacks on industrial control systems, with a focus on SCADA systems, are presented. SCADA environment operations are examined to identify how they differ from information technology environment operations with regard to users and entities. The insights are used to construct detection use cases for SCADA environments and identify relevant data that can be used as metrics to identify insider threats to SCADA environments.

2 User and Entity Behavior Analytics

User and entity behavior analytics is the principal technique used in the information technology domain to detect insider threats. Data about users and relevant entities are collected in a security information and event management (SIEM) system or other central repository to support analytics for identifying anomalies. Ideally, the anomalies should be correlated with malicious activity, but this is not always the case. For example, an engineer might have to connect to a system from a foreign country in the middle of the night due to an outage because the engineer is the only individual who could address the problem. While the pattern is highly anomalous, the event does not correspond to an insider threat. The lack of one-to-one correlations between malicious activities and user and entity behavior anomalies is a fundamental limitation of the technique.

However, if a foreign adversary were to steal the engineer's credentials and attempt to connect from abroad, an anomalous usage pattern similar to the one associated with the vacationing engineer would be recreated. Therefore, security operations staff would have to investigate the anomaly flagged by the analytics system to determine if the identified anomaly is malicious (true positive) or a red herring (false positive). Such false positives are costly because human intervention is required for all anomaly alerts. Even if the system were to be automated to eliminate human actions, blocking legitimate user activity would be very problematic, especially in a critical infrastructure asset. As such, a tradeoff must be established between the sensitivity of detecting real malicious activity (true positives) and the volume of false positives that can be tolerated.

Different user and entity behavior analytics implementations address the tradeoff in different ways. A seminal paper by Shashanka et al. [19] employs several features underlying behavior profiling and anomaly identification:

- Timestamp of first access of the day.
- Timestamp of last access of the day.
- Duration between last and first access.
- Total duration of all electronic flows in the day.
- Number of electronic flows in the day.
- Total bytes downloaded.
- Total bytes uploaded.

Shashanka and colleagues conducted experiments that used the set of features and their associated profiles to monitor access to an internal server. In the 362,791 conversations involving the server, 64 "interesting" events were identified, of which 39 were flagged as alerts (i.e., activities that should be investigated) with 60% confidence. The work does not report the percentage of true positive alerts, but assuming that the confidence was not underestimated, a ratio of at least 40% of false positives would be expected. The ratio of possible true positives to the number of total conversations was reported to be very low (0.006%). Due to this low base rate, extremely high accuracy (significantly better than 99.996%) would be required to lower the false positive rate while still capturing the same (possible) true positives.

Microsoft [16] has adopted a different approach that combines analytics with threat intelligence to match anomalies identified by user and entity behavior analytics to behavior patterns of known attacks in order to improve the confidence in alerts. Behaviors are flagged as anomalies when they differ substantially in the following six situations:

- Across geographical locations, devices and environments (compared with user behavior).
- Across geographical locations, devices and environments (compared with peer behavior).
- Across geographical locations, devices and environments (compared with organization behavior).
- Across time and frequency horizons (compared with user behavior).
- Across time and frequency horizons (compared with peer behavior).
- Across time and frequency horizons (compared with organization behavior).

Similar to Shashanka et al. [19], Microsoft reports that less than 1% of all activities examined were flagged as events. However, Microsoft does not report the proportion of the events that represented alerts or true positives, although they are expected to be less than the number of alerts.

Other commercial solutions exist for user and entity behavior analytics, but some of them are not transparent about the metrics used. Gartner [9], credited by some to be the originator of the user and entity behavior analytics term, categorizes the commercial solutions in the insider threat management quadrant grouping along with data loss prevention and data management products. Every major SIEM platform, including Splunk, QRadar Opentext/Arcsight and Microsoft ATA, is listed as supporting a form of user and entity behavior analytics. In this sense, enterprise applications of user and entity behavior analytics are very mature.

3 SCADA System Application Challenges

An important caveat regarding the maturity of user and entity behavior analytics is that the technology is geared towards enterprise risk. In fact, the risk is heavily skewed towards commodity crime, targeted ransomware, data theft and data sabotage. This is clear from the metrics specified by Shashanka et al. [19]. Total bytes downloaded and uploaded are appropriate metrics in most enterprise risk scenarios. A person stealing data would have abnormally high download rates. A person uploading malware or offensive tools would have anomalous high upload rates. However, these metrics would be grossly inappropriate for detecting a SCADA system operator who maliciously opens a circuit breaker to cause a blackout.

Several characteristics of industrial control systems, and SCADA systems in particular, render direct application of user and entity behavior analytics difficult. First, not many users are individually identifiable. Also, the bulk of data traffic is machine-to-machine communications, implying that most activity is initiated by service accounts instead of human users. Furthermore, many human user accounts are often generic or shared accounts (e.g., admin), especially when identity federation technologies such as Active Directory are not used in the operational technology side. For example, the computer hosting the local human-machine interface at a substation is likely to be logged into a generic account if Active Directory is not used because managing the identities and access of all possible users that could show up in a maintenance context would be cost prohibitive without centrally-managed identity and access.

Second, human activity is often transformed into machine activity at user interaction points such as human-machine interfaces. In the example where a malicious operator opens a circuit breaker, the operator would be logged onto the human-machine interface with their own user account entity. However, the SCADA command to the circuit breaker would be transmitted and processed by machine accounts. This would render it very difficult for commercial tools to correlate the malicious payload activity to a user entity.

Third, baseline human activity is often limited to maintenance, performance adjustments and outage responses. When a managed process is performing well, a human operator typically only monitors the environment. While certain actions are performed to ensure that systems under control operate at peak efficiency, they are not repeated routinely. Consider the case of a substation being taken offline for maintenance. How many times would this have to be done for it to become part of a statistical baseline? This renders baselining across time and frequency horizons very difficult.

Fourth, insider threats in industrial control environments are geared more toward sabotage than data theft. Traditional user and entity behavior analytics are concerned with industrial espionage and personal information leakage. The vast majority of patterns relate to activities such as users reading abnormal files, downloading large volumes of data from secure storage and uploading large volumes of data to external sources. These patterns do not correlate well with industrial sabotage scenarios, especially if the sabotage involves abusing legitimate access.

Fifth, SCADA system operators are unlikely to keep normal business hours. Several metrics used for correlation such as the first/last login times and time/location access baselines are based on the expectation that employees follow regular schedules, working during daytime hours and infrequently at night for overtime. Thus, connections outside of normal work hours would be indicative of individuals in different time zones or with abnormal sleep schedules accessing their accounts. Such assumptions break down when dealing with shift workers that operate physical processes 24/7.

Finally, the attack patterns in industrial control systems are different from those in enterprise networks. Because the attacker goals and the technologies used are different, the tactics, techniques and procedures (TTPs) are different. As such, pre-filtering based on threat intelligence data could introduce errors, unless threat data specific to industrial control environments is considered.

Given these differences, it is clear that the successful application of user and entity behavior analytics in industrial control environments would require customization with regard to detection use case definition as well as feature extraction and baselining.

4 Industrial Control System Incidents

In order to create good insider threat detection use cases, inspiration can be drawn from historical industrial control system incidents. This section details industrial control system incidents caused by insiders and outside actors abusing legitimate access.

Several surveys of historical incidents involving insiders have been conducted. However, the surveys tend to cover only publicly documented incidents. Since incidents are rarely reported, it is expected that the surveys cover a fraction of incidents and, therefore, have significant sampling biases. Public interest in cyber security has increased over time, so more recent incidents tend to be reported to a greater degree. Additionally, major and dramatic incidents get more coverage due to human interest. Also, the focus on events in the United States and coverage by the English media contribute to the bias.

Helmsley and Fisher [11] surveyed industrial control system incidents covering the period from 2000 to 2017 (along with one early incident from 1903). The survey was intentionally non-exhaustive, focusing on events that have been used as talking points. For example, a Turkish pipeline explosion reportedly caused by a cyber attack was discussed extensively in the operational technology community. However, the incident had been debunked at the time of writing [13].

The survey also includes the well-known Maroochy Water Services (Australia) breach that is discussed in more detail below.

A follow-up 2022 report by Grubbs et al. [10] covers the period from 2017 to 2021. Since the report is more recent and covers a shorter period, it benefits from the heightened awareness of cyber incidents. The report draws from wider sources than Helmsley and Fisher [11], including many media sources. The report covers three additional insider threats that are discussed below.

A report sponsored by Rockwell Automation [18] does not cover individual incidents, but presents metrics pertaining to 122 incidents from 1982 to 2022 drawn from the Advisen's (global and proprietary) Cybersecurity Loss Database. While it was not possible to extract detailed information about specific insider threat incidents, the reports provide some valuable insights.

In particular, the report states that insiders played indirect roles in about one-third of the incidents, for example, by falling prey to phishing attacks. Included in the one-third are 12% of the total incidents associated with insiders and 1% associated with external plus internal actors. The attacker personas included former employees (7% of incidents) and current employees or contractors (6%). An additional 4% of incidents involved third-party firms as threat actors. While the incidents likely involve competitors targeting their rivals, they may also include supply chain firms abusing their trusted access.

In terms of impact, the Rockwell Automation survey lists manipulation of view and manipulation of control (42% each) as the principal post-compromise impacts. Loss of productivity and revenue (16%) and loss of availability (6%) are the next two types of impacts. Loss of view, safety, control and protection come next (3% each) along with denial of view and denial of control (3% each). These statistics pertain to all incidents as a group, so it is not possible to determine the exact breakdown of insider threats. However, they provide a useful overview of potential attacker goals.

The first category of insider threat incidents involves current or former employees that engaged in deliberate acts of mischief. The most cited insider incident regarding industrial control systems is the Maroochy Water Services breach of 2000 [21]. The incident was perpetrated by a disgruntled laid-off consultant who discharged wastewater in a park to demonstrate that current employees lacked the knowledge to manage the system. The sabotage involved driving to multiple field sites and using the custom laptop and radio he retained from his previous employment to connect to Maroochy systems, change configuration parameters and issue process control commands.

A similar incident occurred in Kansas in 2019 [17]. In this case, a former employee leveraged a remote login facility he had used when employed to shut down processes associated with disinfection and cleaning. The remote login facility had been set up to enable employees to monitor the facility outside of normal business hours.

A more sophisticated incident occurred in California in 2021 [23]. The actor was an instrumentation and control technology contractor at a water treatment plant. He had installed remote control software on his work and personal computers to remotely monitor readings and perform process control actions. After he resigned his position, he used his personal computer to gain remote access to the water facility and send remote commands to uninstall key software tools that monitored water pressure, filtration and chemical levels.

External actors have also been known to compromise, trick or bribe insiders to obtain privileged access. A famous incident is the Ukrainian electric power system cyber attack of 2015 [7]. The so-called Sandworm attackers leveraged legitimate remote access credentials to the human-machine interface of the industrial control system. They seized control of the mouse from the operator and issued commands that opened circuit breakers, causing a widespread blackout. After the attack, specialized tools were used to remotely wipe devices in information technology and operational technology systems to hinder recovery efforts. A subsequent attack in 2016 on the same target attributed to Sandworm had similar impacts, but the weapon used was malware [5].

The two Sandworm attacks were perpetrated by external actors. However, the same attacks could have been conducted by malicious insiders with trusted access. Therefore, the attacks are relevant to building detection use cases involving the use of stolen credentials and the installation of cyber attack tools and malware.

Another related incident occurred at Pinellas County Utilities (Florida) in 2021 [6]. In this case, a malicious entity gained access using the TeamViewer remote-control software on a control panel that monitored water supply. An alert employee noticed the login, but assumed it was legitimate as employees regularly used the method to access the system and no actions were performed immediately after the access. However, a few hours later, the attacker launched control actions that changed the concentration of a chemical in the water supply to a dangerous level. Fortunately, the operator who was logged at the plant noticed the mouse movements and the ensuing chemical concentration change and immediately reversed the action. Other incidents have involved remote attackers gaining access to unsecured control panels, but this particular incident illustrates that – from the system perspective – the malicious action was performed by the "operator" who was currently logged on.

A hybrid version of this incident allegedly occurred at an undisclosed electric power plant in 2019 [2]. In this case, an external actor bribed an individual with access to replace the mouse attached to a human-machine interface with a compromised mouse that could be controlled remotely. The external actor proceeded to deploy ransomware on the industrial control system, forcing the electric power plant to rebuild its systems, a task that took three months.

The most famous industrial control system incident involved the Stuxnet malware that targeted the uranium hexafluoride centrifuge facility in Natanz, Iran. According to a report [12], a Dutch contractor infiltrated the Natanz facility in 2007 and installed water pumps seeded with the malware. The contractor died under suspicious conditions in 2008 and it is impossible to verify this story.

However, this incident could create a most reasonable insider threat detection use case.

5 Concept of Operations

As discussed above, the use of traditional user and entity behavior analytics in operational technology systems is unlikely to achieve good results because the traditional metrics are misaligned with normal operational technology activities and the types of insider threats that should be mitigated. In order to create user and entity behavior analytics compatible with operational technology, the analytics must be tailored to the concept of operations underlying operational technology environments.

The focus of this work is insider threats in control center operations. As such, the threats involve a malicious SCADA system operator or a malicious actor who has compromised a SCADA system operator account and use the legitimate access to negatively impact operations. Thus, the work is concentrated on Layers 2 and 3 of the Purdue Enterprise Reference Architecture, specifically control systems and manufacturing operations systems.

The following system components are considered:

- **Human-Machine Interface:** A human-machine interface enables a user to visualize SCADA system data and perform control actions such as establishing set points and toggling switches. The human-machine interface also provides visualizations of data maintained by other components such as trends from a data historian.
- **Data Historian:** A data historian maintains historical values of SCADA system data points and values computed from real-time data.
- **Advanced Intelligence and Automation Applications:** In addition to human input, most SCADA systems rely on applications that perform specific tasks using SCADA system data as input. For example, an energy management system may consume real-time data from the electric power grid and automatically perform computations to enable operators to optimize system performance beyond what could be achieved purely by looking at raw data or data trends. Data from the applications can also be fed back to the SCADA system to perform control actions automatically to alleviate the burden on human operators. Another example is performing computations to determine if a gas-to-electricity plant needs to be fired up and send an alert to an enterprise resource planning system that is responsible for initiating the purchase of natural gas. The use cases vary and a number of commercially available components may be used. Many electric utilities have custom applications in this category as well.

The engineering workstation, where new control logic is developed and pushed to various field devices and through which remote maintenance of field devices is performed is not considered in this work. However, it would present an

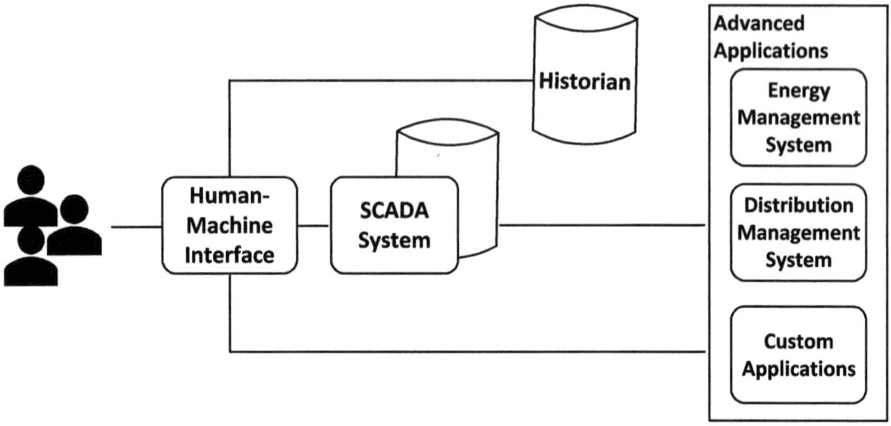

Fig. 1. Control room components and data flows.

interesting use case. Figure 1 presents the control room components considered in this work and the potential data flows between the components.

During normal operations, a human operator is logged into a human-machine interface that presents preconfigured visualizations of system states. This data originates from a SCADA system database with possible enrichment from the data historian and advanced intelligence applications. The SCADA system populates the database through its data acquisition applications that connect to various field devices via SCADA protocols such as Modbus, DNP3 and IEC 61850. The advanced intelligence applications obtain data from the SCADA system database. The historian gathers data on an ongoing basis from the SCADA system and the advanced intelligence applications.

An operator changes the state of the physical system by clicking a graphical element on the human-machine interface. The action is converted by the SCADA system to a command in a SCADA protocol that is transmitted to a field device to effect the change.

A SCADA system comprises the following user entities:

- **Operator User Entities:** Human subjects.
- **Human-Machine Interface Service Entity:** Machine subject.
- **SCADA System Service Entity:** Machine subject.
- **Advanced Intelligence Application Service Entities:** Machine subjects.
- **Historian Service Entity:** Machine subject.

Operator user entities are only expected to interface with the human-machine interface. The human-machine interface service entity primarily interacts with the SCADA system service entity, but it may also interact with the advanced intelligence application service entities and historian service entity. Similarly, the advanced intelligence application service entities primarily interface with the SCADA system service entity, but may also interface with the human-machine interface service entity, historian service entity and among themselves. The historian service entity interacts primarily with the SCADA system service entity, but may also interact with the human-machine interface service entity and advanced intelligence application service entities.

The majority of the interactions are machine-to-machine. However, human insider activity may trigger some machine-to-machine interactions. For example, if a malicious insider toggles a circuit breaker, the SCADA system will contact the field device (machine-to-machine). After the circuit breaker has been toggled, new data is fed to the real-time SCADA system database (machine-to-machine). The change in value may then be input to the energy management system (machine-to-machine) and passed to the historian (machine-to-machine) for trending.

6 SCADA System Use Case Metrics

The metrics of Shashanka et al. [19] are evaluated with respect to normal activity within the concept of operations described above.

With regard to the timestamps of the first and last access of the day and duration of access, operator user entities would be expected to log in and out based on their rotating shifts. Depending on the shifts, it may or may not be possible to baseline the timestamp values. For example, if an operator user entity is assigned shifts on a predictable schedule, estimators based on the shift periods instead of baselines based on hours and days of the week may be suitable. On the other hand, if a shared account is used by different operator user entities in different shifts, it may not be appropriate to baseline the shift periods. All the other entities are not expected to ever log in or log out because they are service entities that would continually access the system as long as the system is up and running.

Regarding the number of electronic flows and sum total of the durations of electronic flows in a day, operator user entities should have one electronic flow to the human-machine interface for the duration of their shifts or a similar pattern if they take breaks. Service entities should have continuous electronic flows between themselves based on the data exchanges. For example, if the human-machine interface does not obtain data from the historian or outputs from the advanced intelligence applications, only a single electronic flow between human-machine interface and SCADA system would be expected. The numbers of electronic flows for the advanced intelligence applications would fluctuate depending on whether they are triggered automatically on a schedule, triggered automatically based on specific conditions or triggered manually by operators via human-machine interface actions.

The distributions of the total numbers of bytes downloaded and uploaded would be relatively flat during the day because most data transfers would be linked to machine-to-machine communications. Even the actions initiated by human operators would be dwarfed by the volume of data exchanged for human-machine interface display when computed on a byte upload basis. The only exception to this would be advanced intelligence applications that are triggered by specific events or by human operators. If they are seldom triggered, an insider triggering the same application multiple times to execute a denial-of-service attack would generate an anomaly based on the metric.

It is now possible to examine the metrics in the context of the attack scenarios under the normal concept of operations.

The times of access were not relevant in the historical incidents. In the case of the Kansas incident, the remote access facility was instituted precisely to connect outside of normal business hours. In the Pinellas County incident and Ukraine (2015) incident, the attacks were observed by operators because they occurred during normal operating hours. It is not possible to determine if the duration of access is relevant based on the historical incidents.

The number of electronic flows and the total duration of electronic flows do not appear to be relevant in most of the historical incidents. Also, in most of the incidents, attackers used tools with established, known legitimate electronic flows to effect changes. The exception is the Maroochy Water Services incident where the attacker effectively added another component in the system to perform his attacks. It could be argued that this was also the case in the Kansas incident because the employee had been terminated. However, this depends on how long the attacker waits before executing the malicious actions. It is likely that the behavior would still be within the baseline. In the Maroochy and Kansas incidents, the volume increases in the electronic flows may not have been statistically significant to trigger alerts compared with the normal volumes of daily flows.

The observed volumes of bytes downloaded and uploaded would not be relevant in all the historical incidents. Because the goal of practically all operational technology environment attackers, insiders included, is to perform sabotage instead of data theft, no statistically-significant change in the number of bytes exchanged would be observed. Analysis of the historical incidents reveals that the impacts are usually achieved via a few human-machine interface clicks. These actions would result in additional packets sent via SCADA protocols that would be dwarfed by the regular polling and data exchange between service components.

Based on the observations, it is clear that a plug-and-play approach using metrics designed for enterprise environments, where data theft is the main concern, is unlikely to yield acceptable results in operational technology environments.

7 Building Detection Use Cases

Since the current plug-and-play detection of insider threats is not aligned with operational technology environments, it is necessary to build appropriate detection use cases and specify the data required for detection.

The first thing to consider is that the goal of the insider is most likely sabotage. Two types of sabotage identified by the Rockwell Automation report [18] are denial of access to a control system and manipulation of a process.

Before developing the detection use cases, it is important to note that detecting sabotage and denial of service are often trivial. After all, if an attacker were to manipulate a circuit breaker to cause a power outage, it would be immediately detected once the lights went out. Therefore, when building detection use cases, the focus should be on identifying whether the adverse effect is caused by an insider or external actor abusing insider access and identify the individual who is involved.

7.1 Denial of Access

The opportunities for denial of access are limited in the control layer. One possibility is for an administrative user to change the configuration of the system to block other users (e.g., by deleting other user accounts). Another possibility is to use a resource exhaustion attack to prevent other users from operating the system.

In the case of administrative access abuse, logging all administrative actions, especially bulk actions, and performing volumetric-based anomaly detection should enable the detection of the denial-of-access use cases. After a system is deployed, administrative activities would be infrequent and mostly associated with change management processes. Large volumes of changes, such as the ones required to lock everyone out of the system, would be unexpected. If a false alert were to be raised, it should be easy to discount the alert without much manual investigation based on operational information.

In the case of resource exhaustion attacks, different attack methods would require different metrics. One type of attack is network-based flooding that consumes the available bandwidth. An attacker intending to target the human-machine interface might attempt to saturate the local-area network. This would require a very large volume of packets because the bandwidth of a local-area network is usually quite high. As such, the pure volumetric detection of bytes downloaded/uploaded would work. Similar detection methods could be applied to attempts that target inter-service communications involving components hosted in the control center server rack, such as the historian, SCADA server and advanced intelligence applications. If an attacker were to target data acquisition from the SCADA system, the packet volumes would be lower because the data links to field devices have smaller bandwidths. However, a human operator should not have electronic flows to field devices, and this would be an effective detection metric.

It is also possible to effect resource exhaustion scenarios using service entities. For example, if a support application that computes optimal power flow could be queried on demand, an attacker could repeatedly trigger the application. This would prompt a data exchange between the SCADA system database and the power flow application to obtain the computed data, significantly increasing their bandwidth usage. In this scenario, volumetric data usage by the human operator may not enable detection. However, a volumetric data usage anomaly correlated with human-machine interface usage logs could enable detection. Many human-machine interfaces do not maintain usage logs. In these instances, additional correlation through sensor fusion [14] could suffice.

The same scenario could be used to exhaust other resources. In the example above where electric power flow computations are invoked, the central processing unit of the server housing the advanced intelligence application could be saturated instead of the network, preventing other services from running on the server. In this use case, there may not be a volumetric anomaly with regard to data usage. However, there would be a volumetric anomaly in human-machine interface logging, assuming of course that logging functionality is present.

7.2 Manipulation of Process

In addition to denial of access, manipulation of process would be of interest by a malicious insider. One option for process manipulation is via direct connections to field devices. This is accomplished using a parallel SCADA/human-machine interface.

Therefore, one detection possibility involves tracking the human-machine interface service entities in the operational technology environment. This tracking should strictly use a "known good" list instead of monitoring electronic flow volumes. However, even with this approach, incidents where known good SCADA/human-machine interface service entities are abused by terminated employees would evade detection. To address this situation, additional correlations between SCADA/human-machine interface service entities and their potential users should be analyzed, for example, via an asset tracking management process.

Another option for process manipulation is abusing an approved human-machine interface. In this case, human-machine interface usage logs could help identify the source of the insider threat. However, as mentioned above, human-machine interfaces may not support logging and additional sensor fusion would be required.

An alternative approach that could be used to improve confidence in insider threat detection is the *post hoc* analysis of operator actions. During normal operations, an operator would not attempt to take the system down or execute other harmful actions. An advanced intelligence application that reverse engineers the effects of operator actions on the overall performance metrics could be developed. The application would scrutinize directional anomalies induced by operator entities (i.e., anomalies that tend to make the performance generally worse instead of generally better) to detect insider threats.

7.3 Summary

Table 1 summarizes the detection use cases for insider threat sabotage scenarios involving denial of access and manipulation of process. The detection metrics for these use cases differ significantly from the ones commonly employed for data theft detection implemented by default in commercial user and entity behavior

Table 1. Detection use cases for insider sabotage.

Use Case	Metrics	Detection
Denial of Access		
Administrative Access Abuse	Administrative activity logs per administrative user entity	Volumetric anomaly
Network Flood Resource Exhaustion – Control Center from User Entity	Bytes downloaded/uploaded per network user entity	Volumetric anomaly
Network Flood Resource Exhaustion – Data Acquisition Links from User Entity	Number of field device electronic flows per network user entity	Existence of any volume except for SCADA network entity
Network Flood Resource Exhaustion – Control Center from Service Entity	Bytes downloaded/uploaded per network user entity	Volumetric anomaly
	Human-machine interface usage logs per operator user entity	Volumetric anomaly
Generic Resource Exhaustion from Service Entity	Human-machine interface usage logs per operator user entity	Volumetric anomaly
Manipulation of Process		
Direct Connection to Field Device	Number of field device electronic flows per SCADA/human-machine interface network user entity	Strict known good list associated with asset tracking management process
Approved Human-Machine Interface Use	Human-machine interface usage logs per operator user entity	Forensics only
Approved Human-Machine Interface Use	*Post hoc* analysis of operator actions relative to overall system performance per operator user entity	Directional anomaly

analytics systems. Implementing some of the detection metrics requires human-machine interface logging functionality that is not universally implemented in operational technology environments. Advanced intelligence applications with *post hoc* analysis functionality are less common. Given the potential negative impacts on critical infrastructure assets, it is important to deploy such insider threat detection functionality in operational technology environments.

8 Conclusions

Off-the-shelf commercial implementations of user and entity behavior analytics designed for information technology environments are not well suited for insider threat detection in operational technology environments. This is because the information technology implementations generally focus on data theft whereas insider threat incidents in operational technology environments primarily involve sabotage. For example, an information technology system might generate an alarm based on a volumetric anomaly in the total number of bytes uploaded, corresponding to data exfiltration by a user. In contrast, in an operational technology environment, insider sabotage may involve a resource exhaustion attack that is manifested by a volumetric anomaly in the number of connections but not in the total number of bytes uploaded. Although the two anomalies are both volumetric in nature, the detection metrics are different. Therefore, it is vital to customize detection use cases to combat insider threats in operational technology environments.

The analysis of historical insider threat incidents in operational technology environments reveals that the two principal insider attacks have involved denial of access to the control systems and leveraging access to control systems to manipulate physical processes. Denial of access to control systems can be detected using traditional data such as activity logs, electronic flows and data flow volumes supplemented by additional human-machine interface data. However, the manipulation of physical processes requires data well beyond what is collected and processed by traditional user and entity behavior analytics. The additional data that is vital for *post hoc* analysis includes current and historical data about process status and trends as well as detailed historical and current data about operator behavior.

Future research will attempt to improve confidence in insider threat detection in operational technology environments by conducting *post hoc* analyses of operator actions. These analyses, which are forensic in nature, are conceptually similar to airplane crash investigations that rely on black boxes to record almost everything. More important is to detect insider threat activity in operational technology environments accurately and consistently in real time and prevent the negative impacts. This will require capturing detailed process, control system and operator behavior data, and developing sophisticated deep learning models. The scientific effort is formidable. Also, obtaining large volumes of the required high-fidelity data is extremely difficult because insider threat attacks are rare and critical infrastructure asset owners are disinclined to share real attack data.

References

1. Al-Mhiqani, M., Alsboui, T., Al-Shehari, T., Abdulkareem, K., Ahmad, R., Mohammed, M.: Insider threat detection in cyber-physical systems: a systematic literature review. Comput. Electr. Eng. **119**(A), 109489 (2024)
2. Archer, Power plant reportedly hit by mouse ransomware attack, Portland, Oregon (2020).(archerint.com/power-plant-reportedly-hit-by-mouse-ransomware-attack)

3. Bao, H., Lu, R., Li, B., Deng, R.: BLITHE: behavior rule-based insider threat detection for smart grid. IEEE Internet Things J. **3**(2), 190–205 (2016)
4. Cheh, C., Keefe, K., Feddersen, B., Chen, B., Temple, W., Sanders, W.: Developing models for physical attacks on cyber-physical systems. In: Proceedings of the Workshop on Cyber-Physical Systems Security and Privacy, pp. 49–55 (2017)
5. Cherepanov, A., Lipovsky, R.: Industroyer: biggest threat to industrial control systems since stuxnet. WeLiveSecurity (2017). www.welivesecurity.com/2017/06/12/industroyer-biggest-threat-industrial-control-systems-since-stuxnet
6. Cybersecurity and Infrastructure Security Agency: Cybersecurity Advisory: Compromise of U.S. Water Treatment Facility, Alert Code: AA21-042A, Washington, DC (2021). www.cisa.gov/news-events/cybersecurity-advisories/aa21-042a
7. Cybersecurity and Infrastructure Security Agency: ICS Alert: Cyber Attack Against Ukrainian Critical Infrastructure, Alert Code: IR-ALERT-H-16-043-01AP, Washington, DC (2021). www.cisa.gov/news-events/ics-alerts/ir-alert-h-16-056-01
8. d'Ambrosio, N., Perrone, G., Romano, S.: Including insider threats into risk management through bayesian threat graph networks. Comput. Secur. **133**, 103410 (2023)
9. Gartner Peer Insights: Insider risk management solutions reviews and ratings, Stamford, Connecticut (2025). www.gartner.com/reviews/market/insider-risk-management-solutions
10. Grubbs, R., Stoddard, J., Freeman, S., Fisher, R.: Evolution and trends of industrial control system cyber incidents Since 2017, Document no. INL/JIOU-21-65119-Revision-0, Idaho National Laboratory, Idaho Falls, Idaho (2022)
11. Hemsley, K., Fisher, R.: History of industrial control system cyber incidents, document no. INL/CON-18-44411-Revision-2, Idaho National Laboratory, Idaho Falls, Idaho (2018)
12. Hollingworth, D.: Dutch engineer revealed as stuxnet agent. Cyber Daily (2024). www.cyberdaily.au/security/10010-dutch-engineer-revealed-as-stuxnet-agent
13. Lee, R.: Closing the case on the reported 2008 Russian cyber attack on the BTC pipeline (2015). www.robertmlee.org/closing-the-case-on-the-reported-2008-russian-cyber-attack-on-the-btc-pipeline
14. Lemay, A., Sadighian, A., Fernandez, J.: Lightweight journaling for scada systems via event correlation. In: ICCIP 2016. IAICT, vol. 485, pp. 99–115. Springer, Cham (2016). https://doi.org/10.1007/978-3-319-48737-3_6
15. Liu, Z., Wang, L.: FlipIt game model based defense strategy against cyberattacks on SCADA systems considering insider assistance. IEEE Trans. Inf. Forensics Secur. **16**, 2791–2804 (2021)
16. Microsoft: Advanced threat detection with user and entity behavior analytics (UEBA) in Microsoft Sentinel, Redmond, Washington (2025). https://learn.microsoft.com/en-us/azure/sentinel/identify-threats-with-entity-behavior-analytics
17. Morgan, L.: Another cyber attack affecting water supply. Cyber Security Hub (2021). www.cshub.com/attacks/articles/another-cyber-attack-affecting-water-supply)
18. Rockwell Automation: Anatomy of 100+ cybersecurity incidents in industrial operations: a research study with recommendations for strengthening defenses in OT/ICS, Document no. GMSN-SP025A-EN-P-August 2023, Milwaukee, Wisconsin (2023)

19. Shashanka, M., Shen, M., Wang, J.: User and entity behavior analytics for enterprise security. In: Proceedings of the IEEE International Conference on Big Data, pp. 1867–1874 (2016)
20. Singh, A., Chatterjee, K., Satapathy, S.: TrIDS: an intelligent behavioral trust based IDS for a smart healthcare system. Clust. Comput. **26**(2), 903–925 (2022)
21. Slay, J., Miller, M.: Lessons learned from the Maroochy water breach. In: Goetz, E., Shenoi, S. (eds.) ICCIP 2007. IIFIP, vol. 253, pp. 73–82. Springer, Boston, MA (2008). https://doi.org/10.1007/978-0-387-75462-8_6
22. Tang, S., Liu, Z., Wang, L.: Power system reliability analysis considering external and insider attacks on a SCADA system. In: Proceedings of the IEEE/PES Transmission and Distribution Conference and Exposition (2020)
23. Toulas, B.: Former employee charged for attacking water treatment plant. Bleeping Computer (2023). www.bleepingcomputer.com/news/security/former-employee-charged-for-attacking-water-treatment-plant
24. Wang, X., Fidge, C., Nourbakhsh, G., Foo, E., Jadidi, Z., Li, C.: Anomaly detection for insider attacks from untrusted intelligent electronic devices in substation automation systems. IEEE Access **10**, 6629–6649 (2022)

Infrastructure Communications Security

Topology-Sensitive Attacks on Electric Power System Communications

Arzhan Tong[1(✉)] and Stephen Wolthusen[1,2]

[1] Royal Holloway, University of London, Egham, UK
arzhan.tong.2023@live.rhul.ac.uk
[2] Norwegian University of Science and Technology, Gjøvik, Norway

Abstract. Certain security guarantees pertaining to power system automation communications based on the IEC 61850 series of standards can be provided by employing mechanisms in the IEC 62351 standard. However, total correctness and, thus, the safety of protocol semantics cannot be guaranteed without message delivery guarantees.

This chapter presents an applied π-calculus model that describes process and bay level communications in the IEC 61850 framework with a focus on sampled value and Generic Object Oriented Substation Event (GOOSE) messages with explicit representations of topology using a formal grammar. The model supports reasoning about attacks, especially related to communications channel properties. Selected attack modes are specified and proofs of the feasibility/infeasibility of denial-of-service and change-in-causality attacks are provided.

Keywords: Electric Power System · Communications · IEC 61850 Protocol · Attacks · Applied π-Calculus

1 Introduction

Modern power systems automation based on the IEC 61850 series of standards allow considerable freedom for interconnecting components as long as the performance requirements are satisfied. In the standard communications model, Generic Object Oriented Substation Event (GOOSE), sampled value (SV) and Generic Substation Event (GSSE) messages are identified as time-critical, although certain indirect dependencies may impact performance.

The hard real-time requirements specified in the IEC 61850-5 standard [8] focus on message transmission time. Any violations result in breaches of total correctness. Therefore, real-time violations must be considered to be attack targets for attacks alongside others such as integrity breaches covered in the IEC 62351-6 standard [9] for process level and bay level communications based on the IEC 61850-8-1 standard [6] and IEC 61850-9-2 standard [7], respectively.

While the IEC 61850-8-1 standard describes a mapping to the IEC 8802-3 (Ethernet) standard, the network topology of a substation automation system typically has to satisfy additional requirements – specifically, the channels should provide adequate redundancy and they cannot be passive. Even at the bay level,

Published by Springer Nature Switzerland AG 2026
J. Staggs and S. Shenoi (Eds.): ICCIP 2025, IFIP AICT 763, pp. 123–145, 2026.
https://doi.org/10.1007/978-3-032-11914-8_6

the channels comprise active components with dynamically selected protocols, especially when using the IEC 62439-3 High-Availability Seamless Redundancy (HSR) Protocol and Parallel Redundancy Protocol (PRP) [10].

In order to prove the feasibility/infeasibility of several classes of attacks, especially attacks on availability, it is necessary to explicitly incorporate the channel topology in the proofs. This chapter presents an applied π-calculus model that describes process and bay level communications in the IEC 61850 framework with a focus on GOOSE and SV messages with explicit representations of topology using a formal grammar. The model supports reasoning about attacks, especially related to communications channel properties. Selected attack modes are specified and proofs of the feasibility/infeasibility of denial-of-service and change-in-causality attacks are provided.

2 Related Work

Modern power systems require extensive automation to satisfy performance and cost objectives from generation to distribution, and the associated automation protocols rely on networked systems to operate properly. The IEC 61850 protocol standards [8,11] are widely used for substation automation in the energy sector. Security mechanisms in the standards as well as others such as the IEC 60870 standard are factored in the IEC 62351 standard [9]. However, research on the security of real-time GOOSE/SV messages (that require transfer times of a quarter of a cycle for P2/P3 performance classes) has focused mainly on detecting malicious activity [2,12] instead of determining if interference is possible *a priori*, with a few exceptions such as the work of Yegorov et al. [13].

The applied π-calculus proposed by Abadi et al. [1] has its origin in the analysis of security protocols in distributed systems with an emphasis on cryptographic primitives. Th applied π-calculus was instrumental in bridging the gap between the abstract nature of the π-calculus and the practical requirements of reasoning about real-world communications systems, especially those involving security-critical interactions. Abadi and colleagues introduced terms in the calculus to represent cryptographic primitives and formal reasoning techniques to prove properties such as secrecy and authenticity.

The work described in this chapter uses the applied π-calculus to model real-time properties by relying on causality and to map operational behaviors and vulnerabilities of time-sensitive industrial communications protocols. Specifically, the model incorporates domain-specific behavior of the IEC 61850 GOOSE and SV message retransmission semantics, buffer management and timing constraints that are crucial to analyzing attacks on systems where performance and reliability are as critical as security. The model also extends the calculus scope to formalize conditions for successful causality breaches similar to those used to make cryptographic guarantees. This is achieved by utilizing dynamic name substitution to capture the ability of an attacker to selectively manipulate message sequences and buffer states.

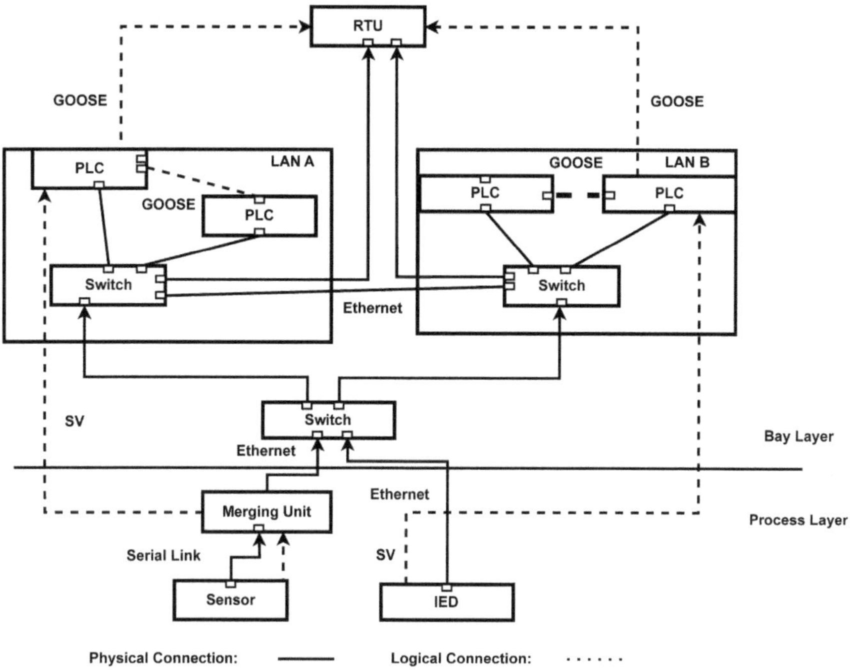

Fig. 1. Substation automation with redundancy in the process and bay layers.

Previous work has focused mainly on detecting attacks, including denial-of-service attacks. Elbez et al. [3] demonstrated methods for detecting denial-of-service attacks by analyzing anomalies in logical traffic patterns. They also relied on EDA4GNeT to detect deviations in traffic behavior indicative of potential attacks [4]. As such, most work emphasizes patterns and statistical deviations, but does not fully consider the limitations imposed on observers by the use of the precision time synchronization regime. While these studies provide insights into logical traffic patterns, they neglect the role of network topology in message propagation.

3 Bay Level Topology

The IEC 61850 standard provides a hierarchical framework for substation automation systems comprising three layers – process layer, bay layer and station layer. While the station layer handles high-level supervisory functions, this work primarily focuses on the process layer and bay layer because they are central to real-time operation and high-speed communications.

The process and bay layers manage interactions between electrical equipment and routing devices through high-speed communications pathways and redundancy protocols that are crucial to ensuring substation reliability and resilience as well as time synchronization. Figure 1 shows a substation automation system representing the process and bay layers with redundancy protocols in place. This is one of several possible representations of a substation automation system.

The process layer located at the bottom of the hierarchy directly interfaces with electrical equipment such as sensors, actuators and transformers. It gathers real-time data and transmits it upward while simultaneously executing commands received from the bay layer. The bay layer positioned above the process layer provides control and protection for substation zones, ensuring that critical operations such as fault isolation occur reliably. Together, the two layers form the operational core of the IEC 61850 topology, where timing precision, redundancy and very low latency communications are pivotal to meeting the performance requirements.

The process layer plays a foundational role by collecting real-time measurements from devices such as sensors and transformers, and transmitting the data to devices in the bay layer. The merging unit (MU), a key component of the process layer, is tasked with digitizing analog signals from the sensors and converting them to high-frequency SV messages as defined in IEC 61850-9-2. The SV messages are transmitted to intelligent electronic devices (IEDs) and programmable logic controllers (PLCs) in the bay layer, where they are used for protection, control and monitoring purposes. Although sensors and merging units can be used together for data collection, it is increasingly common to position intelligent electronic devices in the process layer to collect and transform the data to a suitable format before sending it to the bay layer. This eliminates the need to use a merging unit for data conversion.

The SV data communications format used in the process layer ensures that performance requirements are met by data transmission being highly synchronized and deterministic, which is critical for time-sensitive protection and control tasks. However the performance requirements with regard to latency are more generous because dealing with fault tolerance is not as important. The desired performance is achieved using protocols such as Industrial Ethernet for fast delivery. Figure 1 shows the use of SV messages to send data between nodes before reaching a switch in the bay layer.

The bay layer is responsible for substation protection and control. It functions as an intermediary between the process layer that provides real-time data and the station layer that issues operational commands. The bay layer relies on GOOSE and GSSE messaging for rapid, event-driven communications and optional HSR/PRP redundancy mechanisms to ensure communications link reliability.

GOOSE messaging, the core data exchange format in the bay layer, allows for the instantaneous exchange of status information between intelligent electronic devices. For instance, when a fault is detected, GOOSE messages enable peer-to-peer communications among relays, enabling them to coordinate actions such as tripping circuit breakers. This ensures that critical protection actions occur with minimal latency to meet the stringent performance requirements. Figure 1 shows bay layer nodes communicating via GOOSE messages.

Redundancy mechanism protocols such as HSR and PRP are implemented at the bay layer to ensure continuous communications in the event of communications or device failures. HSR creates a closed-loop network using a ring topology where data is transmitted in both directions, enabling uninterrupted communications even if one path is severed. PRP, on the other hand, provides dual independent communications paths, ensuring seamless failover if one path fails. These mechanisms are vital to maintaining the integrity of GOOSE messaging and other communications tasks in the bay layer, rendering the layer central to substation reliability and resilience.

While HSR is often depicted as operating in a ring topology, the protocol is not inherently restricted to this configuration. The HSR standard and implementations also allow for more complex arrangements such as mesh topologies where multiple paths can exist between devices. This flexibility enables HSR to adapt to various physical and logical layouts depending on substation requirements and constraints.

The primary focus of this work is to analyze ring topologies as a viable and commonly used configuration for HSR. However, it is equally valid to consider mesh topologies under HSR. In a mesh topology, devices are connected via multiple overlapping paths, offering additional robustness and fault-tolerance capabilities beyond a ring topology. Mesh topologies are more complex to manage, but they provide greater reliability by enabling multiple simultaneous communications routes. Such configurations may be chosen in scenarios where network availability is critical and where physical constraints render strict ring topologies impractical.

In addition to redundancy, mechanisms are required to provide synchronization in the bay layer. One of the most important technologies for this purpose is the Precision Time Protocol (PTP) defined by the IEEE 1588 standard [5]. PTP operates at the bay layer to ensure highly accurate time synchronization among the various components, vital to fast acting protection and control. PTP supports synchronization by distributing time references (timestamps) in messages for all devices in the bay layer. This ensures that all responses to events occur within milliseconds (ms). The model developed in this work incorporates slave clocks at individual devices that synchronize with a PTP grandmaster clock typically located in the bay layer.

To simplify the presentation, Fig. 1 incorporates time references, but the use of a PTP profile is required by IEC 62439-3 to permit deterministic SV traffic. PTP is often implemented in conjunction with redundancy protocols such as HSR and PRP according to IEC 62439-3. The redundancy mechanisms provide robust fault tolerance and eliminate single points of failure, ensuring that time synchronization is maintained even under adverse network conditions, including network failures. By integrating PTP with HSR or PRP, substation networks can achieve the reliability and precision levels required in critical infrastructure assets.

3.1 Grammar Specification

The grammar specified in this section is intended to address the gap in the IEC 61850 standard that offers only a functional abstraction whereas the semantics of GOOSE/SV messages are contingent on performance constraints influenced by network topology. While the standard defines a hierarchical logical layout of a network (process and bay layers), it does not provide detailed, fine-grained representations of the interconnections and communications flows between the layers. The simplification may be adequate for general descriptions of substation automation, but it falls short when designing or analyzing specific topologies, especially in systems that incorporate redundancy protocols and detailed component communications.

The grammar creates actionable and fine-grained topologies. It explicitly captures the physical and logical interconnections between layers, devices and network elements. Instead of focusing solely on the roles of the process, bay and station layers, the grammar models how devices such as merging units, intelligent electronic devices and programmable logic controllers interact with each other. This allows for a deep understanding of substation operational structure, including specific data flow paths, implementation of HSR and PRP redundancy mechanisms and PTP inclusion using slave clocks.

Device interactions at the bay level are enabled by GOOSE/SV messaging whose rules and timing constraints must be explicitly defined to ensure that performance requirements are met. For example, GOOSE messages must be delivered with minimal latency typically within 4 ms (2/3 phase) to ensure that fault responses are executed promptly. Similarly, SV messages in the process layer must have data transmitted at precise intervals, ensuring synchronization across devices for protection. A topology that merely models device connections would not support proofs that the requirements are met without incorporating additional semantics describing how data is exchanged and processed.

The grammar provides a straightforward way to construct all the entities, and especially communications channels, for inclusion in an applied π-calculus representation of IEC 61850 communications at the bay level in a substation automation system. The grammar offers a syntactic representation of the system and the applied π-calculus enables formalizations of dynamic processes and interactions. This provides the foundation for verifying fundamental security properties such as availability, confidentiality and integrity and ensuring that fault tolerance is satisfiable.

The grammar is intended to capture constraints imposed by the IEC 61850 protocol as well as subsidiary protocols (e.g., HSR and PRP), and logical communications flows. However, the grammar is limited due to the difficulty of incorporating several loosely coupled standards that shape the structure and operation of substation automation systems. An example is the placement of clocks that is constrained by PTP.

The bay layer is driven by IEC 61850 for communications, IEC 62439-3 for redundancy protocols and IEEE 1588 for time synchronization. These standards, while individually addressing specific aspects of a system, collectively influence how the topology is designed and how devices interact. For example, IEC 61850 defines the logical architecture and redundancy options, IEC 62439-3 specifies redundancy mechanisms such as HSR and PRP in connection with PTP, and IEEE 1588 provides guidelines for precise time synchronization through PTP. The dependencies existing between standards means that the grammar is a partial representation of bay layer topologies and constraints.

```
<Network> ::= <InitialConnections> <NetworkBody>
<NetworkBody> ::= <NetworkSegment> | <NetworkSegment>
                  <NetworkConnection> | <NetworkSegment>
                  <NetworkConnection> <NetworkBody>
<NetworkSegment> ::= <FieldBus> { <SwitchChain> }
<SwitchChain> ::= <Switch> { <Switch> }
<NetworkConnection> ::= 'Switch connects to' <NetworkSegment>
```

Fig. 2. Recursive network structure.

```
<InitialConnections> ::= <SensorConnection> <ActuatorConnection>
                         { <DeviceConnection> } | <IEDConnection>
                         { <DeviceConnection> }
<SensorConnection> ::= 'Sensor connects to' <MergingUnitConnection>
<ActuatorConnection> ::= 'Actuator connects to'
                         <MergingUnitConnection>
<DeviceConnection> ::= <SensorOrActuator> 'connects to'
                       <MergingUnitConnection> | <IEDConnection>
<IEDConnection> ::= 'IED connects to' <Baycomponent>
<SensorOrActuator> ::= <Sensor> | <Actuator>
<MergingUnitConnection> ::= <MergingUnit> , { <ConnectionType> } ,
                            <SlaveClock> { , <SlaveClock> }
<ConnectionType> ::= <HSRConnection> | <PRPConnection> |
                     <StandardConnection>
```

Fig. 3. Mandatory initial substation automation topology.

```
<FieldBus> ::= 'FieldBus' ( <HSRNetwork> | <PRPNetwork> |
               <StandardNetwork> )
```

Fig. 4. Network types.

Figure 2 presents grammar rules that recursively define the network structure. The rules permit single and multiple network segments. Each segment starts with a FieldBus that connects network types in a substation automation system. Switches connect network segments.

Figure 3 presents grammar rules that define the mandatory initial substation automation topology. The topology incorporates sensors, actuators and merging units, as well as recursive network connections.

Figure 4 presents grammar rules that specify FieldBus network types, including HSR, PRP and standard networks.

```
<HSRNetwork> ::= 'HSRNetwork' '(' <HSRConnections> ')'
HSRConnections ::= ComponentConnection { <ComponentConnection> }
                   'connects back to' <FirstComponent>
<FirstComponent> ::= <Baycomponent>
```

Fig. 5. HSR networks.

```
<PRPNetwork> ::= 'PRPNetwork' '(' <PRPConnections> ')'
<PRPConnections> ::= <DualComponentConnection>
<DualComponentConnection> ::= <ComponentPair> 'connects'
                              <PRPInterface>
                              <ComponentPair> 'connects'
                              <PRPInterface>
<ComponentPair> ::= <Baycomponent> 'to' <Baycomponent>
```

Fig. 6. PRP networks.

```
<StandardNetwork> ::= 'StandardNetwork' ( <StandardConnections> )
<StandardConnections> ::= <ComponentConnection> |
                          <ComponentConnection>
                          <StandardConnections>
<ComponentConnection> ::= <Baycomponent> 'connects' <Interface>
```

Fig. 7. Standard network.

Figure 5 presents grammar rules that specify HSR networks. Redundancy is ensured by connecting multiple components in a closed loop.

Figure 6 presents grammar rules that specify PRP networks. Single points of failure are eliminated by creating dual connections between pairs of mid-layer components.

Figure 7 presents grammar rules that specify standard networks. Standard network connections are formed between components using interfaces.

Figure 8 presents grammar rules that specify switches. Each switch connects to multiple components or other switches, ensuring network connectivity.

Figure 9 presents grammar rules that specify various network components along with their roles and connectivity. The components include programmable logic controllers, intelligent electronic devices, remote terminal units (RTUs), sensors, actuators, slave clocks and merging units. Sensors and actuators connect via merging units, enhancing data integrity before data reaches control components.

```
<Switch> ::= 'switch' ( { <SwitchConnection> } )
<SwitchConnection> ::= <Baycomponent> 'connects to' <Switch> |
                       <Switch> 'connects to' <Switch>
```

Fig. 8. Switches.

```
<Baycomponent> ::= <PLC> | <RTU> | <IED> | <Switch>
<PLC> ::= 'PLC' 'connects to' <Baycomponent> ',' <SlaveClock>
          { ',' <SlaveClock> }
<IED> ::= 'IED' 'connects to' <Baycomponent> ',' <SlaveClock>
          { ',' <SlaveClock> }
<RTU> ::= 'RTU' 'endpoint' ',' <SlaveClock> { ',' <SlaveClock> }
<Sensor> ::= 'Sensor'
<Actuator> ::= 'Actuator'
<SlaveClock> ::= <ComponentSlaveClock>
<ComponentSlaveClock> ::= <PLCSlaveClock> | <RTUSlaveClock> |
<IEDSlaveClock> | <MergingUnitSlaveClock>
<PLCSlaveClock> ::= 'PLC Slave Clock' <ID>
<RTUSlaveClock> ::= 'RTU Slave Clock' <ID>
<IEDSlaveClock> ::= 'IED Slave Clock' <ID>
<MergingUnitSlaveClock> ::= 'Merging Unit Slave Clock' <ID>
```

Fig. 9. Network component roles and connectivity.

```
<Interface> ::= <StandardInterface> | <HSRInterface> |
                <PRPInterface>
<StandardInterface> ::= 'Standard Ethernet'
<HSRInterface> ::= 'HSR Interface'
<PRPInterface> ::= 'PRP Interface'
```

Fig. 10. Network interfaces for data transmission.

Figure 10 presents grammar rules that specify network interfaces used for data transmission in substation automation systems.

The topology of a substation automation network is fundamental to how the system operates in terms of communications as well as security. The connections between devices, routes taken by data and mechanisms for redundancy all influence the ability of a substation automation system to meet security guarantees despite myriad variations in their topologies. This is most relevant because even minor topology changes – such as re-routing a link or adding a new device – can violate timeliness and, thus, total correctness.

3.2 Applied π-Calculus Mapping

The applied π-calculus focuses on the essential elements of the grammar, including the constraints imposed by HSR and PRP. HSR ensures fault tolerance using a closed-loop configuration, where data can traverse the network even in the presence of failures. This is modeled using recursive and cyclic process definitions with channels that loop around, encapsulating the looped nature of HSR. In contrast, PRP creates dual independent paths for communications, eliminating single points of failure. This is expressed in the applied π-calculus via parallel composition that allows simultaneous communications along two separate channels. The modeling of these two protocols highlights the flexibility of the applied π-calculus in capturing diverse network behaviors.

Low-level connectivity involves links of sensors, actuators and merging units. These connections are modeled as channels in the applied π-calculus, facilitating synchronous/asynchronous communications between components. Individual components are modeled as individual processes such as sensors, actuators, merging units and intelligent electronic devices. Note that IEC 61850 specifies time bounds instead of precise intervals, limiting the need for exact time representations in the calculus. IEC 61850 defines data classes such as Type 1-A Fast Messages that include GOOSE and trip signals. These must be transmitted within 4 ms or less to ensure near-instantaneous response for high-speed protection. On the other hand, Type 2 Messages, which include periodic monitoring data, can tolerate much larger delays; these are not considered in this work because the focus is on the lower levels of substation automation systems.

The grammar is meant to map the physical connectivity of components such as merging units and intelligent electronic devices as well as a partial logical connectivity to show how communications flow within devices. However, the logical connections described by the grammar are limited to essential communications pathways and redundancy mechanisms. Physical components in the bay layer, such as merging units, intelligent electronic devices and switches, are modeled in the applied π-calculus as processes interacting over channels that represent physical connections. For example, a channel may model how a merging unit interacts with a switch via an HSR ring or a PRP network. The focus is on capturing the topological structure, specifically the device connections and how redundancy mechanisms such as HSR and PRP provide fault tolerance.

Logical components, on the other hand, describe system functionality and behavior, independent of the physical structure. This includes the retransmission logic for GOOSE messages and the timing precision ensured by PTP. Logical components are expressed in the applied π-calculus as layers of interaction or rules applied over the physical channels. For example, the retransmission of GOOSE messages in burst and cyclic phases are modeled as recursive processes running on top of physical connections.

The variability in timing enables precise delays to be abstracted away in the applied π-calculus model while respecting the upper and lower bounds dictated by the data class.

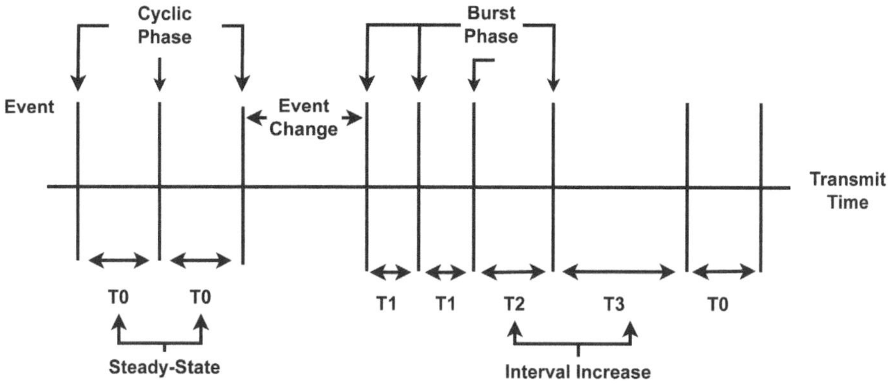

Fig. 11. GOOSE messaging with cyclic and burst phases.

For example, retransmissions in the cyclic phase of GOOSE messages can be modeled recursively without explicitly encoding time delays while implicitly ensuring compliance with Type 1-A timing requirements as shown in Fig. 11. The abstraction helps focus on the logical correctness and interaction patterns of a substation automation system without being constrained by unnecessary timing details. This enables an alignment with the IEC 61850 standard, ensuring that the models are flexible and faithful to the standard while supporting analyses of system behavior and security under adversarial conditions.

4 Attack Model

This section presents attacks on IEC 61850 bay level communications that target network channels. The applied π-calculus model can express numerous attacks that engage process state information. However, the example attacks described in this section are limited because the goal is to capture the effects of a simple denial-of-service attack as a baseline, following which further modeling of causality disruption and simple and state/memory manipulations are provided. Each attack has different requirements on channels. The final attack imposes requirements on the simple process state as well.

Table 1 categorizes attacks based on their primary targets – specifically, whether they disrupt communications channels or manipulate internal process states.

In the network layer, uninterrupted communications deliver critical messages such as GOOSE messages within strict timing constraints. Denial-of-service attacks only need to violate the performance constraints, for example, constraints on trip commands.

In the process layer, attacks leverage device state and memory to manage and process incoming messages. An attacker can exploit the reliance on device state to disrupt functionality. A notable example is an attack that forces a device to

Table 1. Expanded attacks on channels and processes.

Attack Type	Target	Description
Denial-of-Service	Channel	Floods communications channels to overwhelm receiver buffers
Change-in-Causality	Channel	Disrupts order of messages to cause incorrect processing
Replay Attack	Channel	Resends previously captured messages to confuse or disrupt processes
State Manipulation	Process	Alters internal process state to induce incorrect behavior
Message Injection	Channel	Injects fake messages to manipulate system behavior
Eavesdropping	Channel	Intercepts communications to gather sensitive information
Clock Tampering	Process	Modifies clock synchronization to disrupt coordinated operations
Man-in-the-Middle	Channel and Process	Intercepts and alters messages in transit to change content or sequence

remain in a deadlock state by manipulating its state history. In IEC 61850 systems, devices such as protection relays and controllers often use state history to determine whether to transition between operating modes. For example, a protection relay may evaluate the sequence of received GOOSE messages to decide whether to trip a breaker. By carefully injecting messages that reinforce a particular state, an attacker can prevent the device from transitioning to another state, such as tripping in response to a fault condition. More sophisticated attacks can be constructed by combining sub-attacks in causal and temporal order. While this is beyond the scope of this work, it is pertinent to note that the applied π-calculus supports proofs of the feasibility/infeasibility of such complex attacks within the defined semantics. In conjunction with the grammar model that supports changes in device topology, device interactions and protocol behavior, the applied π-calculus provides a stable proof infrastructure for analyzing attack impacts.

Another key advantage of the applied π-calculus is its ability to model processes that interact via communications channels while allowing the interactions to evolve dynamically. Substation automation systems rely on intricate message flows between publishers, subscribers and intermediary nodes such as switches and routers. These flows can change depending on system state, network topology and fault condition. For example, a GOOSE message might be retransmitted repeatedly due to a fault condition while the network re-routes traffic through redundant paths according to HSR/PRP.

At a finer level, the π-calculus can describe the internal behavior of individual processes. Devices in a substation automation system, such as programmable logic controllers and intelligent electronic devices maintain internal state and use buffers to process and manage messages. For example, a protection relay processes incoming GOOSE messages, stores their state history and uses the information to determine whether or not a fault condition exists. The applied π-calculus formally expresses this behavior by modeling message receipt and decision logic as processes. The introduction of state can also enable subtle attacks such as forcing a device to be in a deadlock state by continuously sending it messages. For example, an attacker might inject fake GOOSE messages that reinforce a normal state, preventing a relay from transitioning to a critical state during a legitimate fault. By explicitly modeling this process, the applied π-calculus makes it possible to analyze how an attacker can exploit the state history and device memory to disrupt system behavior, including the behavior of distributed systems without explicit temporal mappings.

To represent state transformation and indirect effects, it may be necessary to explicitly include intermediary nodes such as network components because they are equally relevant as endpoints. For example, a switch can be modeled as a process that listens on one channel and forwards messages on another channel. By introducing delays or modifications at these intermediary points, an attacker can disrupt communications, reorder messages and create inconsistencies between devices. The applied π-calculus provides a clear and formal means to describe the behavior of intermediary nodes and analyze their roles in facilitating or mitigating attacks. The intermediary nodes provide a more realistic view compared with a simple topology that only exhibits direct communications paths.

4.1 Denial-of-Service Attack

In a denial-of-service attack, an attacker injects fake messages into the memory buffer of a device, preventing it from processing legitimate commands. Specifically, the attacker targets device memory capacity by overwriting entries in the buffer with fake or irrelevant data. This requires an interaction with the network channel to send messages to the device buffer. The attacker can send these messages on a separate network channel or on the legitimate channel. For example, a circuit breaker controller might rely on a buffer to queue incoming commands. By continuously injecting messages, the attacker can ensure that the buffer is always full, effectively blocking legitimate trip commands from being processed. This attack exploits the finite memory resources of devices, especially in real-time systems encountered in IEC 61850 environments where devices are designed for speed and determinism instead of robust memory management.

Consider a low-level denial-of-service attack scenario where two nodes, NA and NB, engage in direct communications with each other. The communications use a standard message passing protocol with NA sending messages to

NB while asynchronously waiting and monitoring for acknowledgements from NB on a separate acknowledgement channel. The asynchronous nature of the communications means that the nodes operate in real time.

The denial-of-service attack model demonstrates how an attacker can overwhelm the receiver's buffer with fake data to disrupt communications. In the model, communications between components follow the IEC 61850-8-1 [6] polling request mechanism. Polling requests involve regular queries from one device to another (e.g., a receiver polling a sender for updates). The attacker exploits this periodic behavior by injecting excessive data into the channel, overwhelming the receiver's ability to process legitimate polling responses. Since polling introduces predictable traffic patterns, it becomes an easy target for an attacker seeking to overload the system.

The applied π-calculus specification of node NA is as follows:

$$\begin{aligned}
\mathrm{NA} &= \mathrm{buf_s(data)} \cdot (\mathrm{BurstPhase} \mid \mathrm{ack_r(ack)} \mid \mathrm{Sensor}),\\
\mathrm{BurstPhase\langle data\rangle} &= (\overline{\mathrm{send_s}}\langle\mathrm{data}\rangle \mid \overline{\mathrm{send_s}}\langle\mathrm{data}\rangle \mid \overline{\mathrm{send_s}}\langle\mathrm{data}\rangle)\\
&\quad \mid [\mathrm{s2/NextChannel(data)}] \cdot \mathrm{CyclicPhase\langle data, s2\rangle}\\
\mathrm{CyclicPhase\langle data, s\rangle} &= \overline{\mathrm{s}}\langle\mathrm{data}\rangle \cdot [\mathrm{next_s/NextChannel(data)}]\cdot\\
&\quad \mathrm{CyclicPhase\langle data, next_s\rangle}\\
\mathrm{NextChannel(data)} &= [\mathrm{s2/s1}] \cdot \mathrm{s2\langle data\rangle} \mid [\mathrm{s3/s2}] \cdot \mathrm{s3\langle data\rangle} \mid\\
&\quad [\mathrm{s4/s3}] \cdot \mathrm{s4\langle data\rangle}
\end{aligned}$$

In standard communications, each node has a buffer that stores messages for future processing. The message buffer model has the standard data structure used in IEC 61850 implementations – a queue with the first-in first-out rule. The applied π-calculus specification of buffer NABuffer of node NA is as follows:

$$\begin{aligned}
\mathrm{NABuffer} = {} & \mathrm{s(x1)} \cdot (\overline{\mathrm{buf_s}}\langle\mathrm{x1}\rangle \mid \mathrm{NABuffer}) +\\
& \mathrm{s(x2)} \cdot (\overline{\mathrm{buf_s}}\langle\mathrm{x1}\rangle \mid \overline{\mathrm{buf_s}}\langle\mathrm{x2}\rangle \mid \mathrm{NABuffer}) +\\
& \mathrm{s(x3)} \cdot (\overline{\mathrm{buf_s}}\langle\mathrm{x1}\rangle \mid \overline{\mathrm{buf_s}}\langle\mathrm{x2}\rangle \mid \overline{\mathrm{buf_s}}\langle\mathrm{x3}\rangle \mid \mathrm{NABuffer})
\end{aligned}$$

The applied π-calculus specification of node NB is as follows:

$$\mathrm{NB} = \mathrm{buf\_r(data)} \cdot (\overline{\mathrm{process\_data}}\langle\mathrm{data}\rangle \mid \mathrm{ack\_r}\langle\mathrm{ack}\rangle \mid \mathrm{NB})$$

The applied π-calculus specification of buffer NBBuffer of node NB is as follows:

$$\begin{aligned}
\mathrm{NBBuffer} = {} & \mathrm{send_s}(x1) \cdot (\overline{\mathrm{buf_r}}\langle x1\rangle \mid \mathrm{NBBuffer}) +\\
& \mathrm{send_s}(x2) \cdot (\overline{\mathrm{buf_r}}\langle x1\rangle \mid \overline{\mathrm{buf_r}}\langle x2\rangle \mid \mathrm{NBBuffer}) + 0
\end{aligned}$$

An attacker performing an active attack has access to the name/channel used by node NA to send message updates to node NB. The attacker does not necessarily see the messages sent from node NA to node NB. The objective of the attacker is simply to overload node NB's buffer with fake data to disrupt communications. The attacker intercepts a message on channel X and modifies the message. The applied π-calculus specification of Attacker is as follows:

$$\text{Attacker} = (\overline{\text{send\_s}}\langle\text{fakedata}\rangle + \overline{\text{ack\_r}}\langle\text{fakedata}\rangle) \cdot \text{Attacker}$$

4.2 Change-in-Causality Attack

A change-in-causality attack involves a temporal re-ordering of events (causality reversal) that can cause state de-synchronization, resulting in mismatched states between devices. Such attacks disrupt immediate operations and corrupt the state history used for future decision-making, compounding the impacts over time. As in the case of a denial-of-service attack, the attacker needs to have an active role on the network channel to receive the messages.

The change-in-causality attack in this section involves an intelligent electronic device sending messages to a remote terminal unit, but the attacker reorders the messages received by the remote terminal unit. The assumption is that the attacker performs an active attack with full access to the remote terminal unit.

The change-in-causality attack leverages the IEC 61850 alerts mechanism [6] that uses GOOSE messages. IEC 61850 alerts are event-driven and designed to notify relevant devices of changes in system conditions such as faults and critical data updates. The attacker takes advantage of the asynchronous and event-driven nature of alerts, reordering or delaying them to disrupt the logical flow of communications. The manipulation undermines the causality guarantees that are essential to substation automation operations.

The attack model assumes that data is transmitted from the intelligent electronic device all the way to the remote terminal unit. Also, it assumes the presence of a modern system structure without a merging unit where all data is converted to the right format by the intelligent electronic device.

The applied π-calculus specifications of intelligent electronic device IED, programmable logic controller PLC and remote terminal unit RTU are as follows:

$$\text{IED} = \overline{\text{send\_PLC}}\langle\text{data}\rangle \mid \text{rtu\_ack}(\text{data}) \mid \text{IED}$$

$$\text{PLC} = \text{send\_PLC}(\text{data}) \cdot \text{BurstPhase} \mid \text{PLC}$$

$$\text{RTU} = \text{send\_RTU}(\text{data}) \cdot \overline{\text{process\_data}}\langle\text{data}\rangle \mid \overline{\text{rtu\_ack}}\langle\text{data}\rangle \mid \text{RTU}$$

The applied π-calculus specifications of Attacker, Bufferdata and Select-SendOrNot are as follows:

$$\begin{aligned}
\text{Attacker} &= \big(\text{send_rtu(data)} \mid \overline{\text{send_to_buffer}}\langle\text{data}\rangle\big)\\
&\quad \mid \big([\text{send_rtu/Bufferdata(data)}]\\
&\qquad \mid \overline{\text{send_rtu}}\langle\text{modified_data}\rangle \mid \text{Attacker}\big),\\
\text{Bufferdata} &= \text{send_to_buffer(data)}\\
&\quad \mid [\text{s1/SelectSendOrNot(data1)}] \cdot s1(\text{data1})\\
&\quad \mid [\text{s2/SelectSendOrNot(data2)}] \cdot s2(\text{data2})\\
&\quad \mid [\text{s3/SelectSendOrNot(data3)}] \cdot s3(\text{data3})\\
&\quad \mid \text{Bufferdata}\\
\text{SelectSendOrNot(data)} &= \text{ModifySeqNoAndSend(data)} \mid \text{NoAction}
\end{aligned}$$

In the Attacker process, the attacker intercepts messages sent from the programmable logic controller to the remote terminal unit, which the attacker stores in its own buffer. The terms s1, s2 and s3 correspond to memory locations in the attacker's buffer that store the intercepted messages. A form of name substitution is used for an individual message to decide whether to send it to the remote terminal unity or whether to perform no action. The attacker's buffer runs asynchronously to ensure that it can send an old message in real time. In addition, the attacker rewrites the sequence numbers on the message headers to ensure that they are in sync with the current messages being sent and that the sent messages are not dropped by the remote terminal unit.

The applied π-calculus specifications of BurstPhase, Cyclic Phase and Next-Channel are as follows:

$$\begin{aligned}
\text{BurstPhase}\langle\text{data}\rangle \;=\; &\big(\overline{\text{send_rtu}}\langle\text{data}\rangle\\
&\mid \overline{\text{send_rtu}}\langle\text{data}\rangle\\
&\mid \overline{\text{send_rtu}}\langle\text{data}\rangle\\
&\mid \overline{\text{send_rtu}}\langle\text{data}\rangle\\
&\mid \overline{\text{send_rtu}}\langle\text{data}\rangle\big)\\
&\mid [s2/\text{NextChannel(data)}] \cdot \text{CyclicPhase}\langle\text{data}, s2\rangle
\end{aligned}$$

$$\begin{aligned}
\text{CyclicPhase}\langle\text{data}, s\rangle \;=\; &\overline{s}\langle\text{data}\rangle \cdot [\text{next_s/NextChannel(data)}]\\
&\cdot \text{CyclicPhase}\langle\text{data}, \text{next_s}\rangle
\end{aligned}$$

$$\begin{aligned}
\text{NextChannel(data)} \;=\; &[s2/s1] \cdot s2\langle\text{data}\rangle\\
&\mid [s3/s2] \cdot s3\langle\text{data}\rangle\\
&\mid [s4/s3] \cdot s4\langle\text{data}\rangle
\end{aligned}$$

Once again, the IEC 61850 semantics are employed, specifically, the GOOSE intervals. Unlike the previous example, a different set of intervals is used in the burst phase, corresponding to a different system configuration. The NextChannel process is used to swap channels if one channel is in use.

4.3 Process Layer Attack with State and Memory

In this attack scenario, the attacker observes message exchanges along the communications pathways. The intelligent electronic device IED sends normal or critical voltage data to the programmable logic controller PLC on the appropriate channel based on its criticality. The attacker disrupts the communications flow by intercepting and modifying messages sent between the IED and PLC processes. It is assumed that no integrity protection guarantees are in place.

For example, the attacker can inject a send_plc_critical message into the communications channel while PLCNormal is active, forcing the system to transition to PLCCritical. Once in the PLCCritical state, the attacker can further disrupt the flow by injecting or delaying a send_plc_normal message, preventing the system from stabilizing and causing it to loop indefinitely.

This manipulation of communications pathways alone is sufficient to create a deadlock because the processes rely entirely on the message sequence and timing to coordinate state transitions. The attacker does not need direct visibility into the internal states of PLCNormal or PLCCritical; instead, it relies on the ability to observe, intercept and manipulate messages in the communications channels. For instance, by carefully timing the injection of conflicting messages (send_plc_critical and send_plc_normal), the attacker can ensure that the PLC process can neither complete its task nor transition the system back to normal operation.

The applied π-calculus specifications of IED, PLCNormal, PLCCritical, AttackerCritical, AttackerNormal and MemoryCorruption are as follows:

$$\begin{aligned}\text{IED} = {} & \overline{\text{send\_plc\_normal}}\langle \text{voltagedata, sqNum, stNum}\rangle \\ & + \overline{\text{send\_plc\_critical}}\langle \text{voltagedata, sqNum, stNum}\rangle \\ & \mid \text{IED}\end{aligned}$$

$$\begin{aligned}\text{PLCNormal} = {} & \text{send\_plc\_normal}(\text{voltagedata, sqNum, stNum}) \cdot \\ & \text{PLCNormal} + \\ & \text{send\_plc\_critical}(\text{voltagedata, sqNum, stNum}) \\ & \cdot \text{PLCCritical}, \\ \text{PLCCritical} = {} & \overline{\text{fixvoltage}}\langle \text{voltagechange}\rangle \cdot \text{PLCNormal}\end{aligned}$$

$$\begin{aligned}\text{AttackerCritical} = {} & \text{send\_plc\_critical(voltagedata, sqNum, stNum)}\cdot \\ & \overline{\text{send\_plc\_normal}}\langle \text{data', sqNum', stNum'}\rangle \\ & \cdot \text{AttackerNormal}\end{aligned}$$

$$\begin{aligned}\text{AttackerNormal} = {} & \text{send\_plc\_normal(voltagedata, sqNum, stNum)}\cdot \\ & \overline{\text{send\_plc\_critical}}\langle \text{data', sqNum', stNum'}\rangle \\ & \cdot \text{AttackerCritical}\end{aligned}$$

$$\text{MemoryCorruption} = \overline{\text{memoryblock}}\langle \text{corruptdata}\rangle \cdot \text{PLCCritical}$$

The recursive nature of the definitions ensures that the attacker continues the cycle of conflicting messages, forcing the system into a deadlock state. This manipulation disrupts the communications flow, preventing the processes from reaching their intended states. As in the change-in-causality attack, it is assumed that the attack primarily relies on alerts using GOOSE messages [6] instead of polling requests. The attack also incorporates the ACSI frames from IEC 61850-7-2 and demonstrates how to map these services with an IEC 8802 mapping from IEC 61850-8-1 by including the state number (stnum) and sequence number (sqnum). While the main idea behind the attack is to demonstrate how a deadlock can occur by keeping the programmable logic controller in an inappropriate state, it is also possible to show that the attacker can modify sequence numbers and state numbers to ensure the correct ordering of events and show that the attacker is in a different state than it actually is. This also enables the attacker to evade detection.

5 Security Analyses

This section presents security analyses of the denial-of-service and change-in-causality attack models. The structural congruence property is adequate to provide proofs of successful attacks. It is not necessary to rely on bisimilarity for the proofs due to the simplified definitions used for the assumptions.

5.1 Denial-of-Service Attack Proof

To prove the feasibility of a denial-of-service attack, it is required to demonstrate that an attacker can manipulate the communications pathway to overwhelm the receiver's buffer. Specifically, it must be shown that the attacker can inject excessive or malicious messages into the channel faster than the receiver can process them, thereby exhausting the receiver's buffer capacity. This leads to legitimate messages being dropped or delayed, effectively disrupting the receiver's normal operation.

The proof examines whether the buffer structure and the interactions between the processes provide safeguards against denial-of-service attacks or if the attacker can consistently exploit the vulnerability for a given topology and communications model.

In the following applied π-calculus specification of System, the attacker is scoped within the system and can inject fake messages into the send_s channel:

$$\text{System} = \boldsymbol{\nu}(\text{NA} \mid \text{NABuffer} \mid \text{NB} \mid \text{NBBuffer} \mid \text{Attacker})$$

Scope extrusion, which explicitly exposes the attacker's behavior, is employed in the following applied π-calculus specification of System:

$$\text{System} =(\text{NA} \mid \text{NABuffer} \mid \text{NB} \mid \text{NBBuffer} \mid \boldsymbol{\nu}(\text{Attacker}))$$

where ν implies that the scope of visibility of private names to other processes can be sent outside the original scope. This shares the attacker's behavior with other processes.

Next, the receiver's buffer processes the incoming messages (x_1, x_2) and fake messages are injected by the attacker. This yields three successive applied π-calculus specifications of System:

$$\begin{aligned}\text{System} = {} & (\text{NA} \mid \text{NABuffer} \mid \text{NB} \mid (\text{send\_s}(x_1)\cdot \\ & (\overline{\text{buf\_r}}\langle x_1\rangle \mid \text{NBBuffer}))+ \\ & (\text{send\_s}(x_2)\cdot \\ & (\overline{\text{buf\_r}}\langle x_1\rangle \mid \overline{\text{buf\_r}}\langle x_2\rangle \mid \text{NBBuffer}) + 0)) \\ & \mid \nu(\overline{\text{send\_s}}\langle \text{fakedata}\rangle \cdot \text{Attacker})) \quad \textit{(Sum-L)}\end{aligned}$$

$$\begin{aligned}\text{System} = {} & (\text{NA} \mid \text{NABuffer} \mid \text{NB} \mid \text{send\_s}(x_2)\cdot \\ & (\overline{\text{buf\_r}}\langle x_1\rangle \mid \overline{\text{buf\_r}}\langle x_2\rangle \mid \text{NBBuffer})+ \\ & ((\overline{\text{buf\_r}}\langle x_1\rangle \mid \text{NBBuffer}) + 0)) \\ & \mid \nu(\overline{\text{send\_s}}\langle \text{fakedata}\rangle \cdot \text{Attacker})) \quad \textit{(Sum-L)}\end{aligned}$$

$$\begin{aligned}\text{System} = {} & (\text{NA} \mid \text{NABuffer} \mid \text{NB} \mid ((\overline{buf_r}\langle x_1\rangle \mid \text{NBBuffer})+ \\ & (\overline{\text{buf\_r}}\langle x_1\rangle \mid \overline{\text{buf\_r}}\langle x_2\rangle \mid \text{NBBuffer})) + 0) \\ & \mid \nu(\overline{\text{send\_s}}\langle \text{fakedata}\rangle \cdot \text{Attacker})) \quad \textit{(Sum-R)}\end{aligned}$$

Note that *Sum-L* and *Sum-R* isolate x_1 and x_2 to show that the memory locations are being filled due to send_s. By having the attacker do this, the remaining choice in the buffer process is eventually isolated using *Sum-R*. Repeated injections of fakedata overwhelm the buffer. The 0 represents a buffer overflow where all the memory locations are filled.

Since the buffer reaches a terminal state, there is no further processing and legitimate data is dropped. The denial-of service attack is successful. This yields the final applied π-calculus specification of System:

$$\text{System} = (\text{NA} \mid \text{NABuffer} \mid \text{NB} \mid 0 \mid \nu(\overline{\text{send\_s}}\langle\text{fakedata}\rangle \cdot \text{Attacker}))$$

5.2 Change-In-Causality Attack Proof

To prove the feasibility of the change-in-causality attack, it is required to demonstrate that an attacker can disrupt the logical ordering of messages exchanged between processes. Specifically, it must be shown that the attacker can manipulate the communications pathway by reordering or delaying messages so that the receiver processes events in an incorrect sequence. The result is that processes may transition to incorrect states or fail to respond appropriately to critical events. The proof focuses on whether the communications structure and protocol enable the attacker to reliably alter causality or if there are inherent mechanisms in place that preserve the correct order of messages.

As in the case of the denial-of-service attack, the attacker's behavior is shared across all concurrent processes using scope extrusion. This yields three successive applied π-calculus specifications of System:

$$\text{System} = \boldsymbol{\nu}((\text{RTU} \mid \text{Attacker} \mid \text{Bufferdata} \mid \text{SelectSendOrNot}))$$

$$\text{System} = (\text{RTU} \mid \boldsymbol{\nu}(\text{Attacker}) \mid \text{Bufferdata} \mid \text{SelectSendOrNot})$$

$$\begin{aligned}\text{System} = (&\text{send\_rtu}(\text{data}) \mid \overline{\text{send\_to\_buffer}}\langle\text{data}\rangle \\ &\mid \text{Bufferdata} \mid \text{SelectSendOrNot} \mid \text{RTU})\end{aligned}$$

The attacker in a man-in-the-middle position intercepts a message and sends it to the buffer. This yields the following applied π-calculus specification of System:

$$\begin{aligned}\text{System} = (&\text{send\_rtu}(\text{data1}) \mid \overline{\text{send\_to\_buffer}}\langle\text{data1}\rangle \\ &\mid \text{Bufferdata} \mid \text{SelectSendOrNot} \mid \text{RTU})\end{aligned}$$

Next, the attacker intercepts an additional messages. This yields the following applied π-calculus specification of System:

$$\begin{aligned}\text{System} = (&\text{send\_rtu}(\text{data2}) \mid \overline{\text{send\_to\_buffer}}\langle\text{data2}\rangle \\ &\mid \text{Bufferdata} \mid \text{SelectSendOrNot} \mid \text{RTU})\end{aligned}$$

Next, the attacker leverages SelectSendOrNot, which uses name substitution to decide the fate of messages. A predefined condition is set to decide whether to send the stored messages in order or to send the messages in the wrong order. This yields the following applied π-calculus specification of System:

$$\begin{aligned}\text{System} = (&\overline{\text{send\_to\_buffer}}\langle\text{data1}\rangle \mid \overline{\text{send\_to\_buffer}}\langle\text{data2}\rangle \\ &\mid \text{s1}/\text{SelectSendOrNot}(\text{data1}) \cdot \text{s1}(\text{data1}) \\ &\mid \text{s2}/\text{SelectSendOrNot}(\text{data2}) \cdot \text{s2}(\text{data2}) \\ &\mid \text{SelectSendOrNot} \mid \text{RTU})\end{aligned}$$

The attacker eventually selects a suitable time to send the stored messages. A message is selected from the buffer and the sequence number is modified to avoid detection. This yields the following applied π-calculus specifications of System:

$$\begin{aligned}\text{System} = (&\overline{\text{send\_to\_buffer}}\langle\text{data1}\rangle \mid \overline{\text{send\_to\_buffer}}\langle\text{data2}\rangle \\ &\mid \text{s1}/\text{SelectSendOrNot}(\text{data1}) \cdot \text{s1}(\text{data1}) \\ &\mid \text{s2}/\text{SelectSendOrNot}(\text{data2}) \cdot \text{s2}(\text{data2}) \\ &\mid (\text{ModifySeqNoAndSend}(\text{data1}) \mid \text{NoAction}) \cdot \text{s1}(\text{data1}) \\ &\mid (\text{ModifySeqNoAndSend}(\text{data2}) \mid \text{NoAction}) \cdot \text{s2}(\text{data2}) \\ \mid \text{RTU})&\end{aligned}$$

$$\text{System} = (\text{s1}(\text{data1}) \mid \text{ModifySeqNoAndSend}(\text{data2}) \mid \text{RTU})$$

Due to the attacker's manipulation, the receiver processes data2 before data1. The change-in-causality attack is succesful. This yields the final applied π-calculus specification of System:

$$\text{System} = (\text{process\_data}(\text{data2}) \mid \text{rtu\_ack}(\text{data2}) \mid \text{s1}(\text{data1}))$$

6 Conclusions

This work has been inspired by the argument that an analysis of correctness that includes the security of IEC 61850 bay level communications is reasonably complete only if the performance requirements are part of the security guarantees. Previous research has largely avoided considerations of network topology and infrastructure. By contrast, this work has sought to understand the role of ancillary components in substation automation architectures, especially network topology and infrastructure, and to codify their influences in a common proof framework.

A small subset of attacks mainly focusing on communications channels is described. However, the applied π-calculus model specified in this work is shown to adequately capture the interactions between concurrent and distributed processes. Since process calculi do not offer structuring mechanisms on their own for complex distributed systems, a formal grammar is leveraged to formulate constraints on valid topologies and to provide mappings to the applied π-calculus, including the potential for automation in environments such as ProVerif.

The applied π-calculus analysis can be employed in real-world scenarios to verify that topologies are valid according to protocol standards such as IEC 61850 while also ensuring that the topologies maintain critical security guarantees. By formally modeling communications structures and behavior it is possible to check that all configurations comply with standards and mitigate attacks such as denial-of-service and change-in-causality. The formal analysis can also help reveal subtle gaps in protocol designs where permitted topologies may lead to vulnerabilities that are not immediately apparent from the standards. As such, the applied π-calculus analysis is an important tool for studying security and reliability guarantees in real-time systems beyond the low-level substation automation environments considered in this work.

Future research will focus on seamlessly integrating PTP with redundancy protocols such as HSR and PRP. This is important because PTP ensures precise synchronization across devices that is critical to the proper functioning of protection and control systems, especially in time-sensitive operations. Efforts will also model the interactions of PTP with redundancy mechanisms and explore how synchronization vulnerabilities, such as clock tampering, could impact system reliability. Finally, future research will also extend the grammar and applied π-calculus frameworks to accommodate mesh topologies that offer increased flexibility and robustness by providing multiple redundant paths between devices.

Acknowledgements. This research was supported by the Office of Gas and Electricity Markets (Ofgem), United Kingdom. The authors also wish to thank Tina Wu and Paul Sutton for their assistance with this work.

References

1. Abadi, M., Blanchet, B., Fournet, C.: The applied π-calculus: mobile values, new names and secure communications. J. ACM **65**(1), 1 (2017)
2. Bhattacharya, S., Saqib, N., Govindarasu, M.: ML-based anomaly detection system for IEC 61850 communications in substations. In: Proceedings of the IEEE Power and Energy Society General Meeting (2024)
3. Elbez, G., Nahrstedt, K., Hagenmeyer, V.: Early detection of GOOSE denial-of-service (DoS) attacks in IEC 61850 substations. In: Proceedings of the IEEE International Conference on Communications, Control and Computing Technologies for Smart Grids, pp. 367–373 (2022)
4. Elbez, G., Nahrstedt, K., Hagenmeyer, V.: Early attack detection for securing GOOSE network traffic. IEEE Trans. Smart Grid **15**(1), 899–910 (2024)

5. Institute for Electrical and Electronics Engineers: IEEE 1588–2019: IEEE Standard for a Precision Clock Synchronization Protocol for Networked Measurement and Control Systems. Piscataway, New Jersey (2019)
6. International Electrotechnical Commission: IEC 61850-8-1:2011: Communication Networks and Systems for Power Utility Automation - Part 8–1: Specific Communication Service Mapping (SCSM) - Mappings to MMS (ISO 9506–1 and ISO 9506–2) and to ISO/IEC 8802–3. Switzerland, Geneva (2011)
7. International Electrotechnical Commission: IEC 61850-9-2:2011: Communication Networks and Systems for Power Utility Automation - Part 9–2: Specific Communication Service Mapping (SCSM) - Sampled Values over ISO/IEC 8802–3. Switzerland, Geneva (2011)
8. International Electrotechnical Commission: IEC 61850–5:2013: Communication Networks and Systems for Power Utility Automation - Part 5: Communication Requirements for Functions and Device Models. Switzerland, Geneva (2013)
9. International Electrotechnical Commission: IEC 62351–6:2020: Power Systems Management and Associated Information Exchange: Data and Communications Security - Part 6: Security for IEC 61850. Switzerland, Geneva (2020)
10. International Electrotechnical Commission: IEC 62439–3:2021: Industrial Communication Networks - High Availability Automation Networks - Part 3: Parallel Redundancy Protocol (PRP) and High-Availability Seamless Redundancy (HSR). Switzerland, Geneva (2021)
11. International Electrotechnical Commission: IEC TS 61850-1-2:2020/AMD1:2022: Amendment 1: Communication Networks and Systems for Power Utility Automation - Part 1–2: Guideline on Extending IEC 61850. Switzerland, Geneva (2022)
12. Quincozes, S., Albuquerque, C., Passos, D., Mosse, D.: A survey of intrusion detection and prevention systems in digital substations. Comput. Netw. **184**, 107676 (2021)
13. Yegorov, P., Lackovitch, A., Dean, E., Mustafa, H., Basumallik, S., Srivastava, A.: Analyzing GOOSE security in IEC 61850-based substation using ML, SDN and digital twin. In: Proceedings of the North American Power Symposium (2023)

Keychain-Based Rekeying Function for Securing Device Communications

Rongqi Wang[1,2], Sye Loong Keoh[1(✉)], and Raymond Chan[2]

[1] University of Glasgow, Glasgow, UK
SyeLoong.Keoh@glasgow.ac.uk
[2] Singapore Institute of Technology, Singapore, Singapore

Abstract. The proliferation of Internet-of-Things devices operating at network edges has driven the demand for secure, low-latency and decentralized communications methods. However, in dynamic and resource-constrained environments, conventional solutions relying on centralized key management servers or multiple handshakes introduce significant complexity and overhead.

This chapter describes a keychain-based rekeying function that can be used to devise key management protocols based on chameleon hash functions. It enables lightweight, secure and efficient device-to-device and broadcast communications without relying on a centralized infrastructure. Each message is secured by a unique ephemeral session key derived using a pre-shared master key and chameleon hash, ensuring message authenticity and integrity. The session key can be authenticated and verified easily via chameleon hash collision so that the new session key is securely linked to the previous hash key on the keychain, enabling the verification of the sender and the new session key simultaneously. The protocol avoids expensive handshakes while enabling devices to spontaneously establish secure communications channels. A proof-of-concept implementation over Bluetooth Low Energy demonstrates protocol feasibility and performance. The results indicate that the protocols are particularly suitable for autonomous Internet-of-Things device scenarios, enabling seamless, secure and scalable device-to-device and broadcast communications.

Keywords: Applied Cryptography · Hash Chain · Chameleon Hashing · Internet of Things · Device Communications · Key Establishment

1 Introduction

With the proliferation of the Internet of Things (IoT), increasing numbers of devices such as sensors and actuators are being deployed in computing environments such as smart buildings [17]. The devices operate autonomously and interact with each other seamlessly to perform their tasks. Meanwhile, Internet-of-Things devices located at network edges [24], mobile at times, are now equipped

Published by Springer Nature Switzerland AG 2026
J. Staggs and S. Shenoi (Eds.): ICCIP 2025, IFIP AICT 763, pp. 147–168, 2026.
https://doi.org/10.1007/978-3-032-11914-8_7

with optimized machine learning capabilities [3] to perform advanced tasks such as object detection, obstacle avoidance and facial recognition. In most cases, these devices may not be required to communicate with the cloud to perform their tasks, saving communications bandwidth and reducing latency. This approach is especially useful for proximity-based direct device-to-device and/or broadcast communications [25] that do not involve a third-party such as a cloud server. An example scenario is a smart hotel building in which a roaming robot interacts directly with the passenger elevator to move between floors to provide room service and deliver food.

The direct interactions between Internet-of-Things devices have also raised security challenges, specifically, that the devices cannot rely solely on a key distribution server such as Kerberos [13,25] to distribute session keys between communicating devices. Additionally, since the number of interacting devices can be large, it is difficult for each pair of devices to securely establish a session key spontaneously [26]. Moreover, it is prohibitively expensive to require each device to run a (Datagram) Transport Layer Security (D)TLS server or Constrained Application Protocol (CoAP) Secure [23,30] server locally and then perform a (D)TLS handshake.

This chapter describes the Keychain-Based Rekeying Function (KKF) for creating lightweight authentication and secure data transmission protocols that support device-to-device and broadcast communications. The protocols enable the devices to establish ephemeral session keys with each other without relying on a central infrastructure and subsequently renew their keys in a secure manner. The KKF protocols use chameleon hash functions to create unbounded keychains, enabling the periodic rekeying of communications channels without handshakes. All the devices are assumed to be trusted, provisioned with a secret master key and managed under an administration domain. The latest hash key in the keychain is used as the secret session key to secure the communications channel. Each hash key is derived from a session ID containing the master key and a blinded random nonce. Hence, any entity with knowledge of the master key can derive the hash key. KKF also supports rekeying, which is achieved by verifying a blinded collision nonce such that the new hash key is linked to the previous hash key in the keychain. Only a sender with knowledge of the trapdoor key and the raw random nonce can generate the collision nonce.

The one-on-one device communications protocol is adapted to secure broadcast communications by distributing security parameters to derive consecutive hash keys simultaneously. This enables each broadcast message to be encrypted with a different key that can be verified instantly to authenticate the sender. Devices can generate verifiable ephemeral session keys for each message without prior handshakes, thereby permitting secure, rapidly verifiable and low overhead device-to-device and broadcast communications.

2 Background and Related Work

This section discusses chameleon hashing, hash keychains and authentication schemes for device-to-device communications.

2.1 Chameleon Hashing

Krawczyk and Rabin [21] introduced chameleon hashing as a trapdoor hash function. It possesses the same characteristics as conventional cryptographic hash functions, such as non-repudiation, pre-image resistance and collision resistance under normal circumstances. However, it uniquely enables the holder of the trapdoor key to produce a hash collision while ensuring that such collisions are computationally infeasible for entities without the trapdoor key.

The original hash function has been shown to have key exposure problems where an adversary can derive the trapdoor from the parameters of a single known hash collision [2]. Numerous key-exposure-free approaches have been explored to mitigate this problem [6,8,9].

2.2 Hash Keychains

Hakeem et al. [14] proposed a lightweight key management mechanism for LoRaWAN that applies a hash function iteratively on an initial master key to construct a chain of unique session keys. This approach enables devices to store and update keys without frequently requesting keys from a central server while providing adequate security.

Previous work has employed hash chains in reverse order to associate sensors in a body sensor network and subsequently derive a group key to secure broadcast communications [18,19]. The keychains are bounded in that once all the hash keys have been utilized, new keychains have to be re-created. A variant of the hash keychain was devised that employs a chameleon hash function to create a series of unbounded one-way chameleon hashes that enable recipients to verify the authenticity of senders by computing and comparing the hash collisions [10]. In hash keychaining, the hashes are linked using the collision nonce to establish a chain of hashes that can be verified easily. The methodology has been applied to verify GPS signals from satellites to detect GPS spoofing attacks.

2.3 Device-to-Device Authentication Schemes

Authentication schemes for device-to-device communications are classified into three categories, pseudonymous authentication, group authentication and hybrid authentication.

Pseudonymous Authentication. Pseudonymous authentication uses ephemeral pseudonym certificates to sign messages for unlinkable but accountable communications in vehicular networks. Vehicle devices obtain the certificates and associated keys from a certificate authority and store them locally for future communications. Each communications session typically consumes one key derived from the pseudonym. The large pool of pseudonyms required for continuous communications introduces challenges related to key storage and revocation.

SECMACE+ [20] addresses the challenges by leveraging cloud technology as its vehicular public key infrastructure [11] for large-scale, multi-domain and pseudonymous authentication in vehicular networks. The scheme provides high scalability, availability and strong resilience against denial-of-service attacks. It can handle up to 100 pseudonyms in 56 ms and can be dynamically scaled according to the pseudonym request rate. However, the scheme has strong dependence on a cloud infrastructure to support device-to-device communications, although it is scalable and resilient against benign failures and resource depletion attacks.

Several other pseudonymous authentication schemes using the received signal strength between two communicating parties have been proposed to jointly generate shared keys [27–29]. The received signal strength data is collected via ICMP messages following which randomness is extracted using a Kalman filter. The bitstreams are fed through Mathur quantization to derive common preliminary shared keys. Level-crossing is then applied to increase the randomness rate of the bit key stream, following which the bit key stream is hashed using a universal hash function and SHA256 to check whether the two key digests match. This key establishment scheme reduces the computational complexity of pseudonym generation and revocation. It is used to relay traffic information in vehicle-to-vehicle and vehicle-to-everything communications, enabling vehicles unknown to each other to communicate securely.

Group Authentication. Group authentication enables members of a group to act as authentication providers and verifiers in many-to-many communications. The traditional group authentication scheme requires each member of a group to verify every other member, resulting in a per member complexity of $\mathcal{O}(n)$ where n is the number of group members. Group authentication addresses this deficiency by authenticating all the group members at once. The scheme introduced by Harn [15] involves a group manager that issues unique tokens and shares verification values with all the group members, so that members can verify each other by comparing the verification values with the reconstructed values derived from their tokens. Although the scheme reduces the per member complexity to $\mathcal{O}(1)$, the tokens used in one verification are exposed to all the group members. An enhanced scheme proposed by Hsu et al. [16] uses homomorphic secret sharing to enable secure token reuse in multiple sessions by hiding the tokens during the authentication process.

Hybrid Authentication. Hybrid authentication employs hash functions, digital signatures, message authentication codes and various authentication techniques to achieve optimal computation efficiency, low latency and enhanced security. Camenisch et al. [7] introduced zone encryption that distributes ephemeral zone keys based on geographic locations to authorized vehicles; vehicles in the same zone communicate by sending symmetrically encrypted messages using the ephemeral zone keys. Baee et al. [4] proposed a broadcast authentication scheme that provides key management, authentication and data encryption for vehicle-to-vehicle communications. A trusted authority establishes keys on a daily basis for roadside units and authorized vehicles. Vehicles derive ephemeral keys from the keys received from the trusted authority and roadside units and use the derived keys for authentication and secure communications.

Evaluation. Each type of authentication has advantages and limitations. Pseudonymous authentication offers strong accountability but suffers from high certificate and key management overhead that can disrupt real-time ad-hoc services. Group authentication greatly improves efficiency by enabling all the group members to verify each other, but it places a heavy burden on the group manager to administer tokens and ensure security. Hybrid authentication schemes achieve trade-offs by incorporating various mechanisms, but this adds complexity to system development and implementation.

3 Threat Model and System Assumptions

This section describes the threat model and system assumptions.

3.1 Threat Model

An adversary is assumed to have Dolev-Yao capabilities [12] in that it has full control of insecure public channels used for communications. This includes the ability to intercept, modify, delete and inject broadcast messages at will. In addition, the adversary has complete knowledge of the proposed authentication scheme, including access to the source code.

Under this model, the adversary is capable of launching spoofing, man-in-the-middle and replay attacks:

- **Spoofing Attack:** The adversary forges a message, acts as an authorized device and joins a conversation.
- **Man-in-the-Middle Attack:** The adversary intercepts transmitted messages to gain unauthorized access to message data.
- **Replay Attack:** The adversary replays a previously captured legitimate message to disrupt communications.

3.2 System Assumptions

The security protocol is intended to manage communications involving a group of Internet-of-Things devices that have been commissioned and bootstrapped with keying material. For example, in a building management system, it is assumed that new robots and Internet-of-Things devices brought into the building need to be registered before they can be deployed.

- **Device Trust:** The protocol runs on authorized devices. Each device is provisioned with a common master key that is stored in trusted device storage. The devices are free from malware and have restricted physical access.

Table 1. Keychain-Based Rekeying Function protocol notation.

Notation	Definition
$\mathcal{G}$	Base point of NIST P-256 Elliptic Curve Cryptography
K	Master key
Y	Elliptic curve cryptography public key
y	Elliptic curve cryptography private key (trapdoor)
HK	Chameleon hash key
sid	Session ID for each communications session
r	Random nonce
$\tilde{r}$	Blinded random nonce for distribution
seq	Incremental sequence number
m	Authentication payload
r/	Collision nonce
$\tilde{r}$/	Blinded collision nonce for distribution
h	Hash-based message authentication code
ht	Hash table storing security parameters on a device
M	Message payload
EM	Message encrypted with the latest hash key
`AES_encrypt`	Symmetric encryption function (AES256)
`AES_decrypt`	Symmetric decryption function (AES256)
`Rand`	Random number generation function
`HMAC`	Hash-based message authentication code function (SHA256)

- **Device Accessibility:** Devices are not guaranteed to have access to other network components (e.g., certificate authority or trusted authority) at all times.
- **Network Topology:** A dynamic network topology is expected. Devices may engage in one-to-one communications or group communications anywhere and leave the communications at any time.

4 Keychain-Based Rekeying Function Protocol Design

This section describes the Keychain-Based Rekeying Function (KKF) that securely sends messages between trusted devices. The KKF protocols support two scenarios. In the first scenario, a device communicates with another device using one-to-one communications, where both devices are expected to be in close proximity to each other. In the second scenario, a group of devices communicate with all the surrounding devices using one-to-many (broadcast) communications. Table 1 defines the notation used in the KKF protocols.

The KKF protocols build on the chameleon hash function to form a keychain, which is a series of unbounded one-way hash keys. The latest hash key is used as the secret session key for securing device communications; hence, a communications session has to be rekeyed. The recipient verifies the new hash key by checking its hash collision with the previous hash key, thereby authenticating the sender of the hash key.

Because the protocols are designed for trusted devices to communicate with each other, it is assumed that the devices have been provisioned with a 256-bit master key **K** prior to deployment. **K** should be a randomly generated string created using secure methods to ensure its unpredictability and strength. It is preferably generated via joint computation, where each entity independently generates random input parameters during the setup phase and then securely combines the input parameters to produce a common master key without any single entity having complete knowledge of **K**. The master key is then provisioned into the devices before they are deployed in the field.

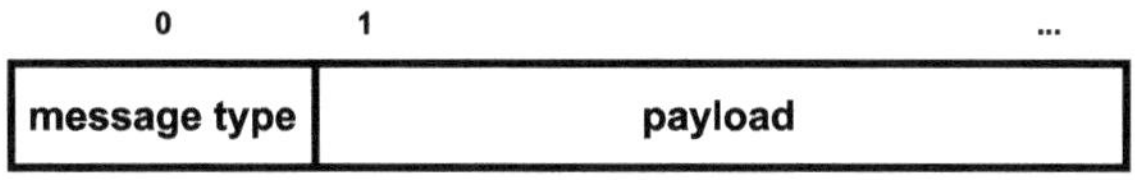

Fig. 1. Data packet structure.

The proposed KKF protocols comprise five phases: key generation, key distribution, rekeying, message protection and message verification. Figure 1 shows the data packet structure used by the KKF protocols. The first byte indicates the message type; it is followed by the message payload.

4.1 One-to-One Communications

The main objective of one-to-one communications is to establish a private communications channel with a specific device by distributing a secret hash key $\mathbf{HK}_n$ as the session key, where $\mathbf{HK}_0$ is the first session key that can be rekeyed or updated periodically with $\mathbf{HK}_1 \ldots \mathbf{HK}_n$. The hash key is used to protect messages exchanged over a public channel.

Key Generation. The device initiating communications first generates a pair of elliptic curve cryptography keys: a private trapdoor key $\mathbf{y}$ and its corresponding public key $\mathbf{Y}$. The keys are derived from the NIST P256 elliptic curve with $\mathbf{y}$ selected as a random scalar from the finite field $\mathbb{F}_p$:

$$\mathbf{y} \in \mathbb{F}_p$$

were p is a large prime number that defines the range of values used in elliptic curve cryptography computations.

Algorithm 1: Initial key generation and key distribution.

Data: Elliptic curve generator $\mathcal{G}$, master key $\mathbf{K}$
Result: Concatenated key distribution data packet
$\mathbf{Y} \leftarrow \mathbf{y} \cdot \mathcal{G}$;
$\mathsf{sid} \leftarrow \mathtt{Rand}(64)$;
$\mathsf{r}_0 \leftarrow \mathtt{Rand}(256)$;
$\mathsf{m}_0 \leftarrow \mathsf{sid}||\mathbf{K}$;
$\tilde{\mathsf{r}}_0 \leftarrow \mathsf{r}_0 \cdot \mathcal{G}$;
$\mathbf{HK}_0 \leftarrow \mathtt{HMAC}(\mathsf{m}_0, \mathbf{Y}) \cdot \mathbf{Y} + \tilde{\mathsf{r}}_0$;
$\mathsf{h}_0 \leftarrow \mathtt{HMAC}(\tilde{\mathsf{r}}_0, \mathbf{HK}_0)$;
$\mathsf{ht}[\mathsf{sid}] \leftarrow \{\mathbf{HK}_0, \mathsf{m}_0, \mathsf{r}_0, \mathbf{Y}, \mathbf{y}\}$;
return $\mathsf{sid}||\tilde{\mathsf{r}}_0||\mathbf{Y}||\mathsf{h}_0$

The public key $\mathbf{Y}$ is computed by the scalar multiplication of $\mathbf{y}$ with the elliptic curve generator $\mathcal{G}$:

$$\mathbf{Y} = \mathbf{y} \cdot \mathcal{G}$$

Key Distribution. Algorithm 1 specifies the initial key generation and key distribution for one-to-one communications. The initiating device first generates a session ID sid, which is a random 32-byte value that uniquely identifies the private session. Next, it creates an initial hash key $\mathbf{HK}_0$:

$$\mathbf{HK}_n = \mathtt{HMAC}(\mathsf{m}_n, \mathbf{Y}) \cdot \mathbf{Y} + \mathsf{r}_n \cdot \mathcal{G} \tag{1}$$

where m_0 is the concatenation of the session ID sid and the master key $\mathbf{K}$, and r_0 is the initial random 32-byte nonce scaled with the elliptic curve cryptography base point $\mathcal{G}$.

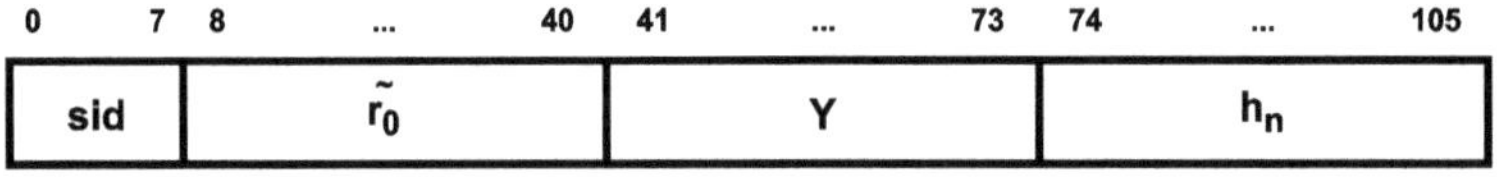

Fig. 2. One-to-one communications key distribution data packet structure.

Note that only trusted devices with knowledge of the master key $\mathbf{K}$ are able to generate $\mathbf{HK}_0$. The integrity of $\tilde{\mathsf{r}}_0$ (i.e., $\mathsf{r}_0 \cdot \mathcal{G}$) and $\mathbf{HK}_0$ is protected by computing a HMAC, i.e., h_0. The generated initial keying materials are subsequently stored in a hash table. The initiator of the communications stores the raw random nonce r_0 in its hash table, but it distributes $\tilde{\mathsf{r}}_0$. Finally, $\mathsf{sid}||\tilde{\mathsf{r}}_0||\mathbf{Y}||\mathsf{h}_0$ is sent to the recipient to establish a secure communications channel using a key distribution data packet structured as shown in Fig. 2.

Algorithm 2: Recipient deriving $\mathbf{HK}_0$ for one-to-one communications.

Data: Elliptic curve generator $\mathcal{G}$, master key $\mathbf{K}$, session ID sid, received blinded nonce $\tilde{\mathsf{r}}_0$ (i.e., $\mathsf{r}_0 \cdot \mathcal{G}$), public key $\mathbf{Y}$, HMAC value h_0
Result: Initial hash key $\mathbf{HK}_0$

$\mathsf{m}'_0 \leftarrow \mathsf{sid}||\mathbf{K}$;
$\mathbf{HK}_0 \leftarrow \mathtt{HMAC}(\mathsf{m}'_0, \mathbf{Y}) \cdot \mathbf{Y} + \tilde{\mathsf{r}}_0$;
$\mathsf{h} \leftarrow \mathtt{HMAC}(\tilde{\mathsf{r}}_0, \mathbf{HK}_0)$;
if $\mathsf{h} = \mathsf{h}_0$ **then**
  $\mathsf{ht}[\mathsf{sid}] \leftarrow \{\mathbf{HK}_0, \mathsf{m}'_0, \tilde{\mathsf{r}}_0, \mathbf{Y}\}$;
  return $\mathbf{HK}_0$
end

The recipient receiving the key distribution data packet derives the secret session key $\mathbf{HK}_0$ using Algorithm 2. With the knowledge of the pre-provisioned master key and by extracting the sid and $\tilde{\mathsf{r}}_0$ from the key distribution data packet, the recipient can compute the hash key $\mathbf{HK}_0$ as shown in Eq. 1. The HMAC h_0 is then verified using $\tilde{\mathsf{r}}_0$ and the generated secret session key $\mathbf{HK}_0$, ensuring that the initial session key $\mathbf{HK}_0$ is authentic and can be used to encrypt the communications channel. Similarly, the recipient maintains a hash table ht for storing security parameters used for rekeying and message verification. The receiver stores the blinded random nonce $\tilde{\mathsf{r}}_0$ in its record because the raw r_0 is not known to the public or the recipient.

Message Protection. Having established a session, the two communicating devices can protect their communications using the established hash key $\mathbf{HK}_0$ as the secret session key. This is subsequently updated with the latest hash key $\mathbf{HK}_n$ upon rekeying where $n \geq 1$.

Algorithm 3: Message protection for one-to-one communications.

Data: Session ID sid, plaintext message M, hash table ht
Result: Encrypted session data packet

if sid *in* $\mathsf{ht.keys}$ **then**
  $\mathsf{ht}[\mathsf{sid}].\mathsf{seq} \leftarrow \mathsf{ht}[\mathsf{sid}].\mathsf{seq} + 1$;
  $\mathsf{EM} \leftarrow \mathtt{AES\_encrypt}(\mathsf{ht}[\mathsf{sid}].\mathsf{seq}||\mathsf{M}, \mathsf{ht}[\mathsf{sid}].\mathbf{HK}, \mathsf{ht}[\mathsf{sid}].\mathsf{r} \cdot \mathcal{G})$;
  $\mathsf{l} \leftarrow \mathtt{len}(\mathsf{EM})$;
  $\mathsf{h} \leftarrow \mathtt{HMAC}(\mathsf{ht}[\mathsf{sid}].\mathsf{seq}||\mathsf{M}, \mathsf{ht}[\mathsf{sid}].\mathbf{HK})$;
  return $\mathsf{sid}||\mathsf{l}||\mathsf{EM}||\mathsf{h}$
end

Algorithm 3 specifies message protection for one-to-one communications. Messages are protected using standard AES encryption by tagging each message with the session ID sid and the message M_n is symmetrically encrypted

Algorithm 4: Message verification for one-to-one communications.

Data: Received session ID sid, encrypted message EM_n, length of encrypted message l_n, HMAC value h_n, hash table ht

Result: Verified data in plaintext

if sid *in* ht.keys **then**
    $\mathsf{M'} \leftarrow$ AES_decrypt(EM_n, ht[sid].**HK**, ht[sid].$\tilde{r}_0$);
    seq $\leftarrow$ $\mathsf{M'}[0:7]$;
    if seq $>$ ht[sid].seq **then**
        $\mathsf{h'} \leftarrow$ HMAC($\mathsf{M'}$, ht[sid].**HK**);
        if $\mathsf{h'} = \mathsf{h}_n$ **then**
            ht[sid].seq $\leftarrow$ seq;
            $\mathsf{M}_n \leftarrow \mathsf{M'}[8 : \mathsf{l}_n - 8]$;
            return M_n
        end
    end
end

together with an incremental sequence number seq using $\mathbf{HK}_n$ as the secret key and $\tilde{r}_n$ as the initialization vector (IV). However, the compressed forms of $\mathbf{HK}_n$ and $\tilde{r}_n$ are 33 bytes long, which exceeds the AES256 specification limits of a 32-byte key and a 16-byte initialization vector. To meet these requirements,

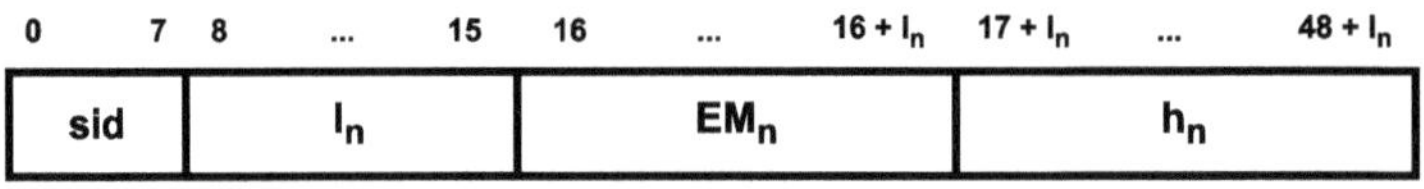

Fig. 3. One-to-one communications encryption data packet structure.

$\mathbf{HK}_n$ and $\tilde{r}_n$ are truncated to 32 bytes and 16 bytes respectively. Figure 3 shows the KKF one-to-one communications encryption data packet structure where l_n denotes the length of the encrypted message.

Message Verification. Upon receiving an encrypted message, the receiver decrypts the data packet using the secret session key $\mathbf{HK}_n$ and $\tilde{r}_n$ as the initialization vector as specified in Algorithm 4. As mentioned previously, the latest hash key and security parameters are stored locally in the device hash table and are retrieved using the session ID sid of the communications channel. Message freshness is verified by checking that the sequence number seq is not smaller than the one stored in the hash table.

Rekeying. It is standard practice to ensure that a secret session key – the hash key $\mathbf{HK}_n$ in this protocol – is short-lived and renewed periodically so that, if the session key is compromised, an adversary does not have access to the content

Algorithm 5: Rekeying process for one-to-one communications.

Data: Elliptic curve generator $\mathcal{G}$, session ID sid, hash table ht
Result: Concatenated key renewal data packet
if sid *in* $\mathsf{ht.keys}$ **then**
  $\mathsf{r}_{n+1} \leftarrow \texttt{Rand}(256)$;
  $\tilde{\mathsf{r}}_{n+1} \leftarrow \mathsf{r}_{n+1} \cdot \mathcal{G}$;
  $\tilde{\mathsf{r}}_n \leftarrow \mathsf{ht[sid].r} \cdot \mathcal{G}$;
  $\mathbf{HK}_{n+1} \leftarrow \texttt{HMAC}(\mathsf{ht[sid].m}, \mathsf{ht[sid]}.\mathbf{Y}) \cdot \mathsf{ht[sid]}.\mathbf{Y} + \mathsf{r}_{n+1} \cdot \mathcal{G}$;
  $\mathsf{r\prime}_n \leftarrow \mathsf{ht[sid]}.\mathbf{y} \cdot [\texttt{HMAC}(\mathsf{ht[sid].m}, \mathbf{Y}) - \texttt{HMAC}(\mathbf{HK}_{n+1}, \mathbf{Y})] + \mathsf{ht[sid].r}$;
  $\tilde{\mathsf{r\prime}}_n \leftarrow \mathsf{r\prime}_n \cdot \mathcal{G}$;
  $\mathsf{EM}_n \leftarrow \texttt{AES\_encrypt}(\tilde{\mathsf{r}}_{n+1} || \tilde{\mathsf{r\prime}}_n, \mathbf{HK}_n, \tilde{\mathsf{r}}_n)$;
  $\mathsf{ht[sid]}.\mathbf{HK} \leftarrow \mathbf{HK}_{n+1}$;
  $\mathsf{ht[sid].r} \leftarrow \mathsf{r}_{n+1}$;
  return $\mathsf{sid}||\mathsf{EM}_n$
end

encrypted with a renewed key. The master key $\mathbf{K}$ is employed to continuously derive ephemeral hash keys that can be verified easily. The master key is neither used for message encryption nor decryption, so exposure to the public is limited. Algorithm 5 specifies the rekeying process based on a chameleon hash chain.

Whenever the secret session key (i.e., latest hash key) needs to be rekeyed for a particular session either periodically or due to key compromise, a new nonce r_{n+1} is generated to derive a new hash key $\mathbf{HK}_{n+1}$. At the same time, a collision nonce $\mathsf{r\prime}_n$ is computed to link the previous hash key $\mathbf{HK}_n$ with the new hash key $\mathbf{HK}_{n+1}$ for easy verification by the receiver. This is done by computing the HMAC-SHA256 values of m_n (i.e., concatenation of sid and $\mathbf{K}$) and compressed $\mathbf{HK}_{n+1}$ using $\mathbf{Y}$ as the key for both computations. The difference between the two HMAC values is then scalar-multiplied with the trapdoor key $\mathbf{y}$ and added to the previous nonce r_n to yield the collision nonce $\mathsf{r\prime}_n$:

$$\mathsf{r\prime}_n = \mathbf{y} \cdot [\texttt{HMAC}(\mathsf{m}_n, \mathbf{Y}) - \texttt{HMAC}(\mathbf{HK}_{n+1}, \mathbf{Y})] + \mathsf{r}_n \tag{2}$$

Note that only the initiator of the communications can derive the new hash key to extend the keychain because it needs the private key (trapdoor) to compute $\mathsf{r\prime}_n$ and it is also the only entity that knows the raw random nonce r_n. The new nonce r_{n+1} and the collision nonce $\mathsf{r\prime}_n$ are first blinded with the elliptic curve cryptography generator $\mathcal{G}$ and then encrypted with the current hash key, following which it is sent to the recipient.

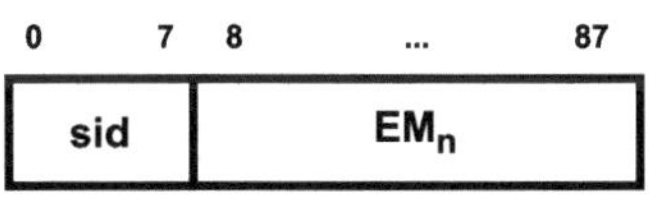

Fig. 4. Rekeying data packet structure.

Algorithm 6: Deriving new hash key for one-to-one communications.

Data: Elliptic curve generator $\mathcal{G}$, session ID sid, encrypted data payload EM_n
Result: New session key $\mathbf{HK}_{n+1}$
if sid *in* $\mathsf{ht.keys}$ **then**
  $\mathsf{M}_n \leftarrow \mathtt{AES\_decrypt}(\mathsf{EM}_n, \mathsf{ht[sid]}.\mathbf{HK}, \mathsf{ht[sid]}.\tilde{\mathsf{r}})$;
  $\tilde{\mathsf{r}}_{n+1} \leftarrow \mathsf{M}_n[0:32]$;
  $\tilde{\mathsf{r}\prime}_n \leftarrow \mathsf{M}_n[33:65]$;
  $\mathbf{HK}_{n+1} \leftarrow \mathtt{HMAC}(\mathsf{ht[sid].m}, \mathsf{ht[sid]}.\mathbf{Y}) \cdot \mathsf{ht[sid]}.\mathbf{Y} + \tilde{\mathsf{r}}_{n+1}$;
  $\mathbf{HK\prime}_n \leftarrow \mathtt{HMAC}(\mathbf{HK}_{n+1}, \mathsf{ht[sid]}.\mathbf{Y}) \cdot \mathsf{ht[sid]}.\mathbf{Y} + \tilde{\mathsf{r}\prime}_n$;
  if $\mathsf{ht[sid]}.\mathbf{HK} = \mathbf{HK\prime}_n$ **then**
    $\mathsf{ht[sid]}.\mathbf{HK} \leftarrow \mathbf{HK}_{n+1}$;
    $\mathsf{ht[sid]}.\tilde{\mathsf{r}} \leftarrow \tilde{\mathsf{r}}_{n+1}$;
    return $\mathbf{HK}_{n+1}$
  end
end

The hash table storing the new session key $\mathbf{HK}_{n+1}$ and the corresponding nonce r_{n+1} is updated in device storage. Figure 4 shows the rekeying data packet structure comprising the session ID sid and encrypted key material EM_n, which is sent to the recipient.

The session key is rekeyed easily upon receiving the rekeying data packet by first decrypting it using the current key to obtain the new blinded nonce $\tilde{\mathsf{r}}_{n+1}$ and the blinded collision nonce $\tilde{\mathsf{r}\prime}_n$. Using the current security parameters in the hash table, the next secret session key $\mathbf{HK}_{n+1}$ is computed using Eq. 1 above where the recipient must successfully decrypt $\tilde{\mathsf{r}}_{n+1}$ and have knowledge of the master key $\mathbf{K}$ that is embedded in the parameter $\mathsf{m} = \mathsf{sid}||\mathbf{K}$ in its local hash table.

The validity of the new hash key $\mathbf{HK}_{n+1}$ is verified easily by ensuring that it is linked to the previous hash key using the blinded collision nonce $\tilde{\mathsf{r}\prime}_n$:

$$\mathbf{HK}_n = \mathtt{HMAC}(\mathbf{HK}_{n+1}, \mathbf{Y}) \cdot \mathbf{Y} + \tilde{\mathsf{r}\prime}_n \quad (3)$$

This ensures that the new nonce is not a spoofed value and that only the entity with the trapdoor key is able to generate the collision nonce. If the hash collision is valid, then the respective hash table records are updated and the new secret session key takes effect. This process effectively chains the previous hash key $\mathbf{HK}_n$ with the new hash key $\mathbf{HK}_{n+1}$, ensuring that the receiver can maintain the continuous flow and integrity of the private session. Algorithm 6 specifies the derivation of the new hash key for one-to-one communications.

4.2 One-to-Many Broadcast Communications

The KKF protocol for securing one-to-one communications can be adapted to support one-to-many communications by broadcasting two sets of security parameters in order to derive consecutive hash keys on the keychain and verify

Algorithm 7: Message protection for one-to-many communications.

Data: Plaintext message M_n, elliptic curve generator $\mathcal{G}$, master key $\mathbf{K}$
Result: Public session data packet
if *not* record **then**
  record.seq $\leftarrow 0$;
  record.r $\leftarrow$ Rand(256);
  record.m $\leftarrow$ record.seq$||\mathbf{K}$;
  record.$\mathbf{Y} \leftarrow$ record.$\mathbf{y} \cdot \mathcal{G}$;
end
$\tilde{r}_{n-1} \leftarrow$ record.r $\cdot \mathcal{G}$;
$\mathsf{r}_n \leftarrow$ Rand(256);
$\tilde{\mathsf{r}}_n \leftarrow \mathsf{r}_n \cdot \mathcal{G}$;
record.seq $\leftarrow$ record.seq $+ 1$;
$\mathsf{m}_n \leftarrow$ record.seq$||\mathbf{K}$;
$\mathbf{HK}_n \leftarrow$ HMAC$(\mathsf{m}_n$, record.$\mathbf{Y})$ $\cdot$ record.$\mathbf{Y} + \mathsf{r}_n \cdot \mathcal{G}$;
$\mathsf{r}\prime_{n-1} \leftarrow$ record.$\mathbf{y} \cdot$ [HMAC(record.m, $\mathbf{Y}$) $-$ HMAC$(\mathbf{HK}_n, \mathbf{Y})$] $+$ record.r;
$\tilde{\mathsf{r}}\prime_{n-1} \leftarrow \mathsf{r}\prime_{n-1} \cdot \mathcal{G}$;
$\mathsf{EM}_n \leftarrow$ AES_encrypt$(\mathsf{M}_n, \mathbf{HK}_n, \tilde{\mathsf{r}}_n)$;
$\mathsf{h}_n \leftarrow$ HMAC$(\mathsf{M}_n, \mathbf{HK}_n)$;
$\mathsf{l}_n \leftarrow$ len(EM);
record.r $\leftarrow \mathsf{r}_n$;
record.m $\leftarrow \mathsf{m}_n$;
return record.seq$||\tilde{\mathsf{r}}_n||\tilde{\mathsf{r}}\prime_{n-1}||$record.$\mathbf{Y}||\tilde{\mathsf{r}}_{n-1}||\mathsf{l}_n||\mathsf{EM}_n||\mathsf{h}_n$

their linkage simultaneously. This eliminates the handshake required by other key exchange protocols. The broadcast message can then be encrypted using the latest hash key on the keychain.

Message Protection. Algorithm 7 specifies the message protection for one-to-many broadcast communications. Two 32-byte random nonces r_{n-1} and r_n are generated along with an incremental sequence number seq. At the start of each communications session, the first two hash keys are generated based on r_0 and r_1 with their respective sequence number seq that is concatenated with the master key $\mathbf{K}$ to create the message m_n. Using these parameters, the hash keys $\mathbf{HK}_{n-1}$ and $\mathbf{HK}_n$ are computed as specified in Eq. 1. The latest hash key $\mathbf{HK}_n$ is then used to encrypt the plaintext message M_n using AES256 with $\tilde{\mathsf{r}}_n$ serving as the initialization vector. For each subsequent message protection broadcast, the sender generates the parameters for the new hash key $\mathbf{HK}_{n+1}$ and broadcasts the parameters of the adjacent pair of hash keys ($\mathbf{HK}_n$, $\mathbf{HK}_{n+1}$) where n is the current hash key index.

In the protocol, the broadcast message is protected using the new hash key that is generated. Because the sender and receivers retain the most recent m_n and $\tilde{\mathsf{r}}_n$, the sender can generate subsequent hash keys, effectively creating a chain of hash keys. Each message is also identified using an incremental seq that is concatenated with the master key $\mathbf{K}$ to detect replay. For each adjacent pair of hash keys, they are verified using Eq. 3 to ensure their authenticity, integrity and validity. To link the keys through hash collisions, the sender uses its trapdoor key $\mathbf{y}$ and the raw random nonce r_{n-1} to derive the collision nonce $\mathsf{r}\prime_{n-1}$ using Eq. 2 above, establishing a relationship between the preceding hash key $\mathbf{HK}_{n-1}$ and the current hash key $\mathbf{HK}_n$.

0 … 7	8 … 40	41 … 73	74 … 106	107 … 139	140 … 147	148 … 148 + l_n	149 + l_n … 180 + l_n
seq	$\tilde{r}_n$	$\tilde{r}'_{n-1}$	Y_n	$\tilde{r}_{n-1}$	l_n	EM_n	h_n

Fig. 5. Broadcast data packet structure.

Each broadcast message thus contains a serialized data packet that includes the sequence number seq, encrypted message EM_n, length l_n of EM_n, HMAC h_n and compressed elliptic curve cryptography points $\tilde{\mathsf{r}}_n$, $\tilde{\mathsf{r}}_{n-1}$, $\tilde{\mathsf{r}}\prime_{n-1}$ and $\mathbf{Y}_n$. Figure 5 shows the broadcast data packet structure.

Algorithm 8: Message verification for one-to-many communications.

Data: Received sequence number seq, random blinded nonces $\tilde{\mathsf{r}}_n$ and $\tilde{\mathsf{r}}_{n-1}$, collision nonce $\tilde{\mathsf{r}}\prime_{n-1}$, public key $\mathbf{Y}$, encrypted message EM_n, HMAC value h_n, master key $\mathbf{K}$, hash table ht

Result: Verified data in plaintext

if $\mathbf{Y}$ *in* ht.keys **then**
    if $\mathsf{seq} <= \mathsf{ht}[\mathbf{Y}].\mathsf{seq}$ **then**
        return None
    end
    $\mathbf{HK}_{n-1} \leftarrow \mathsf{ht}[\mathbf{Y}].\mathbf{HK}$;
else
    $\mathsf{m}\prime_{n-1} \leftarrow \mathsf{seq} - 1 || \mathbf{K}$;
    $\mathbf{HK}_{n-1} \leftarrow \mathtt{HMAC}(\mathsf{m}\prime_{n-1}, \mathsf{record}.\mathbf{Y}) \cdot \mathsf{record}.\mathbf{Y} + \mathsf{record}.\tilde{\mathsf{r}}_{n-1}$;
end
$\mathsf{m}\prime_n \leftarrow \mathsf{seq} || \mathbf{K}$;
$\mathbf{HK}_n \leftarrow \mathtt{HMAC}(\mathsf{m}\prime_n, \mathsf{record}.\mathbf{Y}) \cdot \mathsf{record}.\mathbf{Y} + \tilde{\mathsf{r}}_n$;
$\mathbf{HK}\prime \leftarrow \mathtt{HMAC}(\mathbf{HK}_n, \mathsf{record}.\mathbf{Y}) \cdot \mathsf{record}.\mathbf{Y} + \tilde{\mathsf{r}}\prime_{n-1}$;
if $\mathbf{HK}_{n-1} = \mathbf{HK}\prime$ **then**
    $\mathsf{M}\prime_n \leftarrow \mathtt{AES\_decrypt}(\mathsf{EM}_n, \mathbf{HK}_n, \tilde{\mathsf{r}}_n)$;
    $\mathsf{h}\prime \leftarrow \mathtt{HMAC}(\mathsf{M}\prime_n, \mathbf{HK}_n)$;
    if $\mathsf{h}\prime = \mathsf{h}_n$ **then**
        $\mathsf{ht}[\mathbf{Y}].\mathsf{seq} \leftarrow \mathsf{seq}$;
        $\mathsf{ht}[\mathbf{Y}].\mathbf{HK} \leftarrow \mathbf{HK}_n$;
        return $\mathsf{M}\prime_n$;
    end
end

Message Verification. Algorithm 8 specifies message verification for broadcast communications. The receiver first verifies the sequence number seq and checks the hash collision. Next, it reconstructs m'_n by combining the received seq with the master key $\mathbf{K}$. Using m'_n, m'_{n-1} and the received values $\tilde{\mathsf{r}}_n$, $\tilde{\mathsf{r}}_{n-1}$ and $\mathbf{Y}_n$, the adjacent pair of hash keys $\mathbf{HK}_n$ and $\mathbf{HK}_{n-1}$ are computed using Eq. 1. The authenticity of the message is then verified by first attempting to derive the linkage between $\mathbf{HK}_{n-1}$ from $\mathbf{HK}_n$ using the received blinded collision nonce $\tilde{\mathsf{r}}'_{n-1}$ according to Eq. 3. If a previous record of $\tilde{\mathsf{r}}_{n-1}$ exists, the receiver does not need to extract it and recompute $\mathbf{HK}_{n-1}$ from scratch due to the chain-like structure of the hash keys. These parameters are stored in a separate hash table from the one used for one-to-one communications.

After the hash collision is validated, it is determined that the latest hash key $\mathbf{HK}_n$ is indeed authentic and originates from the sender. The receiver then decrypts the encrypted message using $\mathbf{HK}_n$ as the secret key and $\tilde{\mathsf{r}}_n$ as the initialization vector. The integrity of the message is then verified using the HMAC of the plaintext message M using $\mathbf{HK}_n$ as the key. If any of the verification steps fail, the verification process is terminated and the message received is discarded immediately. Otherwise, the receiver can assume that the message was from an authenticated sender and was not tampered with. The advantage of this approach is that every broadcast message is protected using a new hash key and the authenticity of the key can be verified easily using the collision nonce.

5 Security Analysis

This section discusses data integrity and authenticity of the KKF protocols. Also, it compares the security and privacy properties of the KKF protocols against those of other protocols in the literature.

5.1 Data Integrity and Authenticity

The KKF protocols are secure against spoofing attacks, man-in-the-middle attacks and replay attacks. Spoofing attacks are effectively mitigated via the robustness of chameleon hashes and symmetric encryption. Only authorized devices that possess the master key $\mathbf{K}$ can generate valid hash keys and perform encryption because the blinded random nonces are known to the public. Without access to $\mathbf{K}$, an adversary cannot generate legitimate hash keys $\mathbf{HK}_n$ and subsequently decrypt the messages, preventing it from successfully impersonating legitimate devices. Additionally, without knowledge of the private key (trapdoor) $\mathbf{y}$ and without knowledge of the raw random nonce, it is not possible to link the generated hash key with the previous hash key, thus invalidating the authenticity of the spoofed hash key.

Man-in-the-middle attacks are thwarted by comprehensive authenticity verification and encryption mechanisms. The integrity of transmitted data is guaranteed using HMAC-SHA256, which verifies that the message has not been tampered with during transmission. The chameleon hash function contributes to authenticity verification by binding each message to its corresponding cryptographic session keys and nonces, ensuring that the message originates from a trusted source. Furthermore, the use of AES256 encryption guarantees that, even if an adversary intercepts the encrypted message EM, decrypting the message without the correct symmetric key $\mathbf{HK}_n$ would be computationally infeasible.

Replay attacks are effectively countered by the incremental sequence number seq in each message. Each received sequence number must be greater than the sequence number in the record. This validation ensures that only new messages are accepted, rendering replayed messages obsolete and identifiable as illegitimate. Replacing a previously legitimate message with a replayed message would fail the verification process because the chameleon hash collision and HMAC value would not align correctly. This dual-layered verification mechanism ensures that replayed messages cannot deceive the receiver into accepting unauthorized or tampered communications.

Table 2. Comparison of security and privacy properties.

Properties	Ref [27]	Ref [16]	Ref [7]	Ref [4]	KKF
Authentication	✓	✓	✓	✓	✓
Unlinkability	✓	✓	✓	✓	–
Revocation	✓	✓	✓	✓	✓
Secure Key Update	✓	✓	✓	✓	✓
Scalability	Moderate	Low	High	High	High
Infrastructure Dependency	Low	High	Moderate	Moderate	Low
Authentication Overhead	–	–	284 B/300 B	149 B	154 B/180 B

5.2 Security and Privacy

Table 2 compares the security and privacy properties of the KKF protocols against those of four other protocols in the literature – pseudonymous authentication by Sudarsono and Yuliana [27], group authentication by Hsu et al. [16], zone encryption by Camenisch et al. [7] and hybrid authentication by Baee et al. [4]. All the protocols provide authentication, revocation and secure key updates. However, the KKF protocols do not support perfect unlinkability. The KKF protocol for one-to-one communications relies on session IDs that can be used to trace multiple messages to the same senders. The KKF protocol for one-to-many communications uses a public key that can be updated if needed, but doing so increases the computation and storage overhead.

The KKF protocols rank highly in terms of scalability because they operate independently once the initial setup is complete, without relying on additional infrastructure. In contrast, some of the listed protocols, especially those involving group authentication, depend on external entities such as a group manager, roadside units or trusted authority that limit their scalability. The KKF protocols have light infrastructure dependence because they minimize the reliance on external components after the initial master key distribution.

Table 2 shows the authentication overheads for the listed protocols. Data is not available for the first two protocols involving pseudonymous authentication [27] and group authentication [16]. For zone encryption [7], the authentication overheads are 284 bytes for requests and 300 bytes for responses. The hybrid authentication protocol [4] has overheads of 149 bytes for requests and responses. The KKF one-to-one communications protocol has an authentication overhead of 154 bytes due to the key distribution message, which is 106 bytes to facilitate the derivation of the hash key; subsequent messages only require 48 bytes overhead to indicate the session ID and data length. The KKF one-to-many communications protocol has a 180 bytes authentication overhead because it eliminates a handshake before communications by embedding the authentication parameters in the message itself. The rekeying message has a lower overhead of 87 bytes.

The KKF protocols are better choices in several scenarios. For example, in a smart building where autonomous robots handle tasks such as delivery, security patrols and maintenance, common authentication methods usually depend on a centralized infrastructure, such as an authentication server, trusted authority or roadside unit, that can introduce additional overhead, delays and scalability challenges when multiple devices require real-time authentication. The KKF protocols eliminate the need for additional infrastructure after the initial master key distribution is completed. The decentralized approach enables devices to authenticate and communicate with each other directly, significantly reducing network dependencies and lowering the computational and communications overheads.

Consider a scenario where a robot needs to interact with an elevator in a smart building. In a conventional setup, the elevator would have to check with a centralized server to authenticate the robot before performing any actions. In the case of the KKF protocol, the robot includes the necessary authentication parameters in its request, enabling the elevator to verify message authenticity immediately. This direct interaction boosts the authentication process while ensuring that the system remains operational even when the external infrastructure is compromised or unavailable.

Similarly, in a one-to-many authentication scenario, such as when a security robot broadcasts an alert to the other robots, common approaches might require individual handshakes or rely on a central server to validate the messages. This can introduce overhead and delays, especially in large-scale deployments. The KKF protocol addresses this by incorporating authentication data directly in the broadcast message. As a result, all the nearby devices can instantly verify message legitimacy without communicating with a centralized infrastructure. This approach enhances scalability and responsiveness, rendering the protocol suitable for environments where message timeliness is crucial.

6 Prototype Implementation and Results

A chameleon hash function library in C was developed to implement the KKF protocols. A prototype was implemented utilizing Bluetooth Low Energy (BLE) as the underlying communications medium to assess protocol performance. Because BLE broadcast packets are restricted to 31 bytes in legacy advertisements and most Bluetooth 5.x devices, including Raspberry Pis, do not explicitly support extended advertising that is optional, a General Attribute Profile (GATT) service with "Just Works" was used to simulate communications as in [22]. The GATT server and client nodes were deployed on Raspberry Pi 4 Model B devices with 1.8 GHz ARM Cortex-A72 CPUs and 4 GB RAM, running Ubuntu 24.04.1 LTS with Bluetooth 5.0, Bluez 5.72 and Python 3.12.3.

The computational latency of the KKF protocols was evaluated using an experimental setup involving two Raspberry Pi devices, a transmitter and receiver, placed 1 m apart in an enclosed indoor environment without any intervening obstacles to measure the round-trip times for BLE GATT operations with the message protection protocol.

The receiver ran a GATT service with two characteristics, one for reading and the other for writing. The transmitter was connected to the receiver's GATT service and wrote 16-byte messages for 10^4 iterations using broadcast message protection, one-to-one message protection and plaintext as the control group. The processing times were collected from the transmitter side only to avoid time synchronization problems by measuring the time difference before sending and after reading and processing a message. This included two message protection and two message verification function calls.

Table 3. Bluetooth Low Energy GATT performance results.

Operation	Average Round-Trip Time
One-to-One Message	209 ms
Broadcast Message	210 ms
Plaintext Message	197 ms

Table 3 shows the performance results. The KKF protocols incurred little computational latency when implemented on BLE GATT and it appears that the bulk of latency was due to the inherent BLE communications. For message protection and verification in the KKF protocols, the processing took only 13 ms (= 210 – 197 ms) because the pure BLE communications round-trip time without the security data processing took 197 ms.

The second experiment evaluated the message processing time for key generation, key distribution, rekeying, message protection and message verification in the KKF protocols. The average time taken to process each message type over 10^4 iterations was measured. In the case of message protection, random 16-byte data was generated for each iteration. Processing times were measured using the Python Scalene tool [5].

Table 4. KKF protocol performance results.

Operation	Average Processing Time
Initial Key Distribution	1.713×10^{-3} s
Initial Key Verification	2.289×10^{-4} s
One-to-One Rekeying	1.723×10^{-3} s
One-to-One Rekeying Verification	1.106×10^{-3} s
One-to-One Message Protection	8.168×10^{-4} s
One-to-One Message Verification	1.358×10^{-3} s
Broadcast Message Protection	7.069×10^{-4} s
Broadcast Message Verification	1.134×10^{-3} s

Table 4 shows the KKF protocol performance results. The verification of the hash key (i.e., checking the hash collision nonce) is fast compared with the generation of the collision nonce. This is evident from the results that key verification and rekey verification are more efficient than key distribution and rekeying. However, the broadcast message verification took more time compared with broadcast message protection primarily due to the AES decryption process. The same result is seen for one-to-one message verification. Overall, the results demonstrate that KKF protocol processing is efficient in terms of computational time.

7 Conclusions

The KKF protocols described in this chapter employ chameleon hash keychains to enable lightweight and secure device-to-device and broadcast communications without relying on centralized servers. The message authenticity and integrity properties provided by the protocols are well suited to scenarios where devices in an administrative domain (e.g., smart building or smart factory) are required to interact spontaneously.

A critical aspect of the protocols is the secure management of master keys. Since the master key is pre-shared by all the communicating devices, it must be protected and distributed using a robust technique such as multiparty computation during the initial setup. Additional measures could be employed in dynamic Internet-of-Things environments, where devices join and leave frequently or operate in different geographical areas. For instance, periodically updating the master key would limit the negative impact of a compromised key. This is accomplished by incorporating pseudonym keys [20] or location/zone-based key management [1,7] that enable different subsets of devices to communicate securely in unique cryptographic contexts. Such strategies would also enable controlled traceability that enable authorized entities, such as trusted authorities, to perform auditing and accountability checks as required while maintaining unlinkability for normal communications.

Future work will focus on enhancing the master key distribution and management process to limit the impact of key compromise and ensure security and context-specific communications. Additionally, future work will implement and evaluate the KKF protocols in alternative communications technologies such as Long Term Evolution (LTE) and 5G New Radio Sidelink that offer direct device-to-device communications without network infrastructure dependencies. The Sidelink protocol application could be very useful in real-world scenarios such as vehicular ad hoc networks and industrial Internet-of-Things environments.

References

1. Alawami, M., Kim, H.: LocAuth: a fine-grained indoor location-based authentication system using wireless network characteristics. Comput. Secur. **89** (2020). Article no. 101683
2. Ateniese, G., de Medeiros, B.: On the key exposure problem in chameleon hashes. In: Proceedings of the Fourth International Conference on Security in Communications Networks, pp. 165–179 (2004)
3. Baccour, E., et al.: Pervasive AI for IoT applications: a survey of resource-efficient distributed artificial intelligence. IEEE Commun. Surv. Tutor. **24**(4), 2366–2418 (2022)
4. Baee, M., Simpson, L., Boyen, X., Foo, E., Pieprzyk, J.: ALI: anonymous lightweight inter-vehicle broadcast authentication with encryption. IEEE Trans. Dependable Secure Comput. **20**(3), 1799–1817 (2023)
5. Berger, E., Stern, S., Pizzorno, J.: Triangulating Python performance issues with SCALENE. In: Proceedings of the Seventeenth USENIX Symposium on Operating Systems Design and Implementation, pp. 51–64 (2023)
6. Camenisch, J., Derler, D., Krenn, S., Pohls, H., Samelin, K., Slamanig, D.: Chameleon hashes with ephemeral trapdoors. In: Proceedings of the Twentieth International Conference on Public-Key Cryptography, Part II, pp. 152–182 (2017)
7. Camenisch, J., Drijvers, M., Lehmann, A., Neven, G., Towa, P.: Zone encryption with anonymous authentication for V2V communications. In: Proceedings of the IEEE European Symposium on Security and Privacy, pp. 405–424 (2020)
8. Chen, X., Zhang, F., Susilo, W., Mu, Y.: Efficient generic on-line/off-line signatures without key exposure. In: Katz, J., Yung, M. (eds.) ACNS 2007. LNCS, vol. 4521, pp. 18–30. Springer, Heidelberg (2007). https://doi.org/10.1007/978-3-540-72738-5_2
9. Chen, X., Zhang, F., Susilo, W., Tian, H., Li, J., Kim, K.: Identity-based chameleon hashing and signatures without key exposure. Inf. Sci. **265**, 198–210 (2014)
10. Chu, Y.H., Keoh, S.L., Seow, C.K., Cao, Q., Wen, K., Tan, S.Y.: GPS signal authentication using a chameleon hash keychain. In: Staggs, J., Shenoi, S. (eds.) ICCIP 2021. IFIP Advances in Information and Communication Technology, vol. 636, pp. 209–226. Springer, Cham (2022). https://doi.org/10.1007/978-3-030-93511-5_10

11. Cincilla, P., Hicham, O., Charles, B.: Vehicular PKI scalability-consistency trade-offs in large scale distributed scenarios. In: Proceedings of the IEEE Vehicular Networking Conference (2016)
12. Dolev, D., Yao, A.: On the security of public key protocols. IEEE Trans. Inf. Theory **29**(2), 198–208 (1983)
13. Feng, D., Lu, L., Yuan-Wu, Y., Li, G., Li, S., Feng, G.: Device-to-device communications in cellular networks. IEEE Commun. Mag. **52**(4), 49–55 (2014)
14. Hakeem, S., El-Kader, S., Kim, H.: A key management protocol based on hash chain key generation for securing LoRaWAN networks. Sensors **21** (2021). Article no. 5838
15. Harn, L.: Group authentication. IEEE Trans. Comput. **62**(9), 1893–1898 (2013)
16. Hsu, C., Harn, L., Xia, Z.: An HSS-based robust and lightweight multiple group authentication for ITS towards 5G. IET Intel. Transport Syst. **15**(11), 1454–1460 (2021)
17. Jaidka, H., Sharma, N., Singh, R.: Evolution of IoT to IIoT: applications and challenges. In: Proceedings of the International Conference on Innovative Computing and Communications (2020)
18. Keoh, S.: Efficient group key management and authentication for body sensor networks. In: Proceedings of the IEEE International Conference on Communications (2011)
19. Keoh, S., Lupu, E., Sloman, M.: Securing body sensor networks: sensor association and key management. In: Proceedings of the IEEE International Conference on Pervasive Computing and Communications (2009)
20. Khodaei, M., Noroozi, H., Papadimitratos, P.: SECMACE+: upscaling pseudonymous authentication for large mobile systems. IEEE Trans. Cloud Comput. **11**(3), 3009–3026 (2023)
21. Krawczyk, H., Rabin, T.: Chameleon hashing and signatures. Cryptology ePrint Archive, Paper 1998/010 (eprint.iacr.org/1998/010) (1998)
22. Liu, T., Ramachandran, G., Jurdak, R.: Towards quantum resilient IoT: a backward-compatible approach to secure BLE key exchange against quantum threats. In: Proceedings of the Ninth ACM/IEEE International Conference on Internet-of-Things Design and Implementation, pp. 170–180 (2024)
23. Park, C., Park, W.: A group-oriented DTLS handshake for secure IoT applications. IEEE Trans. Autom. Sci. Eng. **15**(4), 1920–1929 (2018)
24. Rafique, W., Qi, L., Yaqoob, I., Imran, M., Ur Rasool, R., Dou, W.: Complementing IoT services through software defined networking and edge computing: a comprehensive survey. IEEE Commun. Surv. Tutor. **22**(3), 1761–1804 (2020)
25. Shen, X.: Device-to-device communications in 5G cellular networks. IEEE Netw. **29**(2), 2–3 (2015)
26. Singh, A., Awasthi, A., Singh, K.: Lightweight multilevel key management scheme for large scale wireless sensor networks. In: Proceedings of the Third International Conference on Computing for Sustainable Global Development, pp. 3014–3017 (2016)
27. Sudarsono, A., Yuliana, M.: An anonymous authentication with received signal strength based pseudonymous identity generation for VANETs. IEEE Access **11**, 15637–15654 (2023)
28. Sudarsono, A., Yuliana, M., Kristalina, P.: A shared secret key generation between vehicle and roadside based preprocessing method. In: Proceedings of the International Conference on Computer Engineering, Networks and Intelligent Multimedia (2019)

29. Sudarsono, A., Yuliana, M., Kristalina, P., Barakbah, A.: An implementation of shared key generation extracted from received signal strength in vehicular ad-hoc communications. In: Proceedings of the Sixth International Symposium on Computing and Networking, pp. 57–65 (2018)
30. Westphall, J., Loffi, L., Westphall, C., Martina, J.: CoAP + DTLS: a comprehensive overview of cryptographic performance in an IoT scenario. In: Proceedings of the IEEE Sensor Applications Symposium (2020)

Author Index

Published by Springer Nature Switzerland AG 2026
J. Staggs and S. Shenoi (Eds.): ICCIP 2025, IFIP AICT 763, p. 169, 2026.
https://doi.org/10.1007/978-3-032-11914-8